**Ilsup Ahn** is Carl I. Lindberg Professor of
Philosophy at North Park University. He is the
author of *Position and Responsibility* (2009) and
*Religious Ethics and Migration: Doing Justice
to Undocumented Workers* (2013). He is also
a coeditor of *Asian American Christian Ethics:
Voices, Methods, Issues* (2015). He received his
PhD in Social and Religious Ethics from the
University of Chicago.

D1116674

# JUST DEBT

# JUST DEBT

*Theology, Ethics, and Neoliberalism*

Ilsup Ahn

BAYLOR UNIVERSITY PRESS

Unless otherwise stated, Scripture quotations are from the New Revised Standard Version Bible, copyright 1989, Division of Christian Education of the National Council of the Churches of Christ in the United States of America. Used by permission. All rights reserved.

*Cover Design and cover illustration* by Hannah Feldmeier

Library of Congress Cataloging-in-Publication Data

Names: Ahn, Ilsup, author.
Title: Just debt : theology, ethics, and neoliberalism / Ilsup Ahn.
Description: Waco, Texas : Baylor University Press, [2017] | Includes
  bibliographical references and index.
Identifiers: LCCN 2017003701 (print) | LCCN 2017027125 (ebook) | ISBN
  9781481307376 (ePub) | ISBN 9781481307383 (ebook-Mobi/Kindle) |
  ISBN 9781481306935 (web PDF) | ISBN 9781481306911 (hardback: alk.
  paper) | ISBN 9781481306928 (pbk. : alk. paper)
Subjects: LCSH: Debt. | Credit control. | Debt relief.
Classification: LCC HG3701 (ebook) | LCC HG3701.A23 2017 (print) |
  DDC 174—dc23
LC record available at https://lccn.loc.gov/2017003701

To my sister

# Contents

# ACKNOWLEDGMENTS

Writing is a continuous practice of getting into debt, and it must be right for me to begin a book by acknowledging my own indebtedness to those who have helped me to get this volume published. I would first like to express my sincere appreciation to Brandel Library of North Park University and its wonderful staff. I have requested a countless number of inter-library loans, and they supported my research in the best way possible. In particular, Steve Spencer, Theological and Cataloging Librarian, was exceptionally helpful. Deepest gratitude should be given to the Baylor University Press team, especially director Carey Newman for his belief and efforts on behalf of this project. I extend my deepest gratitude to three anonymous readers who offered me an invaluable critique. Thanks to their critical-constructive comments, I was able to revise the original manuscript in a much richer and more critical way. I also would like to express my hearty appreciation to Carrie Watterson and Cade Jarrell, who carefully edited the whole manuscript.

I do not want to disremember my gratefulness to the Stead Center of Garrett-Evangelical Theological Seminary and its director Brent Waters, who invited me to deliver my first public lecture on this project while I was revising the original manuscript. The lecture preparation and presentation in September 2016 indeed enhanced the overall quality of this work. Norman Faramelli and George Crowell of the Monetary Policy Interest Group of the Society of Christian Ethics also greatly encouraged me while I was working on this book project. I am also thankful to two academic journals that gave me permissions to use some portions of my articles in this book. Readers are to be informed that a section on Nietzsche in chapter 1 was published in *The Heythrop Journal* 51, no. 3 (May 2010), and another section on Marx in chapter 2 in *Trans-Humanities* 6, no. 1 (February 2013).

Finally, and above all, I would like to offer my deepest gratitude to my spouse, Jaeyeon (Lucy), and our two sons, Daniel and Joshua. Thanks to her continuous encouragement and support as well as her belief in this project from its early stage, I was finally able to finish it. My spiritual and emotional indebtedness to my parents (Byung Won Ahn and Nang Geun Seo) must also be acknowledged. Their encouraging words and unending blessings have renewed my spirit many times. Finally, I dedicate this book to my sister Hea Jin, who has continuously supported my journey with her unending kindness and generosity.

# INTRODUCTION

What we know about debt and our belief in its economy are the result of humanity's grand and ambitious ideological project whose historical origin goes back to the late eighteenth century in Great Britain. What happened in the late eighteenth century? A bold and new idea was born and quickly adopted by powerful imperial nations, according to which the the economic and financial world should be run by its own rules of the game and thus be separated from the social, religious, and political world. Although this grand and ambitious ideological project was not designed and launched by a certain mastermind, a few individuals have played a major role in the development and advancement of this grand and ambitious historical project. At the forefront of this historical and ideological venture lie Adam Smith's 1776 *The Wealth of Nations* and Jeremy Bentham's 1787 *Defence of Usury*. As is well known, with his innovate concepts such as division of labor, productivity, and free markets, Smith lays an ideological foundation of modern capitalism. In his book, he maintains that since the economic system is freestanding, it should be left with substantial autonomy so that it can regulate itself through its own mechanism, famously known as the "invisible hand." In his *Defence of Usury*, meanwhile, Bentham attacks the notion of legal regulation of usury by arguing that it is nothing but a customary convention that can be reduced to a matter of convenience. (We should note that Smith justified the contemporary usury law, and because of that he was severely criticized by Bentham.) Bentham's idea was not adopted during his lifetime, but, soon after his death, the usury law was repealed in England in 1852, and other European nations quickly followed suit.

How has this grand and ambitious ideological project affected us? The short answer to this question is that due to this ideological project, we come to have a delimited and skewed view on debt and its economy. Regrettably, this biased view has also become the ideological foundation of the neoliberal economy of debt. What is wrong with the neoliberal idea of debt? Why is the neoliberal idea of debt problematic? The neoliberal idea of debt is problematic because it is no longer conceived as a morally relevant issue but a morally neutral and thus amoral contractual matter between the creditor and the debtor based on certain terms of a contract. Because of the grand and ambitious ideological project, debt has been largely reduced to a mere contractual issue, separated from its historical, social, and religious background. As the world of economy and finance was separated from its background world of society, religion, and politics (as Smith and Bentham envisaged), debt and its economy were also severed from the same background world, resulting in the creation of an amoral debt and its economy. This grand and ambitious ideological project was in fact one of the sub-projects of the master project known as the Enlightenment. Supplemented by the key philosophical insight of the so-called social contract theory of the Enlightenment thinkers (Hobbes, Locke, and Rousseau), the modern type of debt as an amoral contractual debt was born, and this becomes a key structural foundation of the rise of neoliberalism.

Why should we then care about the rise of the neoliberal economy of debt? What negative impact has it brought modern society and its people? I answer this question by illustrating some cases. In 2013, *NBC News* reported the story of Raymond Chaney, a sixty-six-year-old veteran from Boise, Idaho, who lives off of Social Security benefits. He borrowed from an Internet payday lender in November 2012 after his car broke down and he did not have money to pay for the service charge of $400.[1] The loan was contracted on the fourteen-day loan terms, but since he could not pay it, he renewed it several times. Within months, Chaney ended up taking out multiple loans from different sites, and by February 2013, his payday lenders took every cent of his Social Security payment. Unfortunately, he was even forced to move out of his apartment because of his unpayable debt. According to the news report, he had borrowed nearly $3,000 and owed $12,000. Owing to his unpayable debt, he became homeless, and he had to live in a rescue mission in Boise. Chaney said to the news reporter, "I'm not dumb, but I did a dumb thing."[2] According to Bob Sullivan, the *NBC News* reporter, twelve million Americans are taking these types of high-interest, short-term loans annually. We have so many people like Chaney in our neighborhood. Although Chaney seems to blame himself for taking out the payday loans, should it be a critical fault for him to borrow $400 to pay for his auto repair? If one should end up losing all of his or her Social Security payment and also being kicked out of his or her apartment as the result of an initial debt of $400 whose interest rate is actually 391 percent (adjusted to annual rate),[3] could we say that he or she is living in a good, just, and decent society?

Combined with globalization, the modern neoliberal debt and its amoralized economy are taking a high human toll in many parts of the world. According to a survey by the UN Economic and Social Commission for Asia and the Pacific, more than eighty-six thousand Indian farmers committed suicide during 2001–2005. Why did so many Indian farmers have to commit suicide? Researchers found out that India's shocking rates of suicide are highest in areas with the most debt-ridden farmers who have small lands (less than one hectare) trying to grow "cash crops" such as cotton and coffee, which are highly susceptible to global price fluctuations.[4] The team from Cambridge University's department of sociology and University College London's department of political science say that high-risk farmers have three characteristics: "those that grow cash crops such as coffee and cotton; those with 'marginal' farms of less than one hectare; and those with debts of Rs 300 or more."[5]

The case of India's alarming suicide rates in its impoverished rural areas helps us see how the amoralized economy of debt is now taking a high human toll on the social and global horizon beyond the individual level. According to the *Daily Mail*, GM (genetically modified) seeds are deeply related to the suicide epidemic in India's rural areas.[6] The typical story goes this way. After many farmers were coerced into growing expensive GM crops, they overborrowed money from local moneylenders. These local farmers, after being sucked into GM debts, bought GM seeds instead of traditional cotton seeds. The price difference is quite alarming, though. These farmers pay £10 for one hundred grams of GM seed, compared to less than £10 for one thousand times more of traditional seeds. Beguiled by the promise of future riches, these farmers borrowed money to buy the GM seeds, but when the harvests failed, they ended up with spiraling debts and no income. According to the *Daily Mail*, although pro-GM experts, lobbyists, and prominent politicians claim that GM crops have transformed Indian agriculture—blaming rural poverty, alcoholism, drought, and "agrarian distress" for the epidemic suicidal rates of rural farmers—the typical case of Shankara, who committed suicide when his harvests failed after switching from farming with traditional seeds, shows that the ethics of debt should not simply be reduced to personal responsibility.[7] The problem of debt has indeed become an important social-ethical issue rather than simply a personal responsibility issue.

The U.S. financial crisis of 2007–2008 is another showcase of how neoliberal debt and its amoralized economy are detrimental to society and why we should engage the matters of debt as a social-ethical issue rather than a personal responsibility problem. There is a general consensus blaming subprime mortgages as one of the key factors that triggered the financial crisis. A subprime mortgage is different from a standard prime mortgage debt by its seductive but potentially disastrous lending tactics. For example, mortgage companies offered lowered interest payments or interest-only mortgages over the first several years to entice prospective low-income households to borrow subprime mortgages. These low introductory "teaser" rates reset later with much higher rates, which subsequently resulted in massive default on the part of vulnerable borrowers. By doing so, the mortgage companies actually violated their own lending standards to raise the total amount of securitized finance by compromising fair loan application procedures such as requesting complete financial documentation, which is commonly known as "no doc loans." During the process, subprime borrowers were told not to worry about higher payments because they could refinance the mortgage later into a more standard fixed-rate loan.[8]

The proliferation of subprime mortgages in the U.S. housing and financial market was not accidental. Barry Ritholtz of the *Washington Post* reports that there were structural reasons behind that. In 1998, the Glass-Steagall Act, which separated regular banks from investment banks, was repealed. This made it possible for banks insured by the FDIC (Federal Deposit Insurance Corporation), whose deposits were guaranteed by the government, to engage in highly risky business. Besides this, in 2004, the Securities and Exchange Commission (SEC) changed the leverage rules, replacing the 1977 net capitalization rule's 12-to-1 leverage limit allowing unlimited leverage for five Wall Street banks, including Goldman Sachs, Morgan Stanley, Merrill Lynch, Lehman Brothers, and Bear Stearns. According to Ritholtz, these banks ramped leverage to 20-, 30-, even 40-to-1.[9] Meanwhile, the Office of the Comptroller of the Currency federally preempted state laws that regulate mortgage credit and national banks. As a result of this federal deregulation, national lenders began to sell increasingly risky loan products in those states, which soon entailed the skyrocketing defaults and subsequent foreclosures.[10]

These three showcases demonstrate how detrimental modern neoliberal debt and its amoralized economy can be to humanity as they are increasingly taking a high human toll on a global scale. They also reveal an important point that an appropriate ethics of debt much needed in today's neoliberal world cannot be the kind of personal code of conduct or simple individual responsibilities such as "do not get into debt" or "pay off your own debt." Whether we recognize it or not, personal finance is increasingly influenced and affected by such structural factors as the neoliberal global economy, deregulation of the financial market, macroeconomic failure, and so on. We are living in a world in which debt must always increase because of the neoliberal capitalist logic of economy. Political philosopher Michael Allen Gillespie succinctly captures the structural problem of the debt-ridden neoliberal global economy:

> Debt in the modern world, as we have seen, is inextricably bound up with the use of capital. The use of capital, however, is possible only if it produces more capital, and this can occur only as part of an ever more widespread and even more efficient organization of production for the transformation of things into commodities. The demand for the continual recycling of capital means that debt must always increase.[11]

Defaulted individual debtors may be blamed for their lack of moral and financial integrity, but if we take the structural aspect of the neoliberal economy of debt into consideration, they may be better viewed as the victims of neoliberal economy and its misguided financial policies rather than merely as financial failures. Paradoxical as it may seem, although neoliberalism proliferates the total amount of debt on a global scale, its immense proliferation of debt also makes it necessary that the problem of debt should not simply be reduced to an individual contractual issue between the debtor and the creditor. When I address the need for an ethics of debt in the age of neoliberalism, I thus refer to the need for a *social* ethics of debt whose parameters transcend the so-called personal domain of individual finance, personal integrity, or contractual duty.

What does it mean, then, for us to develop the social ethics of debt? The entire project of this book is to answer this question, and the brief answer is that the social ethics of debt is established by reanchoring or regrounding the amoralized economy of debt in the social world of culture, religion, and communities. The social ethics of debt strongly holds that debt is the social problem that should be governed by the human arrangement based on moral reflections, critical discourses, and mutual agreements rather than by the mechanical or neutral logic of reciprocity or the inanimate law of market fundamentalism. The social ethics of debt attempts to promote an idea that debt should serve humanity, not vice versa. Unfortunately, humanity has been significantly affected by the exponential growth of debt for several decades, especially since 1980s, a period that has also coincided with the rise of the neoliberal global economy. Represented by such political-economic ideologies as deregulation, free trade, privatization, the rule of the market, and reducing government spending, neoliberalism has fundamentally structured a new planetary system, which sociologist Aihwa Ong metaphorically calls "an economic tsunami that is gathering force across the planet."[12]

The social ethics of debt then thematizes the widespread abuse of debt and its related enormous amount of human suffering and moral injury. In this book, thus, I discuss various human rights violations caused by the abuse of debt and its vicious economy in human societies from ancient Rome to modern Greece, from India to the United States, and from South America to Africa. Even today, human rights violations caused by the abusive economy of debt are still rampant in many parts of the world, and this book directly addresses this issue as an urgent social ethical problem. In confronting the widespread abuse of debt, I try not to lose one of the main focuses of this book, that underneath the global phenomena of the abuse of debt lies an ideological and philosophical underpinning that provides a quasi-moral justification to the creation of an amoral world of debt and its economy. From a critical-ethical perspective, thus, I try to focus on deconstructing this ideological and philosophical underpinning while addressing rampant abuses of debt that have become a hallmark of neoliberalism.

What is this ideological and philosophical underpinning, and what does this have to do with the abuse of debt? The key ideological and philosophical underpinning of neoliberal debt is that as an amoral entity, the problem of debt is exclusively governed by the economic logic of reciprocity. This logic itself becomes a pseudo-moral code of neoliberal debt substituting for any historical, cultural, or religious moral ethos of debt. Such an ideological amoralization of the economic logic of reciprocity lies at the heart of the neoliberal economy of debt. Since debt is commonly contracted between the debtor and the creditor, giving rise to the sense of indebtedness on the part of the debtor, the relationship between the debtor and the creditor is also affected and even shaped by the same amoral spirit of the economy of debt. The abuse of debt then becomes inevitable when the creditor takes advantage of this pseudo-moral code as leverage against the debtor, who cannot but borrow money on risky terms because of the lack of other financial options.

One should note that once the logic of reciprocity is amoralized as a pseudo-morality of the neoliberal economy of debt, all debtors or creditors are treated indiscriminately. The economic logic of neoliberal debt is then effectuated in such a way that it does not matter who the debtor or the creditor is, how the debt has been contracted, or how the debt will be paid back. This logic especially reduces all individual borrowers, who have different personalities, backgrounds, and narratives, to the same group of people identified as debtors without considering their particular situations or contexts. According to this logic, all debtors are indiscriminately equal in the sense they are equally liable to pay their debts and also equally guilty if their debts are unpaid. Of course, this does not mean that I am arguing for discriminatory treatment of debtors according to their social rank, gender, race, or the like.[13] This would be a diabolical infringement of justice. What I am pointing out here is that the neoliberal economy of debt fails to do justice to debt by turning a blind eye to the other core aspect of debt—that is, the story aspect of debt. As illustrated above, almost all debts have their stories, and they should matter in understanding the problem of debt in a more holistic way. Indeed, along with the logic of reciprocity, story comprises two essential aspects of debt (a more detailed description of the story aspect of debt is provided in chapter 6).

In this book I argue that a more holistic social ethics of debt is established by reintegrating these two essential elements of debt: logic and story. From the perspective of a more holistic ethics of debt, the neoliberal concept of debt is problematic because, by neglecting the story aspect of debt, it has enervated the moral ethos of debt, rendering it as a matter of mere contract and mechanical calculation. An amoralized economy of debt has been subject to many forms of the abuse of debt by unscrupulous creditors of the neoliberal world. This abuse has been done sometimes even to the extent of destabilizing the whole economic system itself. The neoliberal concept of debt has also reduced the rich and thick meaning of credit to a mere obverse of debt. The rich moral meaning of credit, which has not only economic and political significance but also religious and symbolic importance, has been radically thinned out by the neoliberal amoralization of debt and its economy. This is the reason why I am arguing that we should reconstruct the social ethics of debt by reanchoring and regrounding the amoralized economy of debt back into the social world of culture, religion, and morals. The story aspect of debt should not be dominated or even colonized by its counterpart—the logic aspect; instead, the logic aspect of debt should be reconciled and reintegrated with the story aspect in a flexible and balanced way.

To develop a more holistic ethics of debt against the backdrop of the neoliberal global economy of debt, I adopt an in-depth interdisciplinary ethical exploration. In my research and reflection, I have come to realize that the construction of a more holistic ethics of debt calls for not only the reanchoring and regrounding of the economy of debt back into the social world of culture, religion, and community, but also the collection and integration of all available moral thoughts and inspirations to cope with the colonizing power of an ever-rising neoliberal economy of debt. Today's neoliberal global society is now constantly challenged to cope with various ethical issues, whose scope and magnitude are incomparable to those of the premodern world in significance and complexity. This changing context requires us to engage them in a different way with a different mindset. For instance, the enormity and ubiquity of neoliberal debt and the myriad forms of its creation and recreation cannot be properly contained or controlled by any single ethical system such as utilitarianism, Kantian deontology, virtue ethics, and so on. The neoliberal problem of debt is too big to be covered by any single ethical paradigm. In this respect, I attempt to engage various ethical traditions and schools to develop a more holistic ethics of debt, which includes not only the ethical ideas of anthropology, philosophy, and economy but also those of religions, especially Abrahamic religions (Islam, Judaism, and Christianity). This book is thus intentionally interdisciplinary in its method, and this method is adopted to establish a more holistic ethics of debt.

This book is composed of two parts. While the first part (chapters 1, 2, and 3) focuses on exploring anthropological and philosophical moral insights for the development of a more holistic ethics of debt, the second part (chapters 4, 5, and 6) engages in Abrahamic religions to appropriate their ethical inspirations. Although each chapter deals with its unique subject matter, all chapters are connected in a way that develops a more holistic ethics of debt. For example, the key anthropological insight of chapter 1 that debt was originally conceived as a form of gift in archaic society becomes a philosophical springboard from which I develop the concept of just debt in chapter 2. The anthropological insight of chapter 1 is further related to chapters 3 and 6, in which I respectively deal with two major questions: How to resolve insolvent debt justly? and Does virtue really matter in developing a more holistic ethics of debt? Chapters 4 and 5 also address key justice issues regarding the problem of debt: Is usury still immoral? and Why should we still, or perhaps even more so, care about the

Jubilee concept in today's neoliberal global society? Despite my stated wish to develop a more holistic ethics of debt, one will find that this book is limited, for instance, in its scope and scale from including a more comprehensive spectrum of religious traditions such as Buddhism and Hinduism. This limitation is simply due to my lack of expertise and capability in those fields. I do hope that other researchers and experts could fill this apparent void, which this book could not satisfy. One needs to be informed as well that the author of this book is a Christian social ethicist of Asian origin who teaches ethics and philosophy in a small liberal arts college in the United States. The primary goal of this book is to develop a more holistic ethics of debt, and, in doing so, I try not to equalize the idea of "holistic" with that of "impartial."

Let me briefly describe how each chapter is composed in light of the common thread of developing a more holistic ethics of debt. In chapter 1, I examine the moral origin of debt through the lens of anthropologists David Graeber's and Marcel Mauss' ethnological and cultural explorations. According to them, the moral origin of debt is deeply related to the moral economy of gift in an archaic society, which is basically the earliest form of society. They help us see that debt was originally conceived as a derivative of the original economy of gift. Debt is fundamentally a problem of human arrangement, not something wholly governed by the so-called scientific economic law of exchange and reciprocity. Based on this anthropological insight, I attempt to deconstruct not only the pervasive *amoral* attitude to the problem of debt but also the widespread abusive economy of debt through a critical engagement with various abusive cases. I also argue that since the institution of gift giving was originally established in the earliest kinship societies to build up social cohesion and solidarity, a more holistic ethics of debt, as a derivative of the moral economy of gift, should be reconstructed in a way to promote the social good of humanity.

In chapter 2 I conceptualize the idea of just debt in conjunction with the critical analysis of the neoliberal phenomenon of "financialization," which has significantly changed the global economy since the 1980s. I first investigate the structural aspect of the global economy of debt by engaging the critical economic theories of Joseph Stiglitz, Thomas Piketty, and neo-Marxist economic theorists with the purpose of uncovering the structural and systemic injustices of the global economy of debt. Against this backdrop, I develop a more holistic ethics of debt by specifically outlining the tripartite qualifications of just debt: "serviceability," "payability," and "shareability." For a debt to be morally constituted, all of these qualifications are to be satisfied. I also develop a new concept of right: the debtor's socioeconomic right to just debt. According to this reconstructive perspective, the creditor's right (to debt payment) turns out to be a prima facie right opposite the debtor's right (to just debt).

In chapter 3 I discuss various cases of debt default and subsequent bankruptcies. By critically engaging in the three categories of debt insolvency—individual, sovereign, and corporate—I develop an argument that, beyond fairness and retribution, what we need in doing justice to various cases of debt insolvency is restorative and relational justice for victimized debtors and affected creditors. On the one hand, no debtor should be under permanent indebted status, and bankruptcy should be designed to give defaulted debtors another chance to start over. On the other hand, no debtors should violate their moral obligation to pay off their debt if they are capable of doing so. In order to do better justice to various cases of debt default, we must also consider that the problem of debt and its default should not be rendered as a mere contractual issue between the creditor and the debtor, because all affected parties and their voices are to be accounted for as well.

In chapter 4 I develop an ethical argument against the widespread rentier economy of debt (such as that of credit card companies) through an in-depth study of Islamic ethics of finance and banking systems. The contemporary movement of Islamic finance is distinguished by two key elements: its ban of all forms of interest, known as *riba*, and its prohibition of what is called *gharar* (speculative transactions). Both concepts render it impossible for Islamic banks to engage in any excessive risk or fraudulent behavior. They also make impossible the use of all conventional derivative instruments in Islamic banking. Since the widespread rentier economy of debt is largely based on and motivated by interest and its premium charge, I hold that governing authorities should critically appropriate key ethical insights of Islamic ethics of finance and banking as they regulate the private sector (commercial or investment banks).

Chapter 5 deals with the ethical issues related to debt relief for HIPCs (heavily indebted poor countries) and the invisible and uncontracted, yet widely acknowledged, ecological debt owed to Third World countries by wealthy creditors such as First World countries and multinational enterprises. In so doing, I critically appropriate Jewish religious traditions and thought, especially the concepts of Sabbath and Jubilee. This chapter has three goals to accomplish: (1) to uncover the ethical insights of the Hebrew concept of Jubilee with regard to the case of HIPCs, (2) to investigate not only the historical origins of debt relief but also its current worldwide civil movement such as Jubilee 2000, and (3) to develop an ethical argument why wealthy First World creditors should consider paying off their ecological debt owed to Third World debtors. By introducing the concept of "debt-for-nature swap" and its exemplary cases, I also illustrate how the Jubilee principle can be creatively implemented in a neoliberal world.

In the final chapter, by responding to the key ethical assessment of the Financial Crisis Inquiry Commission (FCIC) on the cause of the Great Recession of 2007–2008, I attempt to construct a Christian virtue ethics of debt. The 2011 FCIC report identified the essential factors of the financial crisis as credit and housing bubbles, nontraditional mortgages (subprime mortgages), credit ratings, and securitization; it also identified that failure in virtue has been very patent in the crisis, which includes excessive leverage, imprudent risk taking, failure in fiduciary duties, greed, lack of moderation, and fraud. The purpose of this chapter is then to develop a set of moral virtues not only for creditors and debtors but also for those running the financial system as service providers, regulators, and consultants. In so doing, I first critically explore the ideological background of the pervasive lack of virtue in the neoliberal world of finance and then proceed to engage two contemporary theologians, Kathryn Tanner and Stephen H. Webb, who provide a key theological insight in developing a Christian virtue ethics of debt.

## CHAPTER ONE

# THE HISTORY AND TAXONOMY
# OF AMORAL DEBT

## Introduction

Can we imagine a society where there is no debt? Since no one seems to want to be in debt, if we could create a society without debtors, this society would be a lot closer to an ideal one than ours, where all seem to be debtors except for a few lucky ones. We may call this society a debtless society. What is it like to live in this society where no one is in debt? Would a debtless society be a utopia or the kingdom of God? To my knowledge, however, no Western thinkers have yet identified an ideal society as a debtless society, including Karl Marx (1818–1883). Although Western political thinkers have seldom thematized the concept of a debtless society as a viable political vision or goal, Thomas Hobbes (1588–1679) offers us a glimpse of what this society would be like in his book *Leviathan* (1651). It was not his original intention, though, to provide us with a brief but quintessential description of what a debtless society would be like; it was more likely an inadvertent by-product of his philosophical imagination.

Hobbes depicts the society where there is no debt as the state of nature. In the state of nature, men (Hobbes' language) are naturally equal in capacities of mind and body so that even the weakest has enough strength to kill the strongest, "either by secret machination, or by confederacy with others."[1] The state of nature is marked by its lack of a common political power or a governing authority, which effectively leads all its inhabitants to a war-like situation, which he calls "war of every man against every man."[2] The state of nature is further characterized by the total absence of the notions of right and wrong, justice and injustice. According to Hobbes, "Where there is no common Power, there is no Law: where no Law, no Injustice."[3] In the state of nature, force and fraud, the "two cardinal virtues" of war, are prevalent, and its inhabitants are constantly exposed to and motivated by perpetual fear and strife, fed by three psychological causes: competition, diffidence, and glory.[4] In such a condition of war of one against another, Hobbes holds, there is no place for industry, agriculture, navigation, trade; there are no arts, no letters, no civil society, no amenities of civilized living; and, worst of all, there is "continual fear and danger of violent death; and the life of man, solitary, poor, nasty, brutish, and short."[5] I would like to add one crucial item to this "no" list—debt. There is no debt in the state of nature, and thus no one is a debtor to anyone else in this state. Contrary to our initial expectation, according to Hobbes, a debtless society is conceptually illustrated as a violent, unjust, and inhumane society. This society where no one is a debtor to anyone else appears to be far from being a utopia or the kingdom of God.

The absence of attention to debt in the development of the Western political philosophies since the dawn of the Enlightenment and European colonialism is philosophically culminated with the publication of John Rawls' *A Theory of Justice* in 1971. In this hugely influential book, Rawls lays out a conceptual mechanism through which he develops a definitive principle of justice known as "justice as fairness." Drawing on the philosophical insights of the Enlightenment thinkers' social contract theory (Locke, Rousseau, and Kant[6]), he devises a hypothetical situation, known as the "original position," in which a universal principle of justice is hammered out as a result of free individuals' fair and mutual agreement under impartial conditions. He argues that this impartial condition is conceptually possible thanks to the "veil of ignorance." The veil of ignorance is a methodological device that enables all participants of the original position to think from everyone's perspective. According to Rawls, the veil of ignorance makes possible a unanimous agreement on choosing a particular concept of justice by effectively screening individuals' particular aspects, such as their abilities, tastes, positions, and backgrounds, including race, gender, and class. Since these particular aspects would no longer affect the individuals in the original position while they are choosing the principle of justice, it seems evident that the chosen principle of justice will be free from any particular contingencies and thus universal. He also adds that each participant of the original position is not only rational, in the sense of trying best to advance his or her interests in choosing among principles, but also moral, since the idea of a game does not apply here, as each party is not concerned with winning but with getting as many points as possible judged by his or her own system of ends.[7]

Despite the creative methodological breakthrough he develops to uncover the principle of justice from a liberal political tradition, Rawls' original position, like Hobbes' state of nature, is conceived as an ideal type of a debtless society. There is neither a debtor nor an indebted relation in Rawls' original position because the status of a debtor itself is a particular condition to be screened. Of course, one can put himself or herself hypothetically in a debtor's position while he or she is deliberating in the original position, but he or she does so as an impartial individual participant separated from a specific social and structural context of debt. As a result, the principle of justice developed in that hypothetical situation would be only partially conducive to the development of an ethics of debt, or simply inadequate to become a full-fledged ethics of debt due to the lack of a full consideration of social and structural aspects of debt. Since Rawls argues that his theory of justice minds the "basic structure of society," his lack of concern with the problem of debt insinuates that Rawls does not regard debt as one of the key social and structural issues for liberal societies such as the United States and many European countries. Intended or not, the problem of debt has been traditionally marginalized in Western liberal political philosophies and social theories of justice, resulting in the subsequent marginalization of debtors in the structural hierarchy of liberal society.

The first step toward the construction of an ethics of debt is now more than clear. What we need is not only to reconceptualize the problem of debt as a basic social-structural issue in liberal political society but also to demarginalize debtors in the structural hierarchies of both local and global society. As mentioned above, the goal of the philosophical endeavor of developing an ethics of debt should not be about constructing a debtless society. A debtless society can exist only in an imaginative world, and no ethics seems possible where there is no debt; but debt itself is not the source of ethics.

### Deconstructing the *Reductive* Appropriation of Debt

In order to reconceptualize the problem of debt as a basic social-structural issue in liberal political society, we should first demystify debt. Debt has been historically mystified in many different forms by a number of people including philosophers, theologians, politicians, and economists. Among those, two forms are particularly conspicuous: reducing debt to an *amoral* issue and hyperbolizing debt through its *moralization*. I focus on the former in this section, the latter in the following one. The reduction of debt to an amoral issue is enabled when the problem of debt is separated from its historical, cultural, political, or structural context. When debt is entirely decontextualized from its complex context, then no matter what happens to debtors and creditors or between themselves, debt simply becomes a matter of individual responsibility to repay. The moral character of an individual debtor is no longer defined by who he or she is but rather by whether the debtor pays back his or her debt along with the interest in due time. In that decontextualized situation, a debtor is always potentially inferior to his or her creditor in moral character, and if a situation occurs in which a debt is unpaid, the blame always lies in the debtor rather than in the creditor. In that decontextualized situation, there is no chance for a debtor to be recognized as a victim; a debtor is always a potential culprit or defendant, not a potential victim. The potential victim is always the creditor.

In such a decontextualized situation, debt is commonly totalized by economic or business terms, and the moral aspect of the debtor-creditor relation is largely subsumed by legal codes. In that situation, an ethics of debt is significantly reduced or minimized to a level of individual responsibility of debtors. Ethics is largely privatized in this situation. Before attempting to demystify debt, then, we should first investigate how the problem of debt has been reduced to an amoral status. To do this, we need to rely on social-scientific research and its results. North American anthropologist David Graeber argues in his recent book, *Debt: The First 5,000 Years*, that to develop an ethics of debt we should first look at the real history of debt and review the "forgotten debates about debt" instead of trying to approach it from a certain predetermined or privileged vantage point such as the neoliberal economist point of view.

Graeber first points out that the problem of debt has been a major social-structural issue in human history, and the history of debt tells us that it has been an essential factor in defining humanity's moral and religious ethos:

> For thousands of years, the struggle between rich and poor has largely taken the form of conflicts between creditors and debtors—of arguments about the rights and wrongs of interest payments, debt peonage, amnesty, repossession, restitution, the sequestering of sheep, the seizing of vineyards, and the selling of debtors' children into slavery. . . . Terms like "reckoning" or "redemption" are

only the most obvious, since they're taken directly from the language of ancient finance. In a larger sense, the same can be said of "guilt," "freedom," "forgiveness," and even "sin."[8]

He then moves on to deconstruct one of the key conventional economic doctrines, that money was originally invented to replace the inconvenient barter system, relieving ancient people from having to bring their goods to market. Graeber's argument is worth laying out in detail because he effectively demystifies the "great founding myth of the discipline of economics."[9] Graeber begins his argument by pointing out that economists always develop the story of money with a fantasy world of barter.[10] According to Graeber, this economic myth goes back to Adam Smith, who was deeply influenced by the liberal tradition of philosophers such as John Locke, for whom the main goal of government is to protect citizens' private property. Like Locke, Smith believed that property, money, and markets existed before a political government was established as the foundation of human society. According to Smith, when the division of human labor was thoroughly established at the dawn of human civilization, ancient people began to engage in lives of exchanging: "Every man thus lives by exchanging or becomes in some measure a merchant, and the society itself grows to be what is properly a commercial society."[11]

As more people engaged in the exchange of commodities, the need of currency arose, and different commodities such as salt were employed for this purpose. Eventually, precious metals were widely accepted as currency because of traits such as durability and portability. As Smith writes, "It is in this manner that money has become in all civilized nations the universal instrument of commerce, by the intervention of which goods of all kinds are bought and sold, or exchanged for one another."[12] The creation of money boosted the efficiency of the market economy, entailing its further growth. In book 4, chapter 2 of his *Wealth of Nations*, Smith lays out the key tenet of classical liberal market economies by emphasizing the market's capacity to sustain itself and flourish based on its own mechanism, called the "invisible hand." It is worth quoting this rather long passage:

> As every individual, therefore, endeavours as much as he can both to employ his capital in the support of domestic industry, and so to direct that industry that its produce may be of the greatest value; every individual necessarily labours to render the annual revenue of the society as great as he can. He generally, indeed, neither intends to promote the public interest, nor knows how much he is promoting it. By preferring the support of domestic to that of foreign industry, he intends only his own security; and by directing that industry in such a manner as its produce may be of the greatest value, he intends only his own gain, he is in

this, as in many other cases, led by an invisible hand to promote an end which
was no part of his intention. Nor is it always the worse for the society that it
was no part of it. By pursing his own interest he frequently promotes that of the
society more effectually than when he really intends to promote it.[13]

Given that the market system is working best on its own operative principle, the role of government is largely limited to the protection of the
market system rather than its regulation. According to Graeber, the logical
consequence of this argument is that government should limit itself to
guaranteeing the soundness of the currency, if government should play any
role in monetary affairs. Moreover, by making such an argument, Smith
could insist that "economics is itself a field of human inquiry with its own
principles and laws—that is, as distinct from, say ethics or politics."[14] The
result of the distinction between economics and ethics or politics is the
gradual reduction of debt to an amoral status through the separation of
debt from its social, political, and historical context. Indeed, "economics
is then endowed with laws of its own, de-contextualized, de-historicized,
and dissocialized."[15] As economist Gavin Kennedy argues, modern economists, especially those influenced by the Chicago school of economics,
have played a key role in fortifying the separation between economics and
ethics or politics in the name of neoliberalism. These economists have successfully transformed Smith's metaphor into a neoliberal myth.[16]

How does Graeber attempt to demystify debt? In other words, how
does he attempt to deconstruct the neoliberal economists' decontextualizing, dehistoricizing, and dissocializing reduction of debt to an amoral
status? He launches his grand project by asking a fundamental question
as an anthropologist: What *really* happened at the beginning of human
society? Graeber writes:

> In fact, our standard account of monetary history is precisely backwards. We
> did not begin with barter, discover money, and then eventually develop credit
> system. It happened precisely the other way around. What we now call virtual
> money came first. Coins came much later, and their use spread only unevenly,
> never completely replacing credit systems. Barter, in turn, appears to be largely a
> kind of accidental byproduct of the use of coinage or paper money: historically, it
> has mainly been what people who are used to cash transactions do when for one
> reason or another they have no access to currency.[17]

In an interview in the *Green European Journal*, Graeber emphasizes that
debt historically preceded money. Debt existed before money, which was
created for various governmental purposes such as the need for war or
criminal justice. It seems clear that the genealogical origin of money is not
strictly confined to economic necessity. "Money isn't borne out of economic

necessity *stricto sensu*, but rather from state or proto-state needs."[18] What is the moral significance of Graeber's provocative statement that debt exists before the creation of money and the genealogical origin of money is not necessarily economic?

First, although debt is commonly monetized based on the economic logic of exchange and reciprocity, debt is fundamentally a problem of human arrangement, not something wholly governed by the general (economists would rather use "scientific") economic logic of exchange and reciprocity. The amoral attitude toward the subject of debt is problematic because it tends to consolidate a mistaken view that the problem of debt as a monetary affair should be exclusively governed by the general economic logic of exchange and reciprocity. The amoral attitude also allows the general economic logic to become its own moralistic law. This is how debt (*Shuld*) becomes entangled with guilt (*Shuld*). The reduction of debt to an amoral status eventually makes it possible for the general economic logic of exchange and reciprocity to become a dominant and potentially inhumane moral law. Greaber's following statement is particularly pertinent: "The assumption that everything is governed by the concept of exchange and reciprocity leads one to believe that debt is the real root of morality as debt is the result of balance not being restored. Debt, on the contrary, is a drastic departure from the general laws of exchange and reciprocity."[19] The problem of debt is ultimately a matter of people's moral agreement and belief rather than that of a mechanical logic or law.

How do people's moral agreement and belief about debt differ from the general economic logic of exchange and reciprocity? To answer the question, we need to trace back to the first philosophic consideration of debt presented by Anaximander of Miletus (610–546 B.C.E.). Tying debt to the very being of all things, he says, "The beginning of all beings is the unbounded and from there is the coming to be of all things and into there is also their passing away according to necessity and they pay each other their justified debt and penance for their injustice according to the law of time."[20] The injustice Anaximander refers to is the ontological or phenomenological nature of debt that, being limited and bounded, all things cannot but exist only by displacing other things and occupying or embodying the matter that hitherto constituted something else. Since they exist only through displacing, consuming, or destroying another being, all things are in fact in debt. Indeed, for Anaximander, "to be is to be indebted."[21] Michael Allen Gillespie thus writes, "This is the injustice Anaximander refers to, and the injustice that everything must atone for by paying its debt, that is, by passing away, being displaced, destroyed, or consumed by other things."[22] While people's moral agreement and belief about debt are grounded on such a philosophical insight of the very being of all things, the general economic logic of exchange and reciprocity is constituted by economists' narrow focus on the calculative aspect of economic transactions by decontextualizing, dehistoricizing, and dissocializing them.

The general economic logic of exchange and reciprocity of neoliberal economic view is problematic because it tends to reduce the problem of debt to an amoral status. When debt becomes an amoral issue, then it gets much easier for those managers and keepers of the financial market to manipulate debt since they are insulated from any moral and ethical critiques as well as from the government's political interventions. Although classical and neoliberal market economists typically argue that the separation of economics and politics is more efficient in terms of bringing a greater economic good to society and thus the government's hands-off approach to the market economy is more desirable, they seldom attend to the historical fact that the market economy and its system have been largely disrupted by their own guardians and keepers rather than by those in the political sector. The neoliberal economists' fear of government intervention has been proved to be groundless. Moreover, history often demonstrates that politics is the solution to various economic disruptions caused by the unregulated market economy and its agents. Interestingly enough, it was Adam Smith himself who actually was concerned about possible market disruptions by its own agents themselves. Gavin Kennedy correctly points out, "In fact, Smith showed that the main 'interference' with 'free competition' came from the 'merchants and manufactures' themselves, for legislators, and those who influenced them, to legalize or award monopolies and trade protection which were against the public interest in general and the interests of consumers in particular."[23] Unfortunately, Smith's concern has proven to be real and more serious, not just in his time, but more so in the twenty-first century neoliberal capitalist economy.

The case of U.S. financier Bernard (Bernie) L. Madoff is one of the most recent and well-known examples of how the financial market is actually disrupted not by political intervention but by its own agents. In 2009, Madoff was jailed for 150 years for a Ponzi scheme through which he defrauded his clients of billions of dollars. According to Lee F. Monaghan and Micheal O'Flynn, Madoff's Ponzi scheme is not another rotten apple case, because such magnitude (U.S.$65 billion) would not be possible without the background history of deregulation, desupervision, and established institutional mechanisms of mass deception.[24] Monaghan and O'Flynn write, "In short, the growth of Madoff's scheme was inextricably linked to the processes of deregulation and desupervision, which enabled 'control fraud' to flourish within the FIRE [financial, insurance and real estate] sector."[25]

Since the 1980s, neoliberal economic policies have been introduced in the United Kingdom (Margaret Thatcher) and the United States (Ronald Reagan) deregulating the financial markets. Some of these deregulating policies include the Garn-St. Germain Depository Institutions Act of 1982, which not only deregulated savings and loan associations but also allowed banks to provide adjustable-rate mortgage loans, and the Riegle-Neal Interstate Banking and Branching Efficiency Act of 1994, which eliminated previous restrictions on interstate banking and branching. As briefly touched in the introduction, in 1996, the Federal Reserve Board allowed bank holding companies to own investment bank affiliates with up to 25 percent of their business in securities underwriting by shattering the Glass-Steagall Act of 1933. In 2004, the SEC proposed a system of voluntary regulation, which eventually allowed investment banks to hold less capital in reserve and increase leverage.[26]

Madoff's Ponzi scheme is the tip of the iceberg—the iceberg of neoliberal global financialization, which I discuss further in chapter 2. After all, as economists Monaghan and O'Flynn suggest, "The fictitious finance capital . . . necessitates mass deception, secrecy, obfuscation and, eventually, scapegoating," which they also call "Madoffization."[27] Madoff's Ponzi scheme demonstrates that an amoral attitude to the problem of debt is never neutral economically as well as morally. The amoral attitude to the problem of debt espoused by neoliberal economists was an inevitable by-product of their economic doctrine of the separation between economics and ethics or politics. Unfortunately, though, the reduction of debt to an amoral status turns out to be more problematic than conducive to the capitalist economy itself.

At the heart of this reduction lies people's uncritical appropriation of the putative law of the market system operating by the general economic logic of exchange and reciprocity. Although many agents of the economic sector propose the separation between economics and politics, they actually collaborate with the agents of politics through connections and lobbies to promote their own economic benefit instead of upholding the common good of society. In doing so, they transformed debt into an amoral entity so that they could neutralize any moral aspects attached to the widespread manipulation and abuse of debt and its economy by effectively decontextualizing, dehistoricizing, and dissocializing them.

It is important, then, for us to see clearly that everything is not governed by the economic logic of exchange and reciprocity. Debt is not

merely a monetary affair; it is also a human and social affair that should
not be entirely dominated by the rigid law of exchange and reciprocity.
Graeber thus suggests that we should replace "the idea that exchange and
reciprocity are at the heart of human activities by a triad consisting of
three principles—communism, exchange, and hierarchy."[28] Among these,
his concept of communism seems particularly important. He argues that
there are many examples of human behavior that demonstrate that a part
of human relations is founded on the principle of "from each according
to their abilities, to each according to their needs." Communism is distinguished by not involving reciprocity or equivalence. He says, "If you
are in the process of repairing a broken pipe and you ask your colleague,
'pass me the wrench,' the latter doesn't ever respond by 'and what do I get
for it?' even if you are working for Goldman Sachs or Exxon Mobile. . . .
This baseline form of communism constitutes the raw material of sociality,
recognition of our interdependence."[29] The famous parable of the workers
in the vineyard in the New Testament (Matt 20:1-16)[30] is a perfect example
that the economic world does not have to be an amoral world to function.
At the end of the day, all day workers, including those who were hired at
the last minute, have enough to put food on their family table the next day.
No contract was violated, and no one got hurt because of the last-minute
worker's receiving the same wage.

## Deconstructing the *Hyperbolic* Appropriation of Debt

Above I have attempted to dismantle the reductive appropriation of the
economy of debt (done mostly by classical and neoliberal economists) that
transforms debt into an amoral entity by critically engaging Graeber's historical analysis of debt. In this section, I attempt to deconstruct the other
form of this appropriation—the hyperbolic appropriation of the economy
of debt—by critically rereading Friedrich Nietzsche's thesis on the genealogy of morals. The latter is different from the former in that while the
reductive appropriation of debt radically decontextualizes, dehistoricizes,
and dissociates debt from ethics and politics by turning it into an amoral
entity, the hyperbolic appropriation of the economy of debt attempts to
impose the potentially abusive economic logic of exchange and reciprocity
on all human relations and institutions beyond the boundaries of the market in order to exploit, subjugate, or even enslave debtors. In this respect,
the hyperbolic appropriation of the economy of debt is morally problematic because it often functions through a hyperbolic abduction of the rigid
economic logic of exchange and reciprocity.

Friedrich Nietzsche is arguably the first modern Western philosopher who was keenly aware of the potentially abusive economic logic of
exchange and reciprocity and thus tried to uncover its ideological origin
and moral pathology through his method of genealogical critique. In
particular, he was concerned about religion and morality, believing that
Western Christianity is the main culprit to be blamed for its hyperbolic
appropriation of the economy of debt in the fields of religion and morals.
How does he, then, unravel the religious hyperbolic appropriation of the
economy of debt? He first differentiates morals from moralization. While
the former is natural and healthy, the latter is nonnatural and pathological.
For him, Christian morals are incubated by early priests who attempted to
appropriate the rigid and potentially abusive economic logic of exchange
and reciprocity to provide religious and moral meaning to their followers.
It is worth analyzing in detail Nietzsche's *On the Genealogy of Morals* to see
more clearly how the skewed economy of debt would have been allegedly
appropriated by the early priests for their own sake, leaving the Western
world and its descendants in a permanent pathological situation morally
as well as religiously.

Nietzsche develops his theory by beginning with a discussion of the
pervasive moral pathology realized in the forms of "guilt" and "bad conscience." In accounting for the pathology of these moral symptoms, he
illustrates how the hidden economy of debt works. He first distinguishes
the dual aspects of the moral pathology: the bad conscience caused by what
he calls the "internalization of instincts" and the "indebtedness to god."
According to Nietzsche, if natural instincts, which are originally amoral
in themselves, cannot be discharged outwardly because of social codes,
they will eventually turn inward. He summarizes this secular origin of bad
conscience as follows: "Hostility, cruelty, joy in persecuting, in attacking,
in change, in destruction—all this turned against the possessors of such
instincts: that is the origin of the 'bad conscience.'"[31] For him, this aspect
of bad conscience is indeed the moral psychology of a "tamed" person in
a civilized world. He then goes on further to say that there is another origin of bad conscience, which is essentially linked to the genealogy of god
hatched in the "original tribal community." At the dawn of human history,
the living generation began to sense its indebtedness toward the preceding
generations, especially toward the earliest, who were alleged to establish the
tribe as the founding fathers and mothers. Since the tribe could not exist
without the sacrifices and accomplishment of their ancestors, later generations have to "pay them back" with equivalent sacrifices and accomplish-
ments. This duty of ancestral respect is the debt that can potentially grow

as the tribe further flourishes. He epitomizes his argument, saying, "The fear of the ancestor and his power, the consciousness of indebtedness to him, increases, according to this kind of logic, in exactly the same measure as the power of the tribe itself increases, as the tribe itself grows ever more victorious, independent, honored, and feared."[32] Later, Nietzsche holds, the ancestor is transfigured into a god out of this fear, and history has shown that the guilty feeling of indebtedness (*Schuldgefühl*) to god continues to grow for several millennia, and the Christian God becomes the ultimate creditor of human indebtedness.

In section 21 of the second treatise of *On the Genealogy of Morals*, Nietzsche attempts to connect the notion of the moral psychology of bad conscience and the genealogical concept of god through the moralization of debts and duties. Nietzsche develops his argument by stating that the indebtedness to god is "pushed back" into the bad conscience. What does this mean? According to Mathias Risse, to uncover the meaning of "pushing back," we need a third element in addition to the indebtedness toward ancestors and gods, and the early form of the bad conscience: "The joint presence of these two elements by itself does not lead to the moralization of the notions of debts and duty. The third element is Christianity, and it is through the interaction of Christianity with the early form of the bad conscience and the indebtedness that the bad conscience as a feeling of guilt arises."[33] As a result of the interaction with Christianity, the "pushing back" of indebtedness into bad conscience is radically transformed into a much more serious and deep-seated sentiment of guilt. The original form of bad conscience is, then, transformed into a life-denying depressive moral pathology due to the inward "pushing back" of the indebtedness.

Nietzsche's provocative thesis is something that theologians and religious ethicists are to consider regarding its theological or ethical significance, but it is not my interest to engage them here (I have done this in my other work[34]). I am introducing Nietzsche only because his *On the Genealogy of Morals* demonstrates a classic exemplification of how the hyperbolic appropriation of the economy of debt is played out in human history, entailing a detrimental moral threat to humanity. One of the common features of the hyperbolic appropriation of the economy of debt is that debtors are normally exploited, subjugated, and even enslaved by creditors because of the abusive economic logic of exchange and reciprocity. This logic is absolutized by creditors and then imposed on debtors in the name of juridical justice. As we shall see in the following, history has shown us that the hyperbolic appropriation of the economy of debt has been prevalent in virtually every culture and society, and humanity has long been abused by its imposition. Since its cases have always been interlinked with the exploitation, subjugation, and enslavement of humanity, its deconstruction is duly required as we develop an ethics of debt.

Historically, debt bondage and chattel slavery have been the most common and injurious cases of the hyperbolic appropriation of the economy of debt. Debt bondage was "quite normal" in archaic societies,[35] and even though *nexum* (a debt bondage) was abolished in 326 B.C.E. in ancient Rome, "evidence from later Roman history suggests that individuals continued to be reduced to slavery as the result of their inability to pay off their debts."[36] According to Alessandro Stanziani and Gwyn Campbell, chattel slavery and debt bondage coexisted from ancient Rome to the modern world. "In ancient Rome, medieval Afro-Eurasia and the early modern and modern Mediterranean, African and Trans-Atlantic worlds, chattel slavery and debt bondage coexisted and sometimes transmuted one into the other."[37] Recent historical studies also show that contrary to the traditional view that slavery disappeared in medieval times, debt bondage, serfdom, and slavery existed in medieval western Europe.[38]

If one thinks that our modern world is finally free from any types of debt bondage or chattel slavery, one is mistaken. A 2014 global survey conducted by Australia-based rights organization Walk Free Foundation estimates that there are 35.8 million people living in some form of modern slavery.[39] This number is higher than other attempts such as that of the United Nations (UN), which estimates that almost 21 million people are victims of forced labor. Debt bondage is the most common form of slavery in the modern world,[40] and it is typically characterized by the hyperbolic appropriation of the economy of debt. Let me briefly illustrate how debt bondage has to do with the hyperbolic appropriation of the economy of debt. The 1956 Supplementary Convention (Section I, Article I) defines debt bondage as "the status or condition arising from a pledge by a debtor of his personal services or of those of a person under his control as security for a debt, if the value of those services as reasonably assessed is not applied towards the liquidation of the debt or the length and nature of those services are not respectively limited and defined."[41] Debt bondage is basically an immoral institution because at the center of its operation lies an egregious abuse of the economy of debt that takes advantage of the debtors' lack of power and education and also their innocent concession to the abusive debt economy. As is often the case, by rendering the service or labor to repay the debt and the service's duration undefined, creditors put debtors under a permanent enslaved condition. What is worse, the debt is often passed down to subsequent generations, thereby enslaving the debtor's children.

In *Understanding Global Slavery*, Kevin Bales points out that debt bondage is increasingly affecting migrant workers by victimizing them through the vicious abuse of the economy of debt: "This more recent manifestation of debt bondage experienced by migrant workers is similar to that experienced by bonded laborers who work on their creditors' land."[42] Unscrupulous creditors first arrange a spurious debt contract by offering them an advance, but later they render bonded laborers and migrant workers unable to terminate the contract by manipulating the debt contract. Indeed, one of the most common abusive tactics that creditors incorporate is to adjust interest rates upward or simply add interest without informing the bonded laborers. The exorbitant interest rates and the debtors' powerlessness render them vulnerable to the creditors' abusive tactics. In this way, the basic human rights of millions of adults and children are rampantly compromised. In doing so, the creditors' sole purpose is to put the bonded laborers and migrant workers under permanent slave-like conditions.

Unfortunately these creditors commonly menace these debtors either by using physical violence or by mental abuse. When they do so, they justify their immoral behavior by saying that they have the right to do so because the debtors failed to repay their debt. As is evident, however, these creditors blatantly distort the economy of debt for their unjustifiable economic purpose. It was the creditors' unjustifiable plot that actually made these debtors unable to pay their debt. These debtors are not able to pay their debt not because they lack the capacity but because they are set up in such a way. This is a classic paradigm of how the hyperbolic appropriation of the economy of debt works in the real world by dehumanizing and demoralizing debtors. Recent scholarship[43] demonstrates that the hyperbolic appropriation of the economy of debt has been virtually ubiquitous throughout human history. For example, the coolie trade during the nineteenth and early twentieth century exhibits that many immigrants to California from South China were bound to repay their debt at an interest rate of 4–8 percent compounded monthly, causing many to take years to repay their debt.[44] The cases of debt slaves in old Korea, debt servitude or prostitution in Japan during the Edo period (1600–1868), and the slavery among Arabian Gulf pearl divers all share the same aspect of the hyperbolic appropriation of the economy of debt.[45] These cases demonstrate that the debtors are not all the same; a lot of them are actually victims of an unjustly manipulated structure. Thus, what is due to these victims is not moral blame or legal punishment but social justice and public support.

It is also important for us to see that the hyperbolic appropriation of the economy of debt is effectuated in international relations as well. Michael Northcott summarizes how the economy of debt is hyperbolically appropriated in international relations as follows:

> Debt bondage has been the key mechanism for enriching the five richest countries, and for impoverishing the ten poorest. Countries in hock to Western creditors have no choice but to do their bidding: namely, to open up their markets to Western goods; to restrict the production of value-added goods that compete with Western exports; to accept appropriation by foreign conglomerates of their most valuable state assets; and to skew their economies in ways which satisfy the demands of their creditors. We no longer have debtors' prisons for people; we have them for countries instead.[46]

The so-called North-South relations cannot be fully understood without the consideration of the hyperbolic appropriation of the economy of debt on a global scale. The international hyperbolic appropriation of the economy of debt is commonly played out in such a way that when the debtor country is unable to pay its debt, the creditor country takes advantage of the situation by taking over valued natural resources or profitable industrial entities of the debt countries, demanding a so-called restructuring. This global trend is problematic because Southern debt crises largely originated in the political economy of the North. According to Rafael Reuveny and William Thompson, although the North does not necessarily create the debt crises in the South "by design," the economic processes of the North are responsible for creating situations in which Southern debt problems become widespread. Reuveny and Thompson write, "In this respect, Southern debt crises are mislabeled. They are registered most painfully in the South, but they are crises in which both North and South share culpability."[47] Given that the mechanism of Southern debt crises is structurally interlinked with the political economy of the North, the North is thus required to engage Southern debt crises as a morally responsible political party rather than attempting to take advantage of the situation to exploit the South's vulnerable situation.

How is it possible to dismantle the hyperbolic appropriation of the economy of debt? We first need to see that the hyperbolic appropriation is based on two taken-for-granted assumptions. First, all human interactions are forms of exchange. Since exchange is based on the logic of reciprocity, there is no higher logic that governs human interactions than the logic of reciprocity. The logic of reciprocity can be cloaked in different terms such as the reciprocity of "supply and demand," the reciprocity of "give and take," the reciprocity of "borrow and return," and the reciprocity of "credit and debt." The hyperbolic appropriation of the economy of debt is then indispensably related to the absolutizing view that all human interactions are forms of exchange. Dismantling the hyperbolic appropriation would then mean to deabsolutize such a blanket view. Graeber shows us how this deconstructive work can be possible. According to him, we should first engage French anthropologist Claude Lévi-Strauss' structuralism because he lays out an anthropological foundation that human life could be imagined as consisting of three spheres—language, kinship, and economics—and all these three are governed by the same fundamental law of reciprocity.[48] Commenting on Lévi-Strauss' structuralist view on human life, Graeber develops his critical argument, saying, "There are relationships [such as the relation between mother and child] that seem clearly moral but appear to have nothing to do with reciprocity."[49] He succinctly captures his argument as follows: "My point is that such forms of radical equality and radical inequality do exist in the world, that each carries within it its own kind of morality, its own way of thinking and arguing about the rights and wrongs of any given situation, and these moralities are entirely different than that of tit-for-tat exchange."[50]

The second taken-for-granted assumption implied by the hyperbolic appropriation is that there is nothing that cannot be up for exchange or sale. Is it really a moral truth that anything can be up for exchange or sale? While Goethe's *Faust* seems to exemplify that a human soul can be up for exchange or sale, Shakespeare's *The Merchant of Venice* satirizes that even a pound of human flesh can also be up for exchange or sale. What happens is not necessarily what is morally right. For example, it is not morally right for a society to allow commercial trade in human organs. If a certain exchange or sale would damage or deform bodily or spiritual integrity, it is hardly seen to be morally right despite the injured party's nominal agreement. As seen above, various types of debt bondage demonstrate how destructive and dehumanizing this second assumption can be when it is aligned with the dangerous logic of reciprocity. Indeed, because of this alignment, humanity has been deserted, abused, and violated throughout history. Thus, the dismantlement of the hyperbolic appropriation is laid out in a loud and clear voice that not all things are up for exchange and sale, because there are certain things that should never be up for exchange and sale. As is well known, these certain things are exemplified in the form of the so-called negative rights of the Universal Declaration of Human Rights (1948) and other treatises such as International Covenant on Civil and Political Rights (1976). Without doubt, to dismantle the hyperbolic appropriation in a meaningful way, public policy development and its enforcement on both national and global horizons are required. I discuss the public policy issues later in the following chapters.

## Reconstructing the *Moral* Economy of Debt

How could we then reconstruct a moral economy of debt? What is the moral principle for the reconstruction of the moral economy of debt as an alternative to the *reductive* or *hyperbolic* appropriation of the economy of debt, which I deconstructed above? I find a key insight for the reconstruction of the moral economy of debt in Marcel Mauss' *The Gift: Forms and Functions of Exchange in Archaic Societies.* What does Mauss' *The Gift* have to do with the reconstruction of the moral economy of debt? In this book, through a wider anthropological study of archaic societies, Mauss focuses one important set of phenomena called "total phenomenon"—a form of economic system based on gift giving—which is in theory "voluntary, disinterested and spontaneous, but [is] in fact obligatory and interested."[51] Mauss and his research team confine their study to certain chosen areas such as "Polynesia, Melanesia, and to certain well-known codes."[52] The significance of this study lies in its discovery that one of the most important of spiritual mechanisms (or social beliefs) among archaic societies is "the one which obliges us to make a return gift for a gift received."[53]

Mauss then concludes that the spirit of gift exchange may be considered to be characteristic of societies "which have passed the phase of 'total prestation' (between clan and clan, family and family) but have not yet reached the stage of pure individual contract, the money market, sale proper, fixed price, and weighed and coined money."[54] It is not, however, Mauss' point that the archaic economic system of gift giving is no longer relevant to us because modern society has passed the stage of gift exchange. On the contrary, Mauss argues that some elements of this system have survived in modern societies, and it would be erroneous to say that a modern person has become an "economic animal" concerned only with calculation and gain. According to Mauss, although modern Western societies "quite recently turned man into an economic animal . . . we are not yet all animals of the same species."[55]

Mauss goes against "frigid utilitarianism," arguing that the mere pursuit of individual ends is harmful not just to the ends of peace of the whole, but also to individuals themselves. He thus says, "The best economic procedure is not to be found in the calculation of individual needs."[56] How would he respond to the reductive and hyperbolic appropriations of debt? He would definitely go against the reductive appropriation of the economy of debt because economics should not be detached from morality and religion; he would also go against the hyperbolic appropriation of the economy of debt because, as he would agree, not all things are up for economic exchange or sale based on individual needs and calculations.

Mauss concludes his study by suggesting that "we should return to the old and elemental."[57] He clearly believes that there is a better society compared to other types, and we are supposed to strive for that. "Social insurance, solicitude in mutuality or co-operation, in the professional group and all those moral persons called Friendly Societies, are better than the mere personal security guaranteed by the nobleman to his tenant, better than the mean life afforded by the daily wage handed out by managements, and better even than the uncertainty of capitalist savings."[58] According to him, then, the motives of human actions should be "the joy of giving in public, the delight in generous artistic expenditure, the pleasure of hospitality in the public or private feast," rather than those determined by the individualist economy of pure interest.[59]

Regarding the construction of the moral economy of debt, what we could learn from Mauss is that although "the economy of gift exchange fails to conform to the principles of so-called natural economy or utilitarianism,"[60] its function in archaic societies was never separated from the economy of debt. For Mauss, as Yonatan Sagiv points out, "a gift given as a loan, a gift that needs to be reciprocated, can still be called a gift."[61] The close connection between the moral economy of gift exchange and the economy of debt is clearly demonstrated when the receiver or givee is not able to return to the giver with something of equivalent worth. He writes, "The obligation of worthy return is imperative. Face is lost forever if it is not made or if equivalent value is not destroyed."[62] In some cases (e.g., the Kwakiutl, Haida, and Tsimshian), the sanction for this obligation to repay is "enslavement for debt." Mauss thus writes, "It is an institution comparable in nature and function to the Roman *nexum*. The person who cannot return a loan or potlatch loses his rank and even his status of a free man."[63] Why is then the close connection between the moral economy of gift exchange and the economy of debt important in developing a more holistic and authentic ethics of debt, which is distinguished from its reductive or hyperbolic type?

One should first note that the moral economy of gift exchange is not merely interlinked with the economy of debt. There is an order between the two, which may be analogically compared to John Rawls' "lexical order." Just as the first principle of justice should be satisfied prior to the second, in the order of an ethical construction, the moral economy of gift exchange genealogically precedes the economy of debt. In other words, an ethics of debt is conceived as a secondary or a derivative kind to the original moral economy of gift. Mauss does not clearly state this in his book, but he implies this by saying that when the moral economy of gift exchange is not working (when the givee fails to return with something of equivalent worth), the economy of debt kicks in by holding the disgraced givee accountable for his or her inaction or inability.

What does it mean specifically that the moral economy of gift exchange precedes the economy of debt, thereby rendering it possible that an ethics of debt is enabled as a secondary or a derivative kind to the moral economy of gift? The primary significance of this discovery is that the moral ethos of the economy of debt is derived from the underlying ethical ideals or moral values of the economy of gift exchange. What are these underlying ethical ideals or moral values of the economy of gift exchange? Marshall Sahlins offers us an insightful answer to this question. In his article "The Spirit of the Gift," Sahlins argues that Mauss substitutes the exchange of everything between everybody for Hobbes' war of every man against every man.[64] What does this mean? According to Sahlins' interpretation, in an archaic society in which no political authority is yet established, the first consent made among the people is not to authority or even to unity; rather, they consented to adopt total prestation (constant and large-scale gift exchanges) among themselves. This is how the three obligations of archaic society—gift must be given, gift must be received, and gift must be reciprocated—became the social foundation of maintaining peace among themselves.

The moral significance of total prestation is that it helped archaic society to establish and maintain peace rather than to fall into Hobbesian social chaos. Sahlins thus writes, "The gift is alliance, solidarity, communion—in brief, peace, the great virtue that earlier philosophers, Hobbes notably, had discovered in the State."[65] For Sahlins, then, the original ethical ideals or moral values of the archaic economy of gift are fundamentally social in that it prevented archaic society from falling into the Hobbesian "war of all against all" by enabling a necessary social cohesion and solidarity through reciprocal gift giving. "The gift is the primitive way of achieving the peace that in civil society is secured by the State."[66] In this respect, the gift replaces the traditional social contract of Hobbes, Rousseau, and Locke, for whom the social contract had been first of all a pact of society. Sahlins thus says, "Where in the traditional view the contract was a form of political exchange, Mauss saw exchange as a form of political contract. The famous 'total prestation' is a 'total contract.' "[67]

Mauss' anthropological study of gift exchange in archaic society offers us an important anthropological-ethical insight in developing an ethics of debt in that "every exchange, as it embodies some coefficient of sociability, cannot be understood in its material terms apart from its social terms."[68] As a shadow economy of gift exchange in archaic society, debt is expected to embody some coefficient of sociability, which Sahlins exemplifies as forms of social cohesion, solidarity, communion, or social alliance. These social values are what comprise the ethical ideals or moral values of the archaic economy of gift exchange and its shadow economy of debt, and these ideals and values are what anthropologist and sociologist Pierre Bourdieu calls "symbolic capital." Lewis Hyde also succinctly summarizes how gifts contribute to the creation of cohesive society as follows: "If we take the synthetic power of gifts, which establish and maintain the bonds of affection between friends, lovers, and comrades, and if we add to these a circulation wider than a binary give-and-take, we shall soon derive society, or at least those societies—family, guild, fraternity, sorority, band, community—that cohere through faithfulness and gratitude."[69] Thus, if an ethics of debt is conceived as a secondary or derivative kind to the original moral economy of gift, it signifies that the economy of debt is expected to promote such ethical values as social cohesion, solidarity, communion, or social alliance as well. Or, at least, the economy of debt should not violate or disrupt such ethical ideals and moral values.

One, however, should note that there may be some possible challenges to the ethical endeavor of conceiving an ethics of debt as a secondary or derivative kind to the original moral economy of gift. What are these possible challenges? First, the "ambiguity" challenge. According to Pierre Bourdieu, "The major characteristic of the experience of the gift is, without doubt, its ambiguity."[70] He argues that the experience of the gift is ambiguous because it has dual aspects. While the gift can be experienced "as a refusal of self-interest and egoistic calculation" (a gratuitous and unrequited gift), "it never entirely excludes awareness of the logic of exchange."[71] In this respect, he claims that the truth of the gift is always dualistic. The gap between these two truths of the gift may pose a conceptual challenge to our ethical endeavor to conceive an ethics of debt as a secondary or derivative kind to the moral economy of gift. How could we then account for the gap between these two truths of the gift?

According to Bourdieu, this gap is overcome by facilitating and favoring a kind of communal self-deception, which is "a lie told to oneself, as the condition of the coexistence of recognition and misrecognition of the logic of the exchange."[72] By "recognition," he means that everyone recognizes the phenomenon of gift as an exchange; by "misrecognition," he means that everyone also experiences gift as if he or she does not know the rule of exchange. The lapse of time (between the initial gift and the countergift) is important because it helps people (mis)recognize the countergift as a genuine gift (which has nothing to do with the logic of exchange). He thus argues that the gift is one of those social acts whose social logic cannot become "common knowledge." He also adds, "It is a common knowledge that cannot be made public, an 'open secret' which cannot become public knowledge, an official truth, publicly proclaimed."[73] This is why Bourdieu introduces the idea of "collective self-deception" to account for the ambiguous phenomenon of gift. The economy of gift is then captured as the "anti-economic economy," which denotes the denial of interest and calculation.[74] For Bourdieu, the collective self-deception seems inevitable as a "common miscognition" because it renders a "social universe" possible, in which generous conduct (such as gift giving) presents itself as "the only thing to do," not as "the product of a choice made by free will."[75]

Bourdieu's insightful account, bridging the gap between the two truths of the gift, enables us to see more clearly how an ethics of debt is conceived as a secondary or derivative kind to the moral economy of gift. He begins by helping us see that the economy of gift comprises two seemingly opposing elements: "anti-economic" (a true gift should be nonreciprocal) and "economy" (gift giving should be reciprocal). What does he mean by "economic" and "economy?" He means "economic" "in the restricted modern sense of 'economic.'"[76] However, he distinguishes "economy" from "economism." This distinction is critical to differentiate the *moral* economy of debt from the *amoral* economy of debt. According to Bourdieu, while the concept of economy is still "immersed in a social universe," the idea of economism has nothing to do with that.[77] He defines economism as follows: "Economism recognizes no other form of interest than that which capitalism has produced, through a kind of real operation of abstraction, by setting up a universe of relations between man and man based, as Marx says, on 'callous cash payment' and more generally by favoring the creation of relatively autonomous fields, capable of establishing their own axiomatics (through the fundamental tautology 'business is business,' on which 'the economy' is based)."[78] According to Bourdieu, then, while economy signifies the kind of moral economy that is rooted in the social world, economism has nothing to do with the moral aspect of the social world. To summarize, the moral economy of debt is established as a secondary or derivative kind to the moral economy of gift in distinction from the amoral economy of debt because only the former (the moral economy of debt) is associated with the Bourdieusian idea of economy.

It is important to recognize that at the heart of the neoliberal reduction of debt to an amoral status of economism lies an ideological attempt to separate the economy of debt from the moral economy of gift. The neoliberal economists' decontextualizing, dehistoricizing, and dissocializing reduction of debt to an amoral status ultimately purports to consolidate the idea that the economy of debt has nothing to do with the promotion of such ethical ideals and moral values as social cohesion, solidarity, communion, or social alliance. In this respect, Mauss' and Bourdieu's anthropological insights become critical as we attempt to reconstruct an ethics of debt as a form of moral economy, not as an amoral logic of economism.

The second challenge to our effort to reconstruct an ethics of debt as a secondary or derivative kind to the original moral economy of gift is an "excessiveness" challenge. One of Mauss' major theses of *The Gift* is that the exchange of gifts is essentially agonistic. Gift giving can be competitive or even combative. This is clearly illustrated by his examination of the Northwest Coast potlatch. The literal meaning of potlatch is "to feed" or "to consume," and the tribes in the area between the Rocky Mountains and the Pacific coast spend the winter in a continual festival of feasts, fairs, and markets, which also constitute the solemn assembly of the tribe.[79] According to Mauss, however, "What is noteworthy about these tribes is the principle of rivalry and hostility that prevails in all these practices."[80] This rivalry and hostility can even go as far as to fight and kill chiefs and nobles. Mauss characterizes this destructive form of agonistic gift exchange as "usurious and sumptuary," calling it *total services of an agonistic type*."[81]

Georges Bataille's notion of "general economy" is an innovative reflection on the phenomenon of potlatch, which is distinguished from the "restrictive" economic perspective of most economic theory. He specifically suggests that it would be futile "to consider the economic aspects of the potlatch without having formulated the viewpoint defined by *general economy*."[82] Such an excessive aspect of any general economy (which he calls the "accursed share") is destined to result in an outrageous and catastrophic outpouring illustrated by such sacrifices and wars of the Aztecs and the unarmed society of Lamaism. In this respect, Bataille writes, "the gift does not mean anything from the standpoint of general economy; there is dissipation only for the giver."[83] What, then, does this excessive or even destructive aspect of the gift have to do with our attempt to reconstruct an ethics of debt as a secondary or derivative kind to the moral economy of gift? Briefly speaking, when an ethics of debt is reconstructed as a secondary or derivative kind to the moral economy of gift, such excessive and even destructive type of gift is critically screened because the phenomenon of debt fundamentally presupposes the conditionality of limitedness or restrictedness. I would call Mauss' excessive economy of potlatch and Bataille's general economy of gift a type of a hyperbolic economy of gift, and, because of its abusive appropriation of the economy of gift, I hold that such a hyperbolic type is not to be considered the original economy of gift from which an ethics of debt is derived as a secondary or derivative kind of the moral economy of gift.

## Conclusion

Above I have reconstructed an ethics of debt as a secondary or derivative kind to the moral economy of gift. According to this perspective, an ethics of debt is conceived in such a way that it should become a kind of gift or a peculiar gift to the debtor. Anthropologists Graeber and Mauss help us develop a critical perspective that, despite the fact that debt is commonly monetized in today's neoliberal world as if it is wholly governed by the so-called scientific and thus amoral economic logic of exchange and reciprocity, debt was originally conceived in archaic society as part of the moral economy of gift to engender social and symbolic capital that made possible social cohesion and solidarity. As a secondary or derivative kind, the economy of debt then draws on its key moral significance from the moral economy of gift rather than from its own economic logic. Since the moral economy of gift made it possible for archaic society to maintain social cohesion and solidarity, the ethics of debt is also conceived in a way to preserve or promote them.

Since the late eighteenth century, the modern capitalist economy and neoliberalism have increasingly disassociated the moral economy of gift from the economy of debt as they have also disconnected the world of economy from its background world of sociality, morality, and religion. As a result of this grand ideological change, debt is no longer conceived as a kind of gift in today's neoliberal world. This grand historical-ideological project of creating an amoral world of economy and finance, however, has entailed various immoral consequences in the amoralized world of economy and finance. From eastern Europe to South Asia, from West Africa to the Caribbean, from the Mediterranean Sea to the Persian Gulf, countless people have been subjected to various human rights violations such as human trafficking, debt bondage, child labor, and even epidemic suicides due to the various types of the abuse of debt. Indeed, what really transpires in the amoral world of economy and finance is not a continual occurrence of amoral economic behaviors but an increasing manifestation of immoral incidences. It seems now is the time to question the validity of this grand historical-ideological project of creating an amoral world of economy and finance from various critical perspectives, including social sciences, philosophy, economics, and religions.

## CHAPTER TWO

# NEOLIBERAL FINANCIALIZATION AND THE IDEA OF JUST DEBT

## Introduction

As argued in the previous chapter, the constructive effort to develop an ethics of debt should incorporate all the structural aspects of debt, even more so in the case of sovereign debt (known as governmental, national, or public debt), which has been increasingly shaped by global forces such as (post)colonialism, financialization, neoliberalism, and so on. The case of Jamaica's debt crisis is exemplary. Jamaica is one of the most indebted countries in the world, and it spends twice as much on debt repayments as it does on education and health combined.[1] Its national debt currently stands at 140 percent of GDP (gross domestic product), marking one of the highest ratios in the world. About 55 percent of government spending goes toward paying the nation's debt, while 25 percent goes to wages, leaving just 20 percent for everything else, including education, security, and health.[2] In 2013 the IMF (International Monetary Fund) announced a $1 billion loan to "help" Jamaica meet huge debt payments, but, as usual, it came along with four years of austerity, such as a 20 percent real-terms cut in wages.[3] This austerity applied to the already crippled economy severely affected by the financial crisis of 2007–2008.

One may wonder why Jamaica has been suffering from economic austerity for more than four decades. Before Jamaica became independent from Britain in 1962, it had been under Britain's colonial oppression for more than three hundred years. Although Jamaica enjoyed strong economic growth during the first ten years of independence, the oil crisis of the 1970s and the subsequent slowdown in the global economy left Jamaica dependent on foreign debts. When interest rates rose at the start of the 1980s, debt payments skyrocketed from 16 percent of exports in 1977 to a gigantic 35 percent by 1986.[4] The IMF and World Bank imposed large-scale structural adjustment policies, bringing devastating economic impact on many people. Although Michael Norman Manley, a former democratic socialist, returned to office as prime minister in 1989, his government embraced neoliberal policies in marked contrast to the interventionist economic policies of his first government (1972–1980). As it turned out, Jamaica's opening to the neoliberal global economy did not help the country. On the contrary, it exacerbated the country's economic situation. "There has been no progress in cutting hunger, or increasing basic water and sanitation provision. In 1990, 97% of children completed primary school. Now [2013] only 73% do. In 1990, 59 mothers died in childbirth for every 100,000 children born. Now it is 110."[5]

Robert F. Drinan, a Roman Catholic Jesuit priest, writes in his 1993 article after visiting Jamaica and witnessing the bleak economic prospects of its people, "Why can't the industrialized nations be required to give reparation and restitution to those people in colonial lands whose resources they plundered, whose people they deprived of educational opportunities and whose future is now mortgaged by debts of astronomical proportions?"[6] Drinan's critical comment makes more sense if we consider that Jamaica's problems go back much further. Nick Dearden correctly points out, "The island's economy has been shaped by centuries of violence, plunder and slavery. Hundreds of thousands of lives were wasted on sugar plantations, which 'kept the wheels of metropolitan industry turning' in Britain."[7] Regarding Jamaica's national debt, we should not miss an important fact that, by 2013, it has already repaid more money ($19.8 billion) than it has been lent ($18.5 billion), yet its government still owes $7.8 billion due to the huge interest payments.[8] Because Jamaica is classified as an upper-middle-income country with the largest population in the English-speaking Caribbean, it has never been eligible for debt relief. We should note that several other Caribbean countries are also deeply indebted just like Jamaica, and they share the common history that they were once victims of the European colonialism. It is also equally important to note that although the IMF calls its lending program "a rescue package," it is a rescue for Jamaica's creditors, not the poor people who have suffered even worse austerity. As of April 2015, in the third year of an IMF-backed economic program, Jamaica is running the most austere budget in the world, with a primary surplus of 7.5 percent of GDP,[9] which is widely considered "politically unsustainable." Jake Johnston of the Center for Economic and Policy Research concludes his report on Jamaica's debt suggesting that multilateral debt relief for Jamaica would likely free up more resources than would new loans. "Rather than subject the Jamaican people to further decline in living standards on the back of continued austerity, multilateral development banks should work with Jamaica and other creditors to provide meaningful debt relief, freeing up needed resources to invest in the future of the country."[10]

The case of Jamaica's national debt highlights an important aspect of ongoing global debt crises in many parts of the world. Above all, the problem of debt, especially national or sovereign debt, is not only historical but also deeply structural. Given that many poor Third World countries were former colonies of rich First World nations, and the previous historical and economic dependence has been renewed and rebooted in the global context of neoliberalism and financialization, an effort to develop an ethics of debt should certainly address those structural aspects. To be more specific, the First World creditors should ask of themselves first whether they have paid their debts in full to their former colonies before they demand that poor Third World debtors pay their debts. Unfortunately, the legacy of colonialism is still very much alive in the twenty-first century, and at the forefront of this legacy lie the powerful financial agencies of the First World nations.

To address effectively the historical and structural nature of ongoing global debt crises, a new ethics of debt should be able to provide moral principles and ethical guidelines not only to political leaders of each country but also to those who are running financial institutions on a global scale, such as various international financial institutions (IFIs) and other commercial or investment banks. In the following, with a view to developing a new ethics of debt, I critically engage in Karl Marx and Marxists' critique of political economy. Through this critical engagement, I attempt to deconstruct the neoliberal reductionist view on the problem of debt, which regards debt solely as a juridical-economic issue. It is my contention that the problem of debt is more than a juridical-economic issue because the widespread neoliberal abuse of debt calls for global citizens' moral-political engagement. For us to cope with the neoliberal abuse of debt, we should critically appropriate diverse voices of stakeholders including debtors, creditors, policy makers, and regulators. Through this critical and inclusive engagement, the economy of debt is transformed into a *political* economy of debt, and debt is no longer exclusively confined to the debtor-creditor relationship. Ultimately, this chapter offers a moral-political solution to the liberation of debt from the neoliberal exploitation of the economy of debt. In the following, we first engage in the most significant economic change of the past forty years, which has characterized the global economies in the name of financialization.

## Financialization, Rentier Capitalism, and Abusive Economy of Debt

What is financialization? Scholars have different definitions. Greta Krippner, for example, defines it as follows: Financialization is a "pattern of accumulation in which profits accrue primarily through financial channels rather than through trade and commodity production. 'Financial' here refers to activities relating to the provision (or transfer) of liquid capital in expectation of future interest, dividends, or capital gains."[11] Donald Tomaskovic-Devey and Ken-Hou Lin explain financialization by analyzing two interdependent processes: "The first process is financial services firms' increasing importance—in economic, social, and political terms—to U.S. society. The second process is the linked trajectory of nonfinancial firms' increased involvement in financial activity."[12]

According to Gerald Epstein, some writers use the term "financialization" to refer to the growing dominance of capital market financial systems over bank-based financial systems, while others use the term to represent the explosion of financial trading with a myriad of new financial instruments.[13] He defines the term as "the increasing role of financial motives, financial markets, financial actors and financial institutions in the operation of the domestic and international economies."[14] The rise of financialization has fundamentally changed the global economy and politics, and the problem of debt has become one of the most important social and structural issues for many nations and their citizens. As Krippner correctly points out, it is difficult for us to escape the impression that we are living in a world of finance.[15] Financialization has also given birth to a rise of new economic class called "rentiers." John Maynard Keynes refers to the rentier as "the functionless investor" in his *General Theory*, who generates income through the ownership of capital by exploiting its "scarcity-value."[16]

Economist James Crotty argues that financialization in conjunction with neoliberalism and globalization has brought a significant negative impact on the operations of U.S. nonfinancial corporations due to what he calls "neoliberal paradox." Crotty analyzes the paradoxical economic situation as follows. In the 1970s and thereafter NFC (nonfinancial corporation) performance was negatively affected by two major changes: a slowdown in the rate of global aggregate demand growth and increasing market competition and a shift from "patient" finance seeking long-term growth to "impatient" financial markets that raised real interest rates. As a result of this changing environment, NFCs had to pay an increasing share of their cash flow to financial agents.[17] Crotty summarizes this negative changing trend saying, "The combined effect of changes in both sectors lowered NFC profit rates, raised NFC indebtedness, slowed the rate of capital accumulation, and forced NFC top management to switch from the long-term goals and 'high-road' labor relations of the Golden Age to short-term 'survivalist' strategies that involved attacks on white- and blue-collar labor and on key firm suppliers."[18] Increasing financialization pressured NFCs not only to cut wages and benefits to workers but also to engage in fraud and deception to increase apparent profits.[19] Crotty thus concludes his analysis of the neoliberal paradox by calling for the rejection of the neoliberal project:

> It will not be possible for NFCs to lead either advanced or developing nations to stable, egalitarian, long-term prosperity unless the neoliberal project is rejected. . . . The creation of a new "Golden Age" will require a new model of socially embedded economic institutions and state-guided economic growth, one that is appropriate for twenty-first century conditions.[20]

What, then, does the increasing financialization have to do with the abuse and exploitation of the economy of debt on a domestic as well as on a global scale?

Simply put, increasing financialization intrinsically has to do with the manipulation of the economy of debt in three aspects: the dangerous proliferation of debt, the systemic exploitation of vulnerable debtors, and the detrimental concentration of wealth among financial rentiers. First, financialization has funded the exponential growth of debt on a global scale for past decades, resulting in a potential debacle of the whole economy, which actually occurred in 2007–2008. The exponential growth of the derivatives market demonstrates how debt has dangerously proliferated due to the increasing financialization. What are derivatives? They are "financial contracts that are designed to create market price exposure to changes in an underlying commodity, asset or event."[21] The term "derivative" refers to how its value is derived from the performance of an underlying entity, which includes security, commodity interest rate, exchange rate, or even events (known as event derivatives). Although derivatives play a useful and important role in hedging and risk management, as Randall Dodd holds, they can pose several dangers to the stability of financial markets and thereby the overall economy.[22] According to Rex A. McKenzie, "Derivative trading emerges as a major vehicle for speculative capital in risky business transactions that propel the system towards fragility and periodic crises."[23] Today, the size of the derivatives market is astronomical. According to data collected by the Bank of International Settlements, as of December 2014, the total amounts outstanding of over-the-counter derivatives exceeded $630.1 trillion, while the total amounts outstanding of over-the-counter foreign exchange derivatives was $75.8 trillion.[24]

Derivatives are structurally interlinked with debt, as we can see in the case of subprime mortgage lending. To be more specific, derivatives are created when banks issue loans and then sell these financial assets in the secondary loan market. Later these assets are aggregated into large pools and used to create new classes of yield-bearing financial assets, a process that is called securitization. According to Karl Beitel, the securitization process begins when a mortgage originator, such as a private mortgage company or a major bank, issues a new loan to a household while at the same time selling the loan to a government-sponsored entity—such as Fannie Mae, Freddie Mac, or the government-insured Ginnie Mae—or to a Wall Street investment bank (Goldman Sachs, Merrill Lynch, etc.).[25] It is not difficult to conjecture that mortgage companies and banks were motivated to issue more loans to unqualified or less-qualified borrowers with the purpose of selling their debts as derivatives in the secondary markets. It was inevitable that the housing market bubble would burst at one point or another, wreaking havoc on the entire financial market on a global scale.

Second, increasing financialization has been deeply problematic because it not only promotes the exponential growth of private and public debts but also renders many debtors vulnerable to the financial abuse and the exploitation of the economy of debt by unscrupulous financial institutions such as vulture funds. They typically prey on debtors in financial distress by purchasing the now-cheap credit on a secondary market in order to make a huge monetary gain, although it in many cases leaves debtors in a worse state than before. For example, in 1995, a U.S.-based vulture fund, Elliott, purchased $20.7 million worth of defaulted loans made to Peru for a deeply discounted $11.4 million, and then it sued the nation and its Banco de la Nación del Peru in a New York court for the original amount of the loan, plus interest. Elliott won the case with a $58 million settlement, making a $47 million profit, which is about 400 percent return. Elliott, then, applied the same tactic to Argentina. It purchased $630 million of bonds for $48 million (only about 7 percent of face value) when Argentina was about to default in 2001. Elliott soon demanded Argentina pay $2.3 billion, including unpaid interest. It won, again from a New York court, $1.6 billion, but the Argentine government refused to pay. In 2012, Elliott seized the Argentine naval vessel ARA Libertad through its subsidiary, NML Capital, in Ghana. Elliott applied its vulture tactic again in 2008 against Congo.[26]

According to McKenzie, as the key innovation in the era of financialization, derivatives played a major role in leading the Wall Street revolution since the late 1970s, and its end result was a "speculative capitalism" that effectively made all of us gamblers.[27] The 1997 financial crisis of Southeast/ East Asia shows us an example of how the end result of the Wall Street revolution can be detrimental to many innocent people in the world. According to McKenzie, the financial crisis of Southeast/East Asia was brewed up and then exploited by Wall Street agencies. Wall Street departments first created derivatives that fueled speculative positions in the region, enabling the flood of speculative money capital in various derivative forms. These financial products were tailor-made and integrated, and the speculator could buy sophisticated derivatives that, for example, would allow a bigger bet on Thai debt securities with funds borrowed in Japan at low rates and through shorting the Japanese yen.[28] As intended by Wall Street departments, "The unwinding of these derivative positions led to a wholesale dumping of the underlying currencies and securities, leaving markets frozen in illiquidity. Throughout the region, derivative-related forced selling led to the virtual collapse of currencies, securities markets, financial systems, and economies."[29]

While Wall Street investors might have celebrated their huge financial gains, many innocent people in Southeast/East Asia had to suffer because of their sudden financial loss. A collaborative research team of the University of Bristol and Taiwanese researchers conducted their first comprehensive study of the impact of the Asian economic crisis on suicide rates, and they discovered a marked connection between them. According to this social scientific research, "Suicide mortality decreased in the late 1980s and early 1990s but subsequently increased markedly in all countries except Singapore, which had steadily declining suicide rates throughout the study period."[30] They also found out that "the economic crisis was associated with 10,400 more suicides in 1998 compared to 1997 in Japan, Hong Kong and Korea."[31]

Third, increasing financialization is deeply interlinked with the ever-deepening concentration of wealth. A new Oxfam report of 2014 shows how extreme economic inequality has been established, bringing negative impacts on economic growth and poverty reduction in our globalized world. Some of the astonishing discoveries are as follows:

- Almost half of the world's wealth is now owned by just 1 percent of the population.
- The wealth of the world's richest 1 percent amounts to $110 trillion. That's sixty-five times the total wealth of the bottom half of the world's population.
- The bottom half of the world's population owns the same as the richest eighty-five people in the world.
- Seven out of ten people live in countries where economic inequality has increased in the past thirty years.
- The richest 1 percent increased their share of income in twenty-four out of twenty-six countries for which we have data between 1980 and 2012.
- In the United States, the wealthiest 1 percent captured 95 percent of post–financial crisis growth since 2009, while the bottom 90 percent became poorer.[32]

The whopping discrepancy in wealth between the top 1 percent and the bottom of the world's population is not solely an economic matter. As the report clearly points out, this economic inequality is inevitably linked to political degradation because the wealth of superrich people will "capture" such a key political mechanism as policy making. "When wealth captures government policymaking, the rules bend to favor the rich, often to the detriment of everyone else. The consequences include the erosion of democratic governance, the pulling apart of social cohesion, and the vanishing of equal opportunities for all."[33]

It is important to note that the incredible deepening of the concentration of wealth for the past thirty years has coincided with increasing financialization on a global scale. At the heart of this unhealthy, destabilizing, and detrimental trend lies what French economist Thomas Piketty has succinctly captured in his recently published book—*Capital in the Twenty-First Century*—as a law-like formula: $r > g$ ($r$ stands for the average annual rate of return on capital; $g$ stands for the rate of growth of the economy such as the annual increase in income or output).[34] According to Piketty, the ever-deepening concentration of wealth has a "structural character." We can get a glimpse of this structural trend through his analysis of economic data. For example, from the late 1970s to 2010, the increase in the upper decile's share has been relatively steady (from 35 percent in the 1980s, then 40 percent in the 1990s, and 45 percent in the 2000s). What is striking is that this increasing inequality was unaffected by the financial crisis of 2007–2008. As Piketty shows, the level of inequality in 2010 is already significantly higher than the level attained in 2007, proving that the increase of inequality is still continuing.[35]

The structural character of this growing concentration of wealth is deeply related to debt. According to Piketty, one inevitable result of increasing inequality is the virtual stagnation of the purchasing power of the lower and middle classes in the United States, which more than likely motivates modest households to take on debt. Growing household debt is almost unavoidable, "especially since unscrupulous banks and financial intermediaries, freed from regulation and eager to earn good yields on the enormous savings injected into the system by the well-to-do, offered credit on increasingly generous terms."[36] The structural nature of the growing concentration of wealth is then simply translated into the transfer of U.S. national income from the poorest 90 percent to the richest 10 percent since 1980. At the center of this transfer mechanism lie the proliferation debt and manipulation of debtors.[37]

Other economists concur with Piketty's argument that increasing financialization is deeply linked to the detrimental concentration of wealth among financial rentiers. For instance, economists such as Marina Azzimonti and colleagues testify that "the stock of public debt has increased in most advanced economies during the last 30 years, a period also characterized by extensive liberalization of international capital markets," and this period of financialization has coincided with a "sustained increase in income inequality."[38] In his *Price of Inequality*, Joseph Stiglitz develops an argument that socioeconomic inequality not only is bad for the U.S. economy but also has detrimental effects on its democracy. He especially focuses on the problem of "rent seeking" as a major factor that distorts the U.S. economy. According to Stiglitz, rent seeking takes varied forms such as "hidden and open transfers and subsidies from the government, laws that make the marketplace less competitive, lax enforcement of existing competition laws, and statutes that allow corporations to take advantage of others or to pass costs on to the rest of society."[39] Financialization has been deeply related to rent seeking in past decades, as statistics confirm. For example, the composition of the top 1 percent in 2005 was 31 percent executives, managers, and supervisors (nonfinance); 15.7 percent medical; 13.9 percent financial professionals, including management; and

8.4 percent lawyers. It is significant to note that among these the share of finance almost doubled over this period, rising from 7.7 percent in 1979 to 13.9 percent in 2005, and these statistics are based on an income measure excluding capital gains. If capital gains were considered, about half of all capital gains accrue to the top 0.1 percent, and 60 percent of their income for the top four hundred income earners is in the form of capital point (the increased rate of capital gains).[40] This growing inequality thus shows not only how seriously our society has been divided by economic income but also how deeply financialization has been involved with growing inequality.

Above we have seen how increasing financialization intrinsically has to do with the manipulation of the economy of debt in three aspects: the dangerous proliferation of debt, the systemic exploitation of vulnerable debtors, and the detrimental concentration of wealth on financial rentiers. The dramatic 2007–2008 financial meltdown was a global wake-up call to the structural problem embedded in the neoliberal global economy of debt and the financialization it has driven. In an age of global financialization, whose structural problems may be only checked and regulated by the government, public policies, and international laws, it now seems evident that unless a critical and vibrant democratic rule of law is established, humanity as a whole will continue to be exposed to ongoing financial risks and crises. The more practical goal of an ethics of debt becomes clearer. One of the key roles the ethics of debt can and should play is to provide ethical guidelines to all the stakeholders, especially those governing authorities who are responsible for delimiting and regulating financial markets and financiers who are managing and monitoring the system. Of course, ordinary citizens should be informed of these needed ethical guidelines as well since many of them would be directly affected by the laws and regulations it inspires. In the following, I will lay the groundwork for an ethics of debt by focusing on two fronts: first, I critically engage Karl Marx and neo-Marxists regarding their critique on capitalist economy and financialization; second, I develop a new rights theory, proposing the novel concept of the debtor's right to just debt by defining its key qualifications.

## Marx, Neo-Marxists, and the Critique of the Capitalist Economy of Debt

Why should we turn to Karl Marx and his disciples? What do they have to do with the subject matter of this chapter? Marx and his followers are crucial in developing the ethics of debt for two reasons: first, the problem of debt has become one of the most serious economic issues in capitalist countries;

second, Marx and neo-Marxists are arguably the most important critics of the neoliberal capitalistic economic system. Indeed, today's postindustrial capitalist system is indispensably connected with the economy of debt. In analyzing Marx's and neo-Marxists' critiques of the capitalist economy of debt, we first need to differentiate between Marx and neo-Marxists. For Marx, the key subject matter of his critique of the capitalist economy lies in the inevitable downfall of the Western capitalism triggered by the law-like "falling rate of profit"; by contrast, neo-Marxist scholars' main concern is the inevitable collapse of capitalist economy largely caused by ever-growing financialization. Marx and neo-Marxists scholars share a crucial diagnostic consensus that the capitalist economy is embedded with its inherent contradiction that cannot be resolved by its own logic.

We should note first that Marx was aware of the economic quandary of the increasing debt of capitalist firms during a period of expansion and the subsequent falling rate of profit. Marx writes:

> Let us point out that one could also mean by the accumulation of money-capital the accumulation of wealth in the hands of bankers (money-lenders by profession), acting as middlemen between private money-capitalists on the one hand, and the state, communities, and reproducing borrowers on the other. For the entire vast extension of the credit system, and all credit in general, is exploited by them as their private capital.[41]

Thus, this passage from *Capital* shows that Marx was not only aware of the differences between the industrial accumulation of capital and the financial accumulation of capital through a debt/credit system, but he was also critical of the latter. Marx, however, did not fully develop his critique of the problem of increasing debt. The full critique of increasing debt in the capitalist system has, though, been enabled by neo-Marxist economists such as Fred Moseley, John Bellamy Foster, and Fred Magdoff, to name a few. So here I turn to integrating the critical works of Marx and contemporary Marxist scholars, and I analyze the Marxian view on the capitalist conundrum of increasing debt.

According to Marx, the rate of profit would *tend to* decline as a result of technological change (the change of the means of production). For Marx, however, the decline of the rate of profit is neither an accident nor an outcome caused by external sources; it is, rather, the consequence of capitalism's inherent dynamics, which propel the labor-saving technological development that replaces workers with machines. "There are many ways of intensifying labour which imply an increase of constant, as compared to variable, capital, and hence a fall in the rate of profit, such as compelling a labourer to operate a larger number of machines."[42] Marx argues that although technological change increases the productivity of labor at the beginning stage, because of the inherent limits to the increase in profit produced by each worker, labor-saving technological change will ultimately cause the rate of profit to decline. This is why Marx claims that there is an internal contradiction in the economic system of capitalism, which eventually leads to the collapse of capitalism. It is evident for Marx that at the center of this inevitable projection of capitalism lies the internal paradox of capital as such. In this regard, Marx states, "The *real barrier* of capitalist production is *capital itself*. . . . The means—unconditional development of the productive forces of society—comes continually into conflict with the limited purpose, the self-expansion of the existing capital."[43] For Marx, it is apparent that the capitalist mode of production (a historical means of developing the material forces of production) conflicts with its own corresponding relations of social production (a capitalist relationship to capital and the worker's relation to the capitalist).

We should note here that Marx's critique of political economy is more focused on the inherent conflict between the means of production and the relations of social production than it is on the crisis of increasing debt. Although it is true that Marx addresses the problem of debt in his *Capital* (particularly volume 3, part V), it is our contemporary Marxist economists who interconnect Marx's major critique of the capitalistic economic system with the growing problem of debt in global capitalism. Contemporary Marxists argue that although the falling rate of profit in the *industrial market* is temporarily resolved through the proliferation of the *financial market*, because of the growing burden of debt inculcated by the dynamics of the financial market, the capitalistic economic system as such can do nothing but face its sudden collapse, as we almost experienced in the 2007–2008 financial crisis.

Stemming from the theoretical framework provided by Paul Baran and Paul Sweezy's *Monopoly Capital* (1966), John Bellamy Foster and Fred Magdoff, for example, focus on the process of financialization of the capital accumulation process, which first emerged in the recession of 1974–1975. According to Foster and Magdoff, the solution for the owners of capital who came up against the barriers that limit their profitable investment in the *industrial* market (the falling rate of profit) was to expand their demand for *financial* products as a means of maintaining and expanding their money capital. Of course, financial institutions stepped forward with a vast array of new financial instruments (futures, options, derivatives, hedge funds, etc.), and as a result financial speculation has skyrocketed for decades.[44] From the neo-Marxist perspective, thus, financialization is an inevitable process that capitalism must use when propelled by the law of the accumulation of capital. The financialization process, however, cannot be an ultimate solution to the owners of capital. Why not? According to Foster, it is because the financialization of the capital accumulation process is coupled with the speculative growth of the credit-debt system.

Foster substantiates this point by showing that total private debt in the U.S. economy rose from 110 percent of the GDP in 1970 to 293 percent of the GDP in 2007.[45] Additionally, when compared to the 1970s, in which the increase in the U.S. GDP was about sixty cents for every new dollar of debt, by the early twenty-first century, this had declined to about twenty cents for every new dollar of debt.[46] During the period of the financialization of the capital accumulation process, thus, the U.S. economy has witnessed financial instability along with the growth of debt. The financialization process, which Thomas Palley calls "the cult of debt finance," is also characterized by the growing economic bubbles that eventually burst, which induces the even more devastating effect of a deepening economic stagnation. Indeed, the U.S. economy experienced this disastrous aspect of the cult of debt finance in the 2007–2008 financial crisis. The growth of debt, as Foster characterizes it, is like a "drug addiction," because just as in the case of drug addiction, more and more debt is necessary to get the same stimulating effect.

If we use Marx's terms, financialization is depicted as a transformation of "M(money)-C(commodity)-M′(original money plus surplus value)" to "M-M′." The significance of this transformation is that commodities no longer play the central role of producing profits; instead, money simply begets more money with no relation to production. According to Foster and Magdoff, financialization as a response of capital to the stagnation tendency in the real economy (falling rate of profit) inevitably demonstrates a resurfacing of the underlying stagnation endemic to the advanced capitalist economy. With financialization in crisis, there is no other visible way out for monopoly-finance capital. Foster and Magdoff thus write, "The prognosis then is that the economy, even after the immediate devaluation crisis is stabilized, will at best be characterized for some time by minimal growth and by high unemployment, underemployment, and excess capacity."[47] Given that capitalism is unable to handle its inherent problems such as the falling rate of profit, financialization, and stagflation, should we then switch our economic system from capitalism to socialism? Must capitalism be ultimately doomed? Should we agree with Foster, who argues, "In these difficult and dangerous times, there is no alternative to the development of socialist strategies of sustainable human development—on which all our hopes, at every level, must now rest."[48]

Although Marxian critique of the capitalist economy of debt and financialization is not widely accepted by the American public or by those in academia, it is injudicious for us to simply ignore a Marxian diagnosis/ prognosis of capitalism. For example, it is almost surreal to reread Fred Moseley's 2003 prognosis on the American economy. "Finally, Marx's theory also suggests that sooner or later, and very likely within the next decade, the U.S. economy will suffer another serious depression—and perhaps even on the scale of the Great Depression of the 1930s. The combination of a low rate of profit and unprecedented levels of debt will eventually cause widespread bankruptcies of both business and households, which in turn would probably cause the flight of foreign capital, and even worse depression."[49] Moseley's unnerving prognosis also reminds us of Marx's critical comment on the sudden stoppage of the capitalist economy forecasted in *Capital*. "Thus business always appears almost excessively sound right on the eve of a crash. The best proof of this is furnished, for instance, by the Reports on Bank Acts of 1857 and 1858 . . . Business is always thoroughly sound and the campaign in full swing, until suddenly the debacle takes place."[50] The sudden financial breakdown in 2007–2008 seems to be too dramatic to call it an accident. Could the crisis of 2007–2008 become a sufficient reason for us to accept Foster's argument? Is socialism, then, the only alternative to the deeply problematic capitalist system with regard to the quest for sustainable human development? Could there be no other alternative?

Even though Marxian analysis and critique of the internal contradiction of capitalism typified by the falling rate of profit and the financialization of debt should be taken seriously into our consideration, I argue that it is too precipitous to subscribe to the Marxian prescription of replacing capitalism with socialism. Why? First, it is not clear whether socialism could entirely solve the problem of debt. Even if we admit that a socialist system could be exempt from the falling rate of profit and the financialization of debt, we should not come to a hasty conclusion that capitalism would not be able to resolve such problems *politically*. Granting that it is not socialism's goal to build a debtless society, how is debt, then, conceived in a society organized by the principle of from each according to his or her ability, to each according to his or her need? According to this principle, if there is any debtor, it must be society as a whole because in a socialist system debt would arise when society fails to meet the needs of its constituents. As in the cases of the Union of Soviet Socialist Republics and its satellites from the Eastern Bloc, according to Samantha Sparks, at the end of 1986, total debt owed by the Eastern European region including the Soviet Union stood at about $138 billion dollars.[51] This shows the inability of the socialistic system in according the total sum of peoples' various needs to the overall social capacity to produce goods.

It is not my intention, however, to defend capitalism against the socialist critique of capitalism; rather, I am pointing out that the minimalistic philosophy of debt shared by both classical capitalism and the socialist economy is the main problem we have to address. The minimalistic philosophy of debt is clearly outlined by the simple rule of "the debtor should always pay his or her debt to the creditor." Interestingly enough, when it comes to the problem of debt, there seems to be no fundamental difference between the capitalist philosophy of debt and that of the socialists. They basically share the same philosophy of debt. Of course, socialism can be differentiated from capitalism in that Marxian economists condemn the abuse of debt by the capitalists. We should not, however, confound the abuse of debt and debt as such. The critique of the abuse of debt is one thing, and the critique of debt as such is another. Indeed, not all debts are bad or toxic; some debts are desirable and even necessary for the continuous flourishing of humankind. The Marxian approach is right in that it points to the abuse of debt by capitalists, but this should not lead us to the critique of debt as such. In the following section, thus, instead of precipitously choosing to replace capitalism with socialism as a way of resolving the problem of debt, I attempt to develop an ethics of debt with the purpose of overcoming the capitalist abuse of debt while not rushing into the socialist alternative.

## Deconstructing an Amoral Debt

Above we have seen how increasing financialization intrinsically has to do with the manipulation of the economy of debt; we have also seen why the socialist alternative would not become an adequate and sufficient model for our attempt to develop an ethics of debt. How, then, is an ethics of debt possible? How could we develop an ethics of debt that would actually work in the world of finance in an age of financialization? To answer these questions, we first need to investigate how such an unhealthy and unethical financial trend became so prevalent over the past decades on a global scale in the name of financialization. By attempting to answer this question, we may get a better sense of how we are to ethically engage the ever-expanding financialization and the unfettered manipulative economy of debt.

What I have discovered through my research is that at the heart of the manipulative economy of debt lies the Lockean appropriation of debt-linked credit as a financial property. By the Lockean appropriation of debt-linked credit as a financial property, I mean the propertization of a debt-linked credit as if it were no different from other commercial properties that can be purchased, owned, and accumulated without any limit. For John Locke,[52] as David Harvey captures, "individual property is a natural right that arises when individuals create value by mixing their labor with the land: the fruits of their labor belong to them and to them alone."[53] The Lockean appropriation of debt-linked credit as a financial property is problematic because although it is qualitatively different from a commercial property, financiers and rentiers put them together in the same category by transforming a debt-linked financial property into a form of commercial property. How is a debt-linked financial property qualitatively different from a commercial property? Unlike a commercial property whose value is determined by the producer's visible labor according to Lockean labor theory of value, a debt-linked financial property's value is largely governed by the issuer's "symbolic capital" such as creditability and trustworthiness. When one buys money (financial property such as bonds) with money, the buyer believes that the former will grow bigger than it is now. While we would not lend our money to someone we could not trust, we are willing to buy commercial properties from someone we never met before; while we do not have to show our credit score at the shop, we have to when we borrow money from a bank. Besides, while such commercial properties as cars and laptops would not multiply on their own, a debt-linked financial property can multiply on its own through interest. Despite this qualitative difference between commercial and debt-linked financial properties, when they are traded on the market, they are all wrapped up in the same category of property. They are nothing but private property that can be purchased, owned, and accumulated without limit in the liberal capitalist economic system.

From an ethical perspective, the real problem of the Lockean appropriation of debt-linked credit as a financial property is that it has effectively rendered the problem of debt as an *amoral* issue. The moral aspect of debt is largely stripped off by the Lockean appropriation, and as a result of this moral stripping, debt is efficiently transformed into a morally neutral entity in a financial market. Of course, people still can say that there is good debt or bad debt, but the valuation of good or bad is not that different from such categories as a good car or a bad car. This evaluation is largely a nonmoral assessment. Because of the Lockean appropriation of debt-linked credit as a financial property, a huge portion of the derivative market has exponentially grown during the 1990s and 2000s, and at the heart of this financial boom lies what is commonly known as subprime mortgages. During that time, no one called a subprime mortgage a sub-moral debt; it was just considered a "risky" financial property but certainly not an immoral one. Interestingly enough, while auto companies are to recall their vehicles when they discover any risk factors in them, no banks or financiers have recalled their financial products (such as derivatives) because of risk factors. The Lockean appropriation has rendered a debt-linked financial property an amoral entity, and this amoralization of financial property has also successfully neutralized the moral and legal aspect of any risks, letting them have only an economic or financial sense.

The first step toward the reconstruction of an ethics of debt is then to convert an amoralized financial property into a morally conceived financial entity. If this conversion is enabled, the concept of risk will also have a moral and legal aspect as well as its economic or financial sense. One needs to be informed, though, that I am not against the idea of altering a debt-linked credit into a financial property as such;[54] I am only against the immoral appropriation of debt-linked financial properties and unethical management of the financial markets. Let me exemplify how debt-linked financial properties and financial markets are compromised, exploited, and even destroyed by those who would care only for their financial interests.

In 2011, one of the biggest investment banking companies in the world, Goldman Sachs, was sued by Basis Yield Alpha Fund, an Australian hedge fund, who asked for more than $1 billion in damages. Basis argued that Goldman Sachs overcharged for two sets of mortgage-backed securities ($93 million) that it sold them, lying about the securities' expected performance. When Goldman Sachs sold the securities in 2007, it failed to disclose that the firm was actively betting against the securities at the time of the transaction, resulting in the collapse of the company. Basis alleged that Goldman Sachs knew to be junk the securities it was passing on to a client, but sought to profit by shorting the securities. Although Goldman Sachs tried to have the case dismissed, according to Reuters, a New York State appeals court refused to dismiss the lawsuit in January 30, 2014, letting the lawsuit against Goldman Sachs proceed.[55] As of June 14, 2016, Goldman Sachs finally agreed to settle the suit with Basis over the immoral sale of mortgage-linked securities.

In conjunction with the Lockean appropriation of debt-linked credit as a financial property, a deregulatory neoliberal politics has also played an important role in proliferating unhealthy and risky financial operations over the past decades. During this period of financialization and growing inequality, politics has been largely swayed and tamed by neoliberal financiers and their political lobbies instead of checking the unruly tendencies of financialization and the financiers' bubbling appetites for excessive financial profits. The political inability to check neoliberal financialization and its powerful agencies has resulted in the growing socioeconomic inequality in U.S. society. For example, in response to falling bank profits in the early 1990s, two banking deregulation acts were introduced (the 1994 Riegle-Neal Interstate Banking and Branching Act and the 1999 Financial Services Modernization Act), which enabled a steep surge in the proportion of national profits accumulated by banks and bank holding companies.[56] According to Donald Tomaskovic-Devey and Ken-Hou Lin, "Financialization transferred somewhere between 5.8 and 6.6 trillion 2011 dollars in income into the finance sector between 1980 and 2008, about two-thirds as profits."[57] How, then, was this deregulation possible? As Stiglitz takes note, "The bankers have unleashed enormous numbers of lobbyists to persuade any and all who play a role in regulation that they should not be regulated—an estimated 2.5 for every U.S. representative."[58] As a result of political deregulation of the financial market, the excessive financialization of the economy was successfully established, leading "to the point that before the 2008 crisis 40 percent of all corporate profits went to the financial sector."[59] From an ethical perspective, growing inequality and the concentration of wealth in the financial sector are problematic because they not only impede and disintegrate social unity and cohesion but also have a negative impact on productive industry or real economy. Indeed, "financialization actually reduced nonfinancial firms' capital investment in new productive assets and increased the share of their cash flow diverted to the finance sector as increased profits."[60]

## People's Socioeconomic Rights to Just Debt

As seen above, to develop an ethics of debt, we first need to convert an amoral notion of debt into a morally relevant concept. This approach differs from the conventional way of defining the ethics of debt, which tends to focus only on the moral responsibilities of the debtor or the creditor without saying much about the moral nature of debt itself. How is, then, this conversion possible? What is the motivating factor that would actually convert an amoral debt into a morally conceived financial entity? Ironically, it is none other than the phenomenon of financialization as such. How is it so? One of the most significant changes financialization has incurred is that someone else's debt (such as home mortgages) can be anyone else's financial assets through the financial mechanism of derivatives markets. In other words, debt is no longer an exclusive contractual matter between the original debtors and creditors; other financial stakeholders such as investors, financial counselors, and other creditors are now deeply affected by the contract terms of the debt. This realization engenders a new moral perspective according to which the concept of contract is only a necessary but not a sufficient condition for the debtor's moral duty to pay off his or her debt. The moral implication of this realization is that not all contracted debts are morally justifiable. The mere facticity of contract itself should not become the full moral qualification for a justifiable establishment of debt in an age of financialization. In addition to the necessary requirement of contract, the debt itself should also be morally justifiable. What is then the moral criterion that would determine the moral nature of debt? By what standard could we define the concept of just debt? I attempt to answer these questions by presenting the tripartite principles: the principle of serviceability, the principle of payability, and the principle of shareability.

The first qualifying principle of a just debt is serviceability. What does this principle mean? A debt can be legitimate only when it is used directly or indirectly for the sake of those who will pay back after being served. According to this principle, thus, when the creditor decides to lend money to the debtor knowing that the loan money would not be used for the debtor, it is considered to be an unjust debt. For example, when a dictator of a nation loans money from IFIs such as the IMF, which knows that the dictator will not use the loan money for the sake of people but instead embezzle it for his or her own sake, this loan money becomes an unjust debt. According to a 2015 report released by the Jubilee Debt Campaign, 75 percent of export debt owed to the UK is illegitimate, much of it coming from past loans for arms sales to repressive regimes. The report also writes that although the UK government said it was not possible to find out what those loans were originally for, the UK's national archives hold "some scandalous information about UK loans—from tanks used by Indonesian dictator General Suharto against his own people, to warships and helicopters sold to the 1970s military junta in Argentina, which were used to invade the Malvinas (Falkland Islands)."[61] Unjust debt can also be identified in intertemporal relations. For instance, when those who initially contract the debt would not necessarily turn out to be those who have to pay it back later (as we can see in the case of the sovereign debt for consumption), this debt can hardly be legitimate debt. For a debt to be legitimate and just, the borrowed money should serve those who would pay it back later.

The second principle of a just debt is payability. In order for a debt to be moral, it should be first payable for the debtor. On June 25, 2015, in India, sixty-one-year-old Ninge Gowda set his ready-to-harvest sugarcane crop on fire and jumped in, ending his own life. He was a resident of Karnataka's southern sugar bowl district of Mandya and owned a 0.2 hectare in Pandavapura. Gowda's is not an isolated case. One hundred and eight other farmers have committed suicide in the same state between June 1 and July 20.[62] One of the main causes of their tragic deaths was the debt. Gowda had borrowed ₹1.5 ($2,265) from a moneylender at an exorbitant interest rate of 36 percent. Unable to repay the debt while the price of sugarcane dropped significantly, he could not endure the mounting pressure of debt. One of the key factors that render a debt unpayable is high interest rates such as Gowda's 36 percent. With that rate, his debt cannot but be toxic from its origin, which eventually led him to his own death. Contracted though they are, some debts are brazenly toxic and thus immoral.

In her article "Ethical Misconduct and the Global Financial Crisis," Elaine Sternberg argues that subprime mortgages are not the sort of things that can themselves have a moral status. "[A] subprime mortgage can no more be ethical or unethical than a spoon can or a thermometer. The proper objects of moral judgement are not artefacts, but people and their actions."[63] Sternberg's perception of debt as a morally neutral artefact is deeply problematic. While a spoon or a thermometer cannot kill a person unless a murderer used them as a weapon, a toxic debt can kill a person on its own. Social scientists Jason N. Houle and Michael T. Light have recently uncovered a statistical association between state-level foreclosure and suicide rates from 2005 to 2010.[64] During this period, the U.S. suicide rate increased nearly 13 percent from 11.0 to 12.4 per 100,000 people, and this rate was especially pronounced among the middle aged, nearly 30 percent. Due to this increase, middle-aged suicide has become more prevalent than suicide among the elderly, who have historically had higher suicide rates than all other age groups.[65] As we can see in the Caribbean countries' debt crises, unlike such nonmoral artefacts as a spoon or a thermometer, some debts cannot be adequately understood without contextualizing them against their historical and structural backdrops. Indeed, all debts have their unique stories, and they have different levels of a moral status. For a debt to be moral, it is supposed to be payable for the debtor.

The third principle to qualify the concept of just debt is shareability. In a nutshell, shareability means that when the debt turns out to be unpayable due to unexpected events and thus insolvent, creditors should bear at least partial responsibility for the failed loans with debtors. In his article "Risks of Lending and Liability of Lenders," Kunibert Raffer writes, "Although *pacta sunt servanda* (pacts must be respected) is a fundamental legal, economic, and ethical principle, all legal systems recognize circumstances where contractual rights can no longer be enforced, or indeed cease to exist."[66] Although it is the debtor's primary responsibility to pay back his or her debt, external shocks, unexpected catastrophes, or unforeseeable events may change drastically the debtor's situation resulting in the state of insolvency. Indeed, risks always exist in the financial market, and when these risks turn out to be a real situation, the terms of the initial debt contract cannot be fulfilled without any fault caused by the creditors. In a state of insolvency, Raffer holds, shifting all responsibilities onto debtors is not only economically unsound but also ethically wrong.[67] Unfortunately, though, over the past decades since 1970, Organisation for Economic Co-operation and Development (OECD) governments and multilateral institutions made an effort to eliminate any lender responsibility to their commercial banks, while discriminating against Southern sovereign debtors. He writes, "Rigging the market by eliminating risk and giving patently wrong signals to private creditors, the official sector bears great responsibility for the global debt debacle."[68] Since risk and liability render the creditor more responsible for lending decisions, and the principle of shareability ensures the fair distribution of risk and liability on both parties (debtors and creditors), it becomes an integral aspect of just debt.

Above, we have seen what makes debt or a debt contract moral by outlining the three qualifications: serviceability, payability, and shareability. For a debt to be morally established, these qualifications are to be met. The full construction of an ethics of debt, however, may not be possible unless we develop a new concept of right: that is, the debtor's socioeconomic right to just debt in making a debt contract. Regarding the concept of the debtor's right to just debt, three following questions may be asked: First, why do we need to develop the concept of the right to just debt? Second, how could we develop it? Third, what does it mean that debtors have the right to just debt? Ronald Dworkin's distinction between rights and goals appears to give us a helpful guide to answer these questions. According to Dworkin, while the concept of rights is largely associated with the idea of entitlement, the concept of goal is with the state of affairs. Referring to rights, Dworkin says, "It seems natural to say, for example, that freedom of speech is a right, not a goal, because citizens are *entitled* to that freedom as a matter of political morality."[69] On the other hand, as for a goal, he states,

"A goal is a nonindividuated political aim, that is, a state of affairs whose specification does not in this way call for any particular opportunity or resource or liberty for particular individuals."[70]

If we adopt Dworkin's helpful distinction, the debtor's right to just debt is a socioeconomic entitlement in making a debt contract, whereas the promotion of happiness and welfare is a desired state of affairs after which debtors are supposed to strive. If the debtor's right to just debt is politically constituted, then any relevant political decisions are made in such a way to protect the state of affairs in which the debtor enjoys the right. Dworkin writes, "An individual has a right to some opportunity or resource or liberty if it counts in favor of a political decision that the decision is likely to advance or protect the state of affairs in which he enjoys the right, even when no other political aim is served and some political aim is disserved thereby, and counts against that decision that it will retard or endanger that state of affairs, even when some other political aim is thereby served."[71] One may wonder, though, why we should politically ratify this right.

The answer to this question comes from our critical and communal reflection on humanity's experience of the Great Recession that affects many people virtually all over the world. Inculcated by the subprime mortgage crisis and the financial crisis of 2007–2008 it triggered, the Great Recession was the worst global recession since World War II.[72] We need to remember that the Universal Declaration of Human Rights was created in 1948 as humanity's critical and communal response to World War II. There was a consensus in the world community that a more specified list of the rights of individuals are to be universally ratified as a response to the organized human calamities initiated by Nazi Germany. In an age of ever-expanding financialization, as global citizens are increasingly vulnerable to various types of manipulative economy of debt, protecting the debtor's right (individual as well as collective) to just debt is not only morally justifiable but also socioeconomically indispensable because it would better prevent the financial market from unwanted financial crisis and fluctuation caused by unregulated debt defaults. I suggest that since financialization affects almost all global citizens' socioeconomic lives, especially the people of the Global South, and many of them are either actual or potential debtors, the debtor's right to just debt should be recognized by multilateral treaties such as International Covenant on Economic, Social and Cultural Rights (signed in 1966). The covenant's core provisions do not yet recognize this right, but the rapidly changing global economy, especially its financial sector, certainly renders this right as an urgent and legitimate agenda to consider.

The debtor's right to just debt stipulates that the creditors are required to provide a just debt in contracting debt with debtors because each right exists in opposition to a duty. Onora O'Neill's pioneering work on the relation between rights and its corresponding obligations helps us have a more critical view on the relation between the debtor's right to just debt and the creditor's matching obligation to provide it. According to O'Neill, for past decades in the Western world, the ethical development of the rights theory has been largely typified by unbalanced emphasis on the recipient's right, without adequately considering the provider's obligations. For example, various international charters and declarations of rights including the Universal Declaration of Human Rights (1948) have been largely established from a recipient's perspective rather than from that of providers. O'Neill finds it problematic because "we do not yet know whether these universal rights are matched and secured by universal obligations, or by obligations held by some but not by all agents and agencies."[73] She then quickly adds, "It is a matter for deep regret that the Declaration is so opaque about allocating the obligations of justice."[74] For this reason, she develops her ethical position on the priority of obligations over rights.

O'Neill divides the concept of obligations into four categories based on two distinctions: the universal versus the special and the perfect versus the imperfect. While the former is about who holds obligations, the latter division is about to whom obligations are owed. The case of the creditor's obligation to provide just debt is then categorized as one of the *special perfect obligations*, which "require social structures or practices that connect specific agents to specified recipients of action, to whom they owe and for whom they are bound to perform, who are the holders of the equivalent special rights."[75] Indeed, debtor-creditor relationships are established on special terms within which particular obligation bearers are matched with particular right holders. O'Neill writes, "Since special obligations always presuppose special relationships by which agents are allocated to recipients, they are always subject to two levels of ethical vindication or query."[76] An ethics of debt is then established in such a way to allow this ongoing process of "ethical vindication or query" in light of the debtor's rights as well as the creditor's obligations.

One may raise the question, "What about the debtor's obligation and the creditor's right?" Although I have focused on developing the ethical concepts of the debtor's right and the creditor's obligation with regard to the construction of an ethics of debt, this of course does not mean that the proposed ethics of debt simply ignores these paired moral concepts. In a nutshell, according to a new ethics of debt, the debtor's obligation (to pay off the debt) turns out to be the prima facie obligation as opposed to the creditor's obligation (to provide a just debt); in the same manner, the creditor's right (to debt payment) turns out to be the prima facie right in opposition to the debtor's right (to just debt). As argued in the previous chapter, the ultimate purpose of debt is to serve humanity rather than to cheat, abuse, or exploit vulnerable debtors for the sake of the concentration of wealth mainly for oneself.

## Conclusion

For past decades, humanity has witnessed the rise of a new global financial order called financialization, which was unknown to previous generations, and it has come along with a formidable destructive power on a global scale. The financial crisis of 2007–2008 was a global showcase of how ever-expanding financialization can be detrimental to all humanity if it were unjustly manipulated by those who run the system for the sake of concentrating their own wealth. An ethics of debt is developed here as a critical-reflective response to this new global financial order and its possible manipulation from a reconstructionist perspective. The purpose of developing this new ethics of debt is to prevent what O'Neill calls the "avoidable direct and indirect injury." It is important for us to realize that the problem of debt is not just a matter of money and wealth, because it can deeply affect not only individuals' livability but also society's moral foundation and its societal fabric. In this respect, the problem of debt is fundamentally a matter of social justice.

## CHAPTER THREE

# Unpayable Debt and the Ethics of Default and Bankruptcy

## Introduction

In the previous chapter, I have delineated three qualifications of what I call a just debt—serviceability, payability, and shareability. I outlined these qualifications as the *substantive* moral condition in contrast with the *formal* legal requirement of neoliberal debts—that is, the contract. It is my contention that these two conditions are necessary in order for a neoliberal debt to be transformed from its largely amoralized financial unit to a morally conceived financial entity. The attempt to establish the concept of a just debt, however, is only a small step toward the full reconstruction of an ethics of debt. It is important to note that any debts, including the morally justifiable debt, can turn out to be insolvent and thus defaulted because of unexpected and uncontrollable circumstances such as personal accidents or structural economic changes. The purpose of this chapter is, then, to answer the following questions: What are the ethical guidelines when we have to consider such necessary measures as debt default, bankruptcy, or bailout in an age of financialization?[1] How can we provide justice to those who are affected by unpayable debt?

Debt default, bankruptcy, or bailout can be a significant moral issue for several reasons. First, in the case of debt default and bankruptcy, if multiple creditors are involved in maximizing their recovery as measured in dollars and cents, they cannot but face an inevitable issue—that is, how to divide up *fairly* the remaining assets among themselves as they struggle to overcome the financial loss caused by the default. The quest for distributive justice incurred by defaulted debt may also arise among the affected debtors as well. For instance, when a country's sovereign or national debt becomes insolvent on its borrowed money, and so-called austerity measures are brought on the debtor country by IFIs such as the IMF or World Bank, the citizens of the defaulted country suddenly come to face an inevitable question—that is, how to share the imposed financial burdens among themselves equitably? The quest for distributive justice thus becomes an important issue when we attempt to do justice to unpayable debt.

Second, debt default becomes an indispensable social-ethical issue because such thorny issues as punishment, retribution, or rehabilitation ensue while debtors, creditors, and other affected parties are struggling to overcome financial damages. As noted in previous chapters, from ancient Rome to mid-nineteenth-century Europe and from India to the United States in modern society, debtors have been subject to various human rights violations by creditors because of their inability to pay back their debts. Fortunately, most modern democratic societies have transferred the "right to punishment" from the hands of the creditor to the public or juridical authorities in the name of the law and regulations. Through this structural transformation, humanity has significantly reduced unjust human rights violations readily brought on defaulted debtors. Despite this moral and legal development, humanity still has a lot of work to do, especially with regard to providing restorative or rehabilitative justice to many defaulted debtors who should be better termed as victims, rather than as offenders, in today's neoliberal financial system. The usual equation of defaulted debtor as offender and creditor as victim is increasingly untenable because of the structural financial injustices caused by the unbalanced power between the debtor and the creditor, unscrupulous manipulations of financial managers, and the sheer lack of proper legal oversight on the financial system as a whole. The social ethics of debt should thus be able to address not only distributive justice but also restorative or rehabilitative justice on various moral and legal aspects of defaulted debt.

In this chapter, I divide the possible cases of debt default into three categories—individual, sovereign, and corporate—with a view to developing a different set of ethical principles according to each category. One should note that the purpose of this chapter is not to review the history of bankruptcy law to tease out some possible moral principles. It is not the purpose of this chapter either to develop a whole new set of ethical principles on debt default or bankruptcy. There have been more than 150 years of legal development on bankruptcy law in the United States since the authorization of the Bankruptcy Law Consolidation Act of 1849, and these laws reflect their moral and ethical perspective in a given historical context. The scope of my ethical investigation and reflection is thus limited to a more recent and contemporary context that has been largely shaped and influenced by rising global financialization. Overall, in this chapter, I attempt not only to critically inherit valuable moral wisdoms of the U.S. legal tradition on debt default and bankruptcy but also to construct a new ethical approach minding the changing global context of our financial world.

### The Case for Individual Debt Default and Bankruptcy

Regarding the case of individual debt default, the most fundamental ethical problem is how we could morally justify the concept of bankruptcy itself. Bankruptcy did not even exist in ancient society, such as ancient Greece. The first bankruptcy statute was passed in England in 1542 by Henry VIII aiming at "improving the efficiency of debt collection and at introducing justice among creditors."[2] According to Jukka Kilpi, the interests of debtors started to surface, and the most remarkable milestone was the enactment of the Bankruptcy Act of 1705, which for the first time made debt discharge part of the procedure. In the United States, on the federal level, a significant bankruptcy law was enacted in 1898 whose emphasis fell heavily on relieving the debtors' burden.[3] According to the current U.S. law, debtors are allowed to choose between Chapter 7 and Chapter 13. While the former, eligible only to those who have little or no disposable income, is a liquidation bankruptcy designed to wipe out general unsecured debts, the latter is designed for debtors with regular income to pay back at least a portion of their debts through a repayment plan.

From Immanuel Kant's deontological moral perspective, the legal provision of bankruptcy may sound controversial because one should always keep his or her promise in order to fulfill the categorical imperative. In his *Groundwork*, he articulates the categorical duty to pay debts as follows:

> For the universality of a law that everyone believing himself to be in need can make any promise he pleases with the intention not to keep it would make promising, and the very purpose of promising, itself impossible, since no one would believe he was being promised anything, but would laugh at utterances of this kind of empty shams.[4]

If the moral injunction to pay one's own debt were an absolute moral law, bankruptcy as a legal process to resettle one's debt would not be available to defaulted debtors. In his book *The Ethics of Bankruptcy*, however, Jukka Kilpi argues that Kant's deontological exemplification of keeping one's promise to pay his or her debt back is a prima facie moral duty, not an absolute moral injunction. Kilpi states:

> But this duty is, indeed, a *prima facie* duty. There are circumstances in which the obligation is void even if the other party, who has received the promise, wants us to keep it. I do not mean only circumstances in which it is impossible to perform the required act. We have not even a *prima facie* duty to perform impossible acts, because a duty to perform an act which cannot be done is inherently contradictory.[5]

What, then, about the cases in which debtors are proved to be fraudulent, reckless, or negligent? These conditions seem to demonstrate that the debtor's insolvency is largely self-induced. Should he or she be eligible for debt resettlement by filing for bankruptcy? According to Kilpi, the case of fraud is clear. Since the distinctive attribute of fraud is to cause intentionally financial damage to lenders, it deserves punishment. The punishment may include the exclusion of the fraudulent debtor from discharge "because it is part of the nature of punishments that they may violate the offender's autonomy."[6] The case of recklessness is more complex because seeking high returns from risky ventures is not necessarily blameworthy. If, however, the debtor does not conduct his or her affairs in the ways he or she let the creditor believe, in other words, there was a dishonest disclosure of intentions, the debtor is liable for punishment. According to Kilpi, excessive risk may be enough to warrant moral blame for recklessness if the debtor broke the standards of caution agreed on in the contractual context, or again if the debtor has intentionally misrepresented the risk.[7] The case of negligence is somewhat different from the two previous cases in that it is hard for us to blame the contractual parties only for not being competent and prudent enough. In that case, bankruptcy is allowed since it "brings the pain to an end, and confines it to those who have sought exposure to it."[8] Kilpi concludes his moral investigation of punishable debt default by saying that bankruptcy should be arranged in such a way to relieve the financial misery of honest defaulted debtors who did not want to cause harm because, partly, empirical evidence shows that hardships imposed on honest debtors do not bring any additional benefits.[9]

Kilpi's basic philosophical position on the case of individual bankruptcy is grounded in what he calls "a modest Kantian notion of autonomy."[10] As seen above, his philosophical effort to do justice to unpayable debt is largely focused on an individual agency's moral liability and legal culpability, which is indispensably tied to the concept of autonomy. The autonomy-based ethics of individual bankruptcy has some advantages ,such as holding each individual debtor accountable for his or her action according to the moral criteria of fairness, equality, and respect. His approach, however, presupposes that individual debtors are wholly responsible for their financial affairs. This presupposition is increasingly untenable due to the rising neoliberal globalization that has also been intricately intertwined with deepening financialization. For past decades, countless numbers of global citizens have fallen victim to financial misery as a result of the global structural change that induced growing indebtedness and debt default. The following case of Feliciano's indebtedness provides us with a different scenario of people's indebtedness, default, and bankruptcy, which cannot be captured by Kilpi's modest Kantian notion of autonomy and neo-Kantian liberal paradigm of justice.

My name is Feliciano and I grew up in a rural village. Like many people in my community we were not able to study very much. I went to school for only a little more than a year. But later, my wife and I moved to the big city of Oaxaca. I got work doing construction. I worked hard and am one of the lucky ones. I became a Master of Construction. I oversaw workers. I supervised them when they built small buildings and private family homes. It was a lot of responsibility to make sure everybody was working hard and seeing that things were built well. It gave me a lot of pleasure to see a building go up from start to finish. When we first started out in Oaxaca we lived in a tin shack in a housing subdivision. By 1994 we had built a small house of brick and we were happy to have a home and a future for our three children. But the real turning point for us was the devaluation of our currency, the peso, in December of 1994. Within days, a peso became worth a half-peso on the international market. Construction came to a standstill and many works were suspended. For six months I was without work. The costs of construction tripled. Prices fluctuated greatly from one day to the next. In the early part of 1995, there was 85% less construction than in the previous year. Those who had worked received lower salaries than they had previously. Before, I was hired to supervise an entire job. Now I worked by the day. This past year the price of materials has been stable—competition among those who sell materials has made this so. Salaries have not increased but the cost of living has continued to rise monthly over these past three years. Today [in 1997] there is an increase in construction in Oaxaca, but most of it is in the hands of large businesses. They bring their own architects and supervisors and many of the workers are from outside Oaxaca. They buy their materials from factories or basic sources, so the local middlemen are bypassed. Only those who work for the government or for a big business can afford to buy the houses that are being built. Education costs continually climb higher. School uniforms cost double what they cost three years ago. All food, electricity, water, bus fares, and other living expenses constantly go up.[11]

We should first note that Feliciano's financial misery was deeply affected by global structural changes such as the international free trade agreement (e.g., the North American Free Trade Agreement) and the volatile exchange rates (devaluation of Mexican peso) as well as the rising dominance of multinational corporations and franchised businesses. Being unprotected and disenfranchised, Feliciano could not cope with the unjust structural changes of global economy, which was largely run by powerful nations and privileged private sectors across the globe. His indebtedness has nothing to do with fraud, recklessness, or negligence, which Kilpi laid out above. Feliciano's case illustrates that the modest notion of Kantian autonomy can no longer be an effective conceptual scheme in doing justice to such bankruptcies. Given that so many global citizens, especially those in underdeveloped countries, are potentially vulnerable to the kind of financial misery Feliciano has suffered, we need a different conceptual paradigm to provide better justice to those financial victims of ever-increasing globalization and financialization.

The new paradigm should be able to do better justice to those victimized defaulters in today's neoliberal global economy, as we are focusing on restoring their damaged capabilities and dignity rather than on serving a Kantian notion of autonomy. We may find this new paradigm in the works of Martha Nussbaum, who develops a new way of conceptualizing justice known as the "capabilities approach." What is the capabilities approach to justice? According to Nussbaum, the concept of capabilities is an indispensable aspect of dignified human life, and the political goal of the capabilities approach to justice is to secure the "threshold level" of each of ten central human capabilities for each individual in human society: (1) life; (2) bodily health, nourishment, and shelter; (3) bodily integrity; (4) the use of the senses, imagination, and thought; (5) emotional attachment and development; (6) practical reasoning; (7) affiliation and the social bases of self-respect and nonhumiliation; (8) other species; (9) play and recreation; and (10) control over one's political and material environment.[12]

What, then, does Nussbaum's capabilities approach to justice have to do with our quest for doing justice to unpayable debt? We should note that, for many victimized debtors such as Feliciano, unpayable debt is indeed the greatest socioeconomic barrier to a life of human dignity. Their sense of human dignity is often seriously infringed on and violated by unpayable debt. To provide justice to these victimized debtors, then, we are to appropriate Nussbaum's capabilities approach with the purpose of restoring their damaged capabilities. Appropriating Nussbaum's insight, thus, I argue that the right to a "fresh start" should become one of central human capabilities, and those victimized debtors should be able to free themselves from the burdens of unpayable debt as a socioeconomic right.

Although Nussbaum has formulated the ten central human capabilities as an account of minimum core social entitlements, none of them seems specifically refer to the concept of a fresh start. The tenth item on the list, "control over one's environment," may be the closest one, but her specification does not seem to address this directly. Despite this limitation, though, she makes it clear that the list itself is "open-ended and subject to on-going revision and rethinking, in the way that any society's account of its most fundamental entitlements is always subject to supplementation (or deletion)."[13] As argued above, the rising globalization and financialization make the right to a fresh start an even more important legal entitlement, especially for those who would be victimized by the unjust structural forces of global economy. How does the right to a fresh start become one of the central human capabilities?

For two reasons, the right to a fresh start should become one of the central human capabilities. First, without access to this right, as Nussbaum points out, "an intuitive idea of life that is worthy of the dignity of the human being" is not possible.[14] It is not difficult to imagine that debtors like Feliciano would not be able to function properly in a permanently indebted situation, because no one can properly function as a dignified human under constant harassment and poverty due to unpayable debt. Especially if this situation is imposed on the debtor not as a result of his or her own fault but as a result of the structural injustices of the global economy and politics, the right to a fresh start should be considered a legal entitlement to restore his or her damaged dignity. Paradoxical as it may seem, the neoliberal global economy and financialization actually render this right as an urgent and imperative one. Second, we should note that unpayable debt affects not just the victimized debtor but also others who are related to victimized debtors. Karen Gross calls these people the debtor's "community" that includes the debtor's "family, friends, and co-workers."[15] In a bankruptcy context, she argues, "the greatest attention should be paid to the debtor's community for, as the host community, it has the greatest nexus with the debtor."[16] Going back to Feliciano's case, the most significantly affected community members are his innocent children. The obstruction of their father's right to a fresh start will negatively affect these children's future, exacerbating the vicious cycle of injustice begetting injustice. To sever this vicious cycle, the right to a fresh start should be established as one of the central human capabilities.

Regarding the right to a fresh start, one of the most urgent and important problems we are facing now in the United States is the exponential increase of student loan debt.[17] There is compelling evidence that the exponential increase of student debt has more to do with a structural reason than with individual misconduct. According to the *Economist*, student debt in the United States as of August 2015 totals $1.2 trillion (the second-largest consumer obligation after mortgages), up more than threefold over the past decade.[18] The *Wall Street Journal* also reports that nearly seven million U.S. citizens have gone at least a year without making a payment on their federal student loans, which suggests a widening swath of households are unable or unwilling to pay back their school debt. This means that about 17 percent of all borrowers with federal loans are severely delinquent; this number rises if we include borrowers currently in school who are not yet required to repay. There are also millions of other borrowers who are months behind but have not hit the 360-day threshold that the government defines as a default.[19] The case of forty-five-year-old Jody Sofia helps us get a glimpse of what this debilitating mass phenomenon would really mean to those who are affected by that. Jody borrowed $92,500 to get a degree from Florida Coastal School of Law, but she is now in default. Due to the interest rate, her outstanding balance has ballooned to almost $144,000, and she spends her days fielding calls from government-contracted debt collectors. Derailed by illness and having to care for ailing parents, she did not take the bar exam and never got a legal job after graduating from Florida Coastal in 2004. Since, when private companies cannot recover the money, the Treasury Department garnishes Social Security, tax refunds, or wages, it has garnished almost $20,000 from Sofia's tax refund. If Sofia were to utilize repayment programs based on income to pay the student debt, her loans may be forgiven after at least twenty years. She said, "There's something really wrong with this system. . . . The government is spending all this money for these people to constantly call you. How effective is that?"[20]

As two-thirds of student loan balances are held by borrowers older than thirty, the numbers of borrowers from 2004 to 2014 has increased by 89 percent, and more than forty-three million borrowers owe an average of nearly $27,000 each,[21] one may wonder why there has been a phenomenal growth of student debt in the United States. We should note that there are several structural factors that have fueled the exponential increase of student debt for past decade. First, the enactment of BAPCPA (The Bankruptcy Abuse Prevention and Consumer Protection Act of 2005). According to Michael Greenstone and Adam Looney of the Brookings Institution,

"Student loans may have become relatively more available because of changes in the laws protecting creditors, which may have encouraged lenders to offer loans to a broader set of less creditworthy borrowers."[22] Second, the effect of financialization. Just as with mortgages, student loans are also sold as securities in the financial market, and this motivates debt-servicing companies to lend more money to students. Kelly Holland writes, "The total of private student loans outstanding grew rapidly from $55.9 billion in 2005 to $140.2 billion in 2011, fueled in part, perhaps, by the growing market for asset-backed securities backed by student loans, known as SLABS."[23] Third, the exponential growth in enrollment in for-profit colleges. Senator Tom Harkin (D-Iowa), chairperson of the Health, Education, Labor and Pensions Committee, released a report on July 30, 2012, that detailed predatory recruiting, sky-high tuition, low retention rates, and little job placement.[24] For instance, in 2001, 766,000 students were enrolled in for-profit higher education schools, but this number went up to 2.4 million in 2010. The median debt of the average for-profit college graduate was $32,700 compared to $24,600 for the average private nonprofit college graduate. It also unveiled billions in taxpayer dollars diverted to marketing, executive salaries, and profits. In fiscal year 2009, while the thirty companies examined devoted 22.4 percent of all revenues ($4.1 billion) to marketing, advertising, recruiting, and admissions staffing, they spent only 17.7 percent ($3.2 billion) on student instruction. Greenston and Looney's following observation is right: "The increase in enrollment in for-profit colleges, whose students rely more on federal aid and student loans, may have shifted the composition of students toward groups more likely to take out student loans."[25] Fourth, the rentier capitalism of debt servicing companies. According to Janet Lin, Education Management, which operates for-profit colleges and whose largest shareholder is the Goldman Sachs Group Inc., settled with the government in November 2015 for almost $100 million over alleged illegal student-recruitment practices, without admitting wrongdoing. Janet Lorin also helps us see how rentier capitalism is deeply involved in the student loan business. For example, FMS Investment Corp., a unit of Ceannate Corp., was paid $227 million by the Department of Education from October 2011 through September 2015. According to Lorin, "Firms typically earn monthly fees by loan status: $2.85 for those in repayment, $1.05 when borrowers are in school, and 45 cents when they're delinquent 361 days or more."[26]

Above we have seen that there is a structural reason behind the phenomenal increase in student loan debt and its increasing default rates. Many of these defaulted student borrowers are better termed as victims of structural injustices rather than financial delinquents or offenders. Unlike other consumer debts such as credit card debts, as Wenli Li says, "student loans are analogous to investment in physical capital such as an MRI machine purchased by a clinic."[27] The default on student loans thus causes collateral damages to affected debtors, leaving them in almost permanent debt. This is why I argue that the right to a fresh start should be conferred to these victimized debtors as we recognize it as one of the central human capabilities. Of course, each individual should be responsible for his or her life, including financial matters; but if he or she were victimized by the structural injustices of financial system or outdated and inadequate legal institutions, the right to a fresh start should be allowed to him or her. This right should also be allowed to those who might have incurred financial misery out of their own mistakes, incompetence, or negligence. Even those who were involved in fraud, after serving their punishment, are to be given a chance at a fresh start.

## The Case for Sovereign Debt Default and Bankruptcy

Debt default is not delimited to individual debtors. It can also happen to corporate entities, including sovereign nations. As Chris Jochnick states, "Sovereign debt is not only the most urgent economic issue facing many countries but perhaps the leading cause of human rights violations in the developing world."[28] There is a growing consensus among scholars that human rights and human dignity are given priority over payment in a conflictual situation "between two fundamental legal principles: the right of creditors to interest and repayments, and the human right recognized generally (not only in the case of loans) by all civilized legal systems."[29] Jochnick, for instance, argues that "under international law, human rights predominate over conflicting obligations, including debt servicing."[30] Fantu Cheru also writes that if such fundamental human rights as "the right to food," "the right to education," and "the right to health" are jeopardized by debt servicing, demanding and servicing such debt payment is illegitimate.[31] In a similar manner, Christian Barry also writes that sovereign debt raises serious human rights concerns if debt servicing significantly limits the ability of countries to manage their affairs effectively. He then illustrates the case of Tanzania, which spent nine times more on debt service than on health in 2000 even though 1.6 million of its citizens lived with AIDS.[32] Regarding the question of how to provide justice to unpayable debt in the context of a sovereign government, we thus have an overarching principle that human rights should not be violated in servicing debt. We, however, should go further in developing an ethics of debt concerning the case of sovereign insolvency because, as Jack Boorman holds, the real issue is how we are to achieve the overarching principle in a more practical sense.[33]

In his article "The Ethics of Debt Default," James Buchanan provides us with realistic guidelines, arguing that the governmental moral duty to honor debt obligations is not grounded in an idea that the modern state is a "moral unit" in the sense of an extended family. He writes, "The modern state is clearly not a 'moral unit.' . . . Any argument based on moral community seems, at best, neutral with reference to the whole question of adherence to public debt contracts."[34] Instead, he supports a contractarian approach to the ethics of governmental debt default. In developing his position on governmental indebtedness, he focuses on an important difference between individual debt and sovereign debt in that the person who chooses (those who initially contracted the governmental debt) is not necessarily visited with the consequences (those who have to pay back later). To address this intertemporal difference in developing a principle of justice for the case of governmental indebtedness, he applies the Rawlsian concept of the "veil of ignorance." He sets up the question as follows: "We must imagine an individual who is placed behind an intertemporal veil of ignorance, such that generational position cannot be identified. Will a group of several persons in this position reach agreement on the issue of public debt to finance recurrent public consumption?"[35] Buchanan argues that intertemporal agreement might be possible on the authorization of debt financing for several cases, such as extraordinary and temporary demands on the collectivity (wars and disaster reliefs) as well as public capital investment; but he claims that the debt financing of ordinary public consumption should be regarded as immoral by the contractarian standard.[36] Overall, he develops a contractarian moral argument that debtor countries should abide by their promises because of the moral legitimacy of law. This argument, he acknowledges, "loses some of its force, however, when default risk premiums are included in yields."[37]

Buchanan's contractarian approach, however, is not comprehensive enough to do justice to the case of sovereign insolvency. Regardless of the legitimate or illegitimate status of the governmental debt contract, default on sovereign debt can occur, and this situation always comes along with a set of difficult but practical questions: Who will take on the burden? How much should each related party pick up? How could we come to a fair decision on sharing financial burdens and losses? Distinct from individual default cases, any governmental debt default cannot help being more complex and multifaceted because there are multiple agencies (e.g., citizens of the debtor country and the multitude of creditors) whose interests are at stake from the beginning stage of assessing and restructuring the outstanding debt to the final stage of paying back the restructured debt. The problem of sharing the unwanted financial burden is an indispensable aspect of doing justice to sovereign insolvency and bankruptcy. What, then, is the guiding moral principle for governmental debt default and its restructuring process?

In doing justice to the case of sovereign insolvency, we need to realize that there is a tripartite relational dimension that renders the case of sovereign insolvency distinct from the case of individual bankruptcy. The tripartite relational dimension is outlined as follows: first, the relation among the citizens of the defaulted country who should bear the financial burden; second, the relation among the members of the creditor group who should bear the financial loss; third, the relation between the defaulted country and the interested creditors, who should negotiate how to cope with the financial crisis. I develop an ethics of sovereign insolvency by respectively engaging the tripartite relational dimension with a different set of moral principles. As we shall see, these different dimensions call for different criteria of justice.

## The First Dimension: Justice among the Citizens of the Defaulted Country

On June 30, 2015, Greece became the first developed country to fail to make an IMF loan payment. Greece has received three bailouts from the Eurozone countries and the IMF: €110 billion in 2010, €109 billion in 2011, and €86 billion in 2015. These financial bailouts came along with the usual austerity measures, including tax increases, pension cuts, and tight limits on public spending. Citizens erupted into violence protesting against these draconian austerity measures. According to the *Guardian*, Nicolaos Danizis, a sixty-year-old shipyard worker who participated in a Communist-led demonstration outside Parliament said, "These latest measures have been cooked up by outsiders and are totally outrageous. They are aimed not at the rich but at the poor. What we are saying here today is that they will pass only over our dead bodies."[38] In his article "Who Is to Blame for Greece's Crisis?," Mohamed el-Erian argues that although the Greek government, its private creditors, the EU government, and the IMF are to be blamed for Greece's recent financial crisis, the real victims of this historic tragedy are "the most vulnerable segments of the Greek population, who will become much worse off, today and for many years to come, as jobs disappear, savings evaporate, and livelihoods are destroyed."[39]

The case of Greece's sovereign debt default and the subsequent bailout demonstrate that the allocation of social and financial burdens among the citizens of the debtor country becomes a crucial issue in doing justice in the case of sovereign insolvency. I formulate the ethical principle of this issue by critically appropriating John Rawls' distributive theory of justice, especially his concept of the "difference principle." In his 1971 book *A Theory of Justice*, Rawls develops a conceptual mechanism through which diverse individuals can agree on a principle of justice that is presumably fair to all regarding the overall distribution of rights and valued primary goods. In so doing, he devised a hypothetical conceptual situation called the "original position" enabled by another conceptual scheme called the "veil of ignorance." The veil of ignorance basically makes it possible for all participants in the original position to screen their particularities such as abilities, tastes, positions, and social backgrounds in hammering out the ideal principle of justice. Thanks to this mechanism, individuals who gather in the original position are able to make a fair agreement under impartial conditions. The ingenuity of this conceptual breakthrough is that, in the original position, everyone thinks from everyone's perspective, and therefore any agreement made in that situation will be fair to all. One of the theoretic shortcomings of this method, however, is that it does not allow room for any affective elements of individual participants. One is to engage in a rational discussion in the original position solely based on the concept of "disinterested rationality." Feminist philosopher Martha Nussbaum thus criticizes this aspect: "Rawls's parties themselves lack benevolence and an intrinsic love of justice; these sentiments, however, are represented by the Veil of Ignorance. In the Well-Ordered Society, by contrast, people learn principle-dependent sentiment and motives."[40]

What are these two principles of justice that Rawls uncovers through his neo-Kantian conceptual mechanism? While the first principle is about an equal right to basic liberty, the second principle addresses the social and economic inequalities and their arrangement. He devises the "difference principle" in such a way as to allow social and economic inequalities with the condition that they benefit the worst-off members of society. He writes, "Social and economic inequalities are to be arranged so that they are both: (a) to the greatest benefit of the least advantaged, consistent with the just savings principle [difference principle], and (b) attached to offices and positions open to all under conditions of fair equality of opportunity."[41] Rawls' difference principle, despite its conceptual limitation, is an insightful idea that may be applicable to the first relational dimension (relations among the citizens of the defaulted country) of the sovereign insolvency. Of course there is a significant difference between the hypothetical original position in which participants are to develop the principle of justice for distributing social and economic goods, and the real world of the defaulted state in which citizens are to formulate the principle of justice to allocate social and economic burdens fairly among themselves. Despite the contextual and conceptual differences, I argue, we can develop the following Rawlsian principle of justice for a fair distribution of social and economic burdens caused by the sovereign insolvency. I call this principle the "difference principle of liability," which I formulate as follows: "The distribution of social and economic debt liabilities is to be arranged in such a way that it should least burden the least advantaged."

From the perspective of the difference principle of liability, Greece's debt crisis does not seem to be fairly managed by the Greek government. Instead of taking up the least burden, the least advantaged of the Greek society seem to undertake too much financial burden imposed on them under the banner of financial austerity. The highly publicized problem of tax evasion by the rich is a good example of how the Greek government should have rearranged the financial burden following the Rawlsian insight of distributive justice. According to the *Washington Post*, "The size of Greek tax evasion accounted for roughly half the country's budget shortfall in 2008 and one-third in 2009."[42] Haris Theoharis, Greece's secretary-general for public revenue (he has resigned from his position because of death threats) said in an interview with the *Guardian*, "The problem is that it's still too easy for contractors, people in the professions and some big companies not to declare all or part their earnings."[43] He also claims that "direct and indirect taxation should bring in an average of €50bn a year."[44] His thwarted plan to target the rich and well-connected to ease the austerity measures imposed largely on the least advantaged reflects what the difference principle of liability would call for in Greek society.

## The Second Dimension: Relations among the Members of the Creditor Group

Could we apply the Rawlsian distributive justice model to the second relational dimension (relations among the members of the creditor group) of the sovereign insolvency? In an original position composed of the members of the creditor group, I contend, they would come to the following set of agreements, which I would call the "principle of equal proportionality":

(1) all creditors agree to a fair sharing of financial losses caused by the sovereign insolvency and (2) the fair sharing is determined by the equal proportional distribution of the financial losses among the members of the creditor group. The Rawlsian concept of the difference principle, however, would not apply to the second relational dimension, because all members of the creditor group have already acknowledged the potential risks as well as the potential benefits when they made debt contracts with sovereign nations. The Rawlsian egalitarian distributive justice is still relevant because it offers us a critical conceptual edge on how we should respond to the two main problems within the second relational dimension—the problems related to the priority structures of creditors and the problems related to the so-called holdout—whose answers are not fully available yet.

In an article prepared for discussion group of the ILA (International Law Association) Sovereign Insolvency Study Group (2007–2012) hosted by the legal department of the IMF, Kunibert Raffer raises an important question: "Without any legal preference so far, one would have to ask whether there should be any preference ranking rather than symmetric treatment of all creditors."[45] According to Raffer, IFIs' assumed preferential status is morally as well as legally ungrounded. He first investigates various statutes of different IFIs, and he uncovers that their claim for preferential status is not supported by their own original statutes. For example, he writes, "The IMF could be party in any insolvency court or insolvency proceeding by arbitration. No right to preference of any kind exists. The loan loss reserves the IMF has established—officially called precautionary reserves—allow haircuts from an economic point of view."[46] He adds, "No article of the Bank's or IDA's [International Development Association] statues can be stretched to justify preference. By contrast, their Articles of Agreement still contain obligations that prove the founders' intention to subordinate these claims."[47] One of the reasons why Raffer opposes the IFIs' preferential claim is that, protected by preferential entitlement, IFIs may engage in unlawful or immoral financial transactions. He exemplifies two cases: the IBRD had continued lending to Suharto's Indonesia, knowing that a third or at least a quarter of all loans would disappear, whereas the IMF had also lent to Argentina knowing that the program offered no solution. He thus writes, "Demands for full repayment of loans that knowingly damaged the borrower has been 'supported' by the claim to enjoy preferred creditor status."[48] Raffer, however, makes an exception for justifying preference. "If the IMF—or any other IFI—fulfills the role of financing debtor countries during sovereign insolvency procedures, this— only this—money would naturally have to be exempt."[49] Raffer's argument against the IFIs' preferential status is not only reasonable but also morally justifiable because it satisfies the principle of equal proportionality.

The second problem in doing justice to the creditors of sovereign insolvency is the case of the "holdouts." In December 2001, Argentina defaulted on its sovereign debt, which amounted to $93 billion.[50] After its default, Argentina engaged in two restructurings in 2005 and in 2010. The second debt restructuring in 2010 resulted in the restructuring of around 93 percent of the foreign debt that had been defaulted on in 2001, but the remaining 7 percent of the holdout creditors (mainly vulture funds) refused to join the process (vulture fund NML Capital paid $49 million on the secondary market for bonds worth $832 million and sought the payment in full of original nominal amounts plus interest—$1.3 billion, which amounts to a return of 1,600 percent[51]). While the majority of the creditors accepted repayments of around 30 percent of face value and deferred payment terms, the holdout creditors later sued Argentina to prevent Argentina from making payments on the restructured bonds, which Argentina had been servicing. Judge Griesa of the Southern District of New York found in favor of the vulture fund (NML Capital—a subsidiary of Elliott Management) granting an injunction against Argentina.[52] His judgment was affirmed by the Court of Appeals and the Supreme Court of the United States. As a result of this ruling, it became illegal for Argentina to pay its restructured creditors without also making concurrent ratable payments to the holdout creditors. On July 30, 2014, Argentina entered into technical default.[53] From the perspective of the principle of equal proportionality, the holdout case of the NML Capital vulture fund demonstrates not only a blatant moral violation solely motivated by its own financial profits but also the detrimental abuse of law completely ignoring the spirit of international laws. This becomes a reason why the international community steps up its multilateral and international collaborations to develop legal guidelines or a binding international convention to stop vulture funds from continuing to abuse the rule of law.

The Third Dimension: Relations between the Defaulted
Country and the Creditors

Above, regarding the quest for justice to the case of sovereign insolvency, we have explored two relational dimensions—the relations among the citizens of the defaulted country and the relations among the creditors. How can we provide justice to the third relational dimension (the relationship between the defaulted country and its creditors) of sovereign insolvency? Regarding this question, feminist economist Julie A. Nelson offers an important perspective that the problem of debt, including sovereign debt, is fundamentally a *relational* problem rather than a rational problem. According to Nelson, originating in the work of legal scholars Ian Macneil and Stewart Macaulay, the "relational theory of contracts" sees contracting as taking place within a context of ongoing social relationships of cooperation for mutual gain.[54] The debt contract, thus, should be depicted as a relational rather than a rational issue. She writes, "Written contracts, relational contract theorists point out, are only the beginning of a relationship and the actual terms of the contract are often forgotten—or never even fully understood. Renegotiation, this literature points out, is the rule rather than the exception."[55] Thus, when we attempt to do justice to various cases of sovereign insolvency, the type of justice we need to develop is a relational one rather than mechanical or mathematical, which has no room for renegotiation.

Focusing on the relational aspect of the sovereign debt, Matt Peterson and Christian Barry develop two principles—the "principle of assistance and rescue" and the "principle of contributory fault"—in answering the following question: "Who should bear the costs of a country's decision to borrow when that country cannot repay its debts without causing severe deprivation among its people? Should they be borne entirely by the government—and ultimately the people—of that country or should they be pushed in whole or in part on to others?"[56] First, resonating Peter Singer's famous argument that affluent people have the responsibility to assist the global poor,[57] Peterson and Barry develop the principle of assistance and rescue. According to them, we need to consider not only how heavily burdened the population of a country would be in absolute and relative terms if that country were to pay its debts or absorb the full burden of its financial losses, but also how costly it would be for others to offset the costs so that debt restructuring could be available to the defaulted country.[58] Reflecting Iris Marion Young's social connection model of responsibility, they also develop the second principle (the principle of contributory fault), arguing that those who contribute to the financial deprivation of the defaulted country should be also held accountable. Although they do not invoke the name, the second principle reflects the key philosophical tenet of Iris Marion Young's social connection model of responsibility, which she summarizes as "all those who contribute by their actions to structural processes with some unjust outcomes share responsibility for the injustice."[59] Based on these two philosophical principles,

Peterson and Barry argue, "Even in cases where countries have behaved irresponsibly, we should not conclude that their present and future citizens should pay the full costs."[60] The real question is, then, how can we implement the relational justice principles, grounded in Singer's assistance principle and Young's social connection model, to the uncharted territory of sovereign debt default?

It is my contention that the answer to this question lies in the development of sovereign bankruptcy code. Currently we have no equivalent mandatory bankruptcy procedure for the case of sovereign debt default; however, there has been a concerted effort to develop such an idea. Perhaps the most significant effort was done by the IMF first deputy managing director Anne Krueger (2001–2006) in 2002. In her 2001 speech and subsequent 2002 paper—"A New Approach to Sovereign Debt Restructuring"—Krueger broke the taboo at the IMF and brought about a long-needed change in its policy on sovereign insolvency. She first acknowledges that "there is a consensus that the present process for restructuring the debts of a sovereign is more prolonged, more unpredictable and more damaging to the country and its creditors than would be desirable."[61] This is the reason why she proposed the SDRM (sovereign debt restructuring mechanism). Although the proposal contains progressive aspects such as collective action clauses, which would restrict the ability of creditors (such as vulture funds) to enforce their claims in national courts, it was broadly criticized.

Raffer, for instance, argues that because the SDRM reflects strong institutional self-interest on the part of the IMF, its design is unfair, especially to private creditors and debtors. He summarizes his critique of the SDRM as follows, pointing out its lack of procedural justice of mutuality: "The IMF's executive board alone decides on the most important issues under the SDRM: sustainability (and thereby the amount of debt reduction) and the adequacy of the debtor's economic policy. These decisions cannot be challenged."[62] For this reason, Raffer suggests that the more desirable sovereign debt restructuring should be modeled after the U.S. Bankruptcy Code Chapter 9 (municipalities) rather than Chapter 11 (corporations) in that Chapter 9 allows overindebted municipalities to present a plan. It is beyond the scope of this chapter to compare the U.S. Bankruptcy Code Chapter 9 and Chapter 11 in detail, but it is critical to note that the future direction of international legal agreement on sovereign bankruptcy should be based on the concept of relational justice, which would allow the collective bargaining process of negotiation between the debtor countries and the creditors.

## The Case for Corporate Debt Default and Bankruptcy

Just like individual debtors, corporate entities often face impending finan-cial crises that may lead them to the state of default. Unlike individual debtors' default cases, those of corporate entities are much more complex because many stakeholders are involved in liquidating or reorganizing processes with their vested interests. Some of these stakeholders include secured creditors (often a bank), unsecured creditors (banks, suppliers, and bondholders), and stockholders (owners of the company). As one can imagine, when the remaining assets are to be divided among these inter-ested parties by corporate default, there arises a crucial need to sort out how to allocate the remaining assets among these parties. This is one of the key justice issues regarding the case of corporate insolvency. First of all, what is the current legal understanding of corporate bankruptcy?

According to the U.S. SEC, companies have two options, Chapter 11 and Chapter 7 of the Bankruptcy Code. While Chapter 11 is used to "reorganize" its business and try to become profitable again, Chapter 7 is used to stop all operations and "liquidate" the company's assets to pay off the debt.[63] Most publicly held companies file under Chapter 11 rather than Chapter 7 because they can still run their business while controlling the bankruptcy process. Chapter 11 makes it possible for companies to rehabilitate the faltering business, and sometimes they do successfully work out a plan to return to profitability. If not, they finally liquidate their assets to pay off debt. When a company files for Chapter 11, the U.S. Trustee, the bankruptcy arm of the Justice Department, appoints one or more committees to represent the interests of stakeholders such as credi-tors, bondholders, and stockholders to develop a plan of reorganization to get out of debt. This plan is then accepted by the stakeholders and must be confirmed by the court. However, although creditors or stockholders may vote to reject the plan, the court has the authority to disregard this vote and still confirm the plan if it finds the plan fair to creditors as well as stockholders.[64] What we should note is that the SEC's role is generally limited to two tasks: (1) to review the disclosure document to determine whether the company is telling investors and creditors the important information they need to know and (2) to ensure that stockholders are represented by an official committee, if appropriate.[65]

When companies are in serious indebtedness with no possibility of continuing their business operations, they file under Chapter 7 to liqui-date their assets. In that case, administrative and legal expenses are paid first, and the remainder goes to creditors. When the value of the collateral, which is to be returned to secured creditors, is not sufficient, the secured creditors will be grouped with other unsecured creditors for the rest of their claim. Bondholders and other unsecured creditors should file a claim if there is enough money left for them to receive some payment. Placed at the end of the line, stockholders generally do not receive anything in return for their investment. In a case in which creditors are paid in full with some money still left, stockholders will be notified and given an opportunity to file claims.[66] This payment order is commonly called the "absolute priority rule" (APR).

What, then, does it mean to do justice to the case of corporate insolvency? What does ethics have to do with unpayable debt in the context of corporate insolvency? The most influential ethical theory on the case of corporate insolvency seems to be the utilitarian approach. For example, Jacques Boettcher and colleagues write, "The ethics of bankruptcy as a whole is judged using the *utilitarian* criterion: the extent to which the firm's stakeholders are benefited overall and the least harm is done to them."[67] He goes on to say, "We thus use the *utilitarian* norm—when an action provides the greatest benefit and the least harm to all of those who have a stake in the outcome—to decide if a corporate bankruptcy is ethically justified."[68] Based on the utilitarian perspective, Boettcher and colleagues therefore develop the so-called stakeholder theory of corporate bankruptcy. The concept of stakeholder theory was first developed by economist Edward R. Freeman to replace Milton Friedman's stockholder theory. According to Freeman, corporate managers bear a fiduciary relationship to stakeholders. He defines stakeholders as "suppliers, customers, employees, stockholders, and the local community, as well as management in its role as agent for these groups."[69]

By integrating Freeman's stakeholder theory with utilitarian ethics, Boettcher and colleagues first develop an argument that since the human cost is generally greater and the dismantled parts of a firm are normally not as valuable as the intact firm in liquidation, bankruptcy reorganization can be an ethical way for a business to serve the best interests of its stakeholders: employees, suppliers, creditors, shareholders, and the community.[70] They also claim, "We strongly believe that an ethical bankruptcy should be one that can provide the greatest benefits and least harm to the various stakeholders. Bankruptcy as an institution is ethically justified as an attempt to give the honest debtor a second chance."[71] William Fitzpatrick and Samuel DiLullo also incorporate the notion of stakeholder in engaging the management of corporate bankruptcy. According to them, although bankruptcy has focused on protecting the rights of creditors, the change in modern bankruptcy statutes has transformed the status of debtors from mere criminals to entities deserving rehabilitation, altering the legal rights and investment security of a variety of bankruptcy stakeholders.[72] Dinah Payne and Michael Hogg also endorse the stakeholder theory of corporate bankruptcy: "Making the decision as to what strategy to follow when the business is failing is a difficult one, especially if it is management's intention to act in good faith. In reviewing the moral considerations of filing chapter 11 bankruptcy, one should undertake a stakeholder analysis to determine the impact of a decision on relevant stakeholder groups."[73]

From an ethical perspective, the legal appropriation of the stakeholder theory of corporate bankruptcy is certainly a positive movement, especially with regard to doing justice to unpayable corporate debt. This positive direction, however, is largely delimited because of its theoretical alignment with utilitarianism. It is my contention that for us to do better justice to the case of corporate insolvency, the stakeholder theory of corporate bankruptcy should be realigned with and reconstructed by more procedurally justifiable ethical theories such as Jürgen Habermas' discourse ethics by decoupling its current philosophical tie to utilitarianism. Why is this so? Why discourse ethics? What practical outcomes or meaningful change would this philosophical reconstruction bring about?

In a nutshell, this philosophical reconstruction will provide better justice to the case of corporate insolvency. The most important difference between utilitarian stakeholder theory and the discourse ethics appropriation of stakeholder theory lies in the former's tendency to focus on the final outcome (the utilitarian distribution of the remaining assets), while the latter would rather emphasize the procedural aspect of justice (whether all affected parties actually participate in the decision-making process). The critical weakness of utilitarian stakeholder theory lies in the fact that the agential aspect of justice may not be fully exercised because of its methodological emphasis on outcome. Unlike utilitarian theories, which draw on the moral justification of an action from the outcome, Habermas' discourse ethics attempts to draw on moral justification from all affected parties' engaged discourse and possible agreement. It is worth looking at what the basic tenets of Habermas' discourse ethics are.

According to Habermas, in a radically pluralistic society such as the Western world, the traditional moral norms have been largely deconstructed and replaced by a new way of attaining moral justification. To be more specific, instead of relying on traditional or metaphysical notions, people in today's postconventional society draw on their moral justification by engaging in public discourse with those who are affected by their behaviors. Habermas calls this new way of arriving at moral justification as the discourse principle ("D"), which he defines as follows: "Only those norms can claim to be valid that meet (or could meet) with the approval of all affected in their capacity as participants in a practical discourse."[74] Later in his *Between Facts and Norms*, he extends this moral theory into the area of law and politics. For instance, legal discourse should now heed the procedurally regulated bargaining among politically contested groups. He thus says, "More specifically, the negotiation of compromises should follow procedures that provide all the interested parties with an equal opportunity for pressure, that is, an equal opportunity to influence one another during the actual bargaining, so that all the affected interests can come into play and have equal chance of prevailing."[75] It is critical to understand that the only law counted to be legitimate is a set of legal norms that can be rationally accepted by all affected citizens through a discursive process of opinion and will formation.[76]

How, then, does Habermasian procedural justice better serve the case of corporate insolvency compared to utilitarian stakeholder theory? Why should we choose agent-focused procedural justice over outcome-based utilitarian justice with regard to the case of doing justice to corporate insolvency? We should first take a note of an important fact that the current bankruptcy laws (Chapter 11 and Chapter 7) greatly underscore the role of a bankruptcy judge. Boettcher and colleagues write, "The *judge* is the sole determiner in the bankruptcy process and he or she has considerable power over the case. . . . From the ethics perspective, the *judge*, as one of the many participants in the bankruptcy process, should also make efforts to protect the greatest benefits for most of the stakeholders and do the least harm to them, not only in the near future, but also in the longer term."[77] It is evident that the main agent to create a utilitarian outcome in corporate insolvency is the bankruptcy judge rather than those whose interests are directly or indirectly affected by the judge's decision. Of course, the judge is assisted by selected trustees who are supposed to represent the stakeholders' diverse interests. However, according to the *Handbook for Chapter 7 Trustees* (published by the U.S. Department of Justice), "The principal duty of the trustee is to collect and liquidate the property of the estate and to distribute the proceeds to *creditors*. A chapter 7 case must be administered to maximize and expedite dividends to *creditors*."[78] The *Handbook* seems to show that in the case of corporate insolvency the interested voices of debtors are not valued equally with those of creditors. Indeed, we could see here an almost logical interconnection between the utilitarian indifference to the agential aspect of justice and the heavy reliance on the role of bankruptcy judge and the predetermined task of trustees in current bankruptcy laws.

It is thus my contention that if the bankruptcy laws would better serve the interests of *all* related stakeholders, instead of letting the judge decide the case on their behalf, we should let stakeholders be more proactive and participatory by allowing them to engage in the liquidating process through a more open discourse. This is what a discursive and procedural justice is calling for. According to this new paradigm of justice, the judge's role is redefined to facilitate the discourse with a goal of fulfilling procedural justice rather than to calculate stakeholders' maximal utilitarian outcome in light of such legal codes as the APR. The need for a philosophical paradigm change (from utilitarian justice to procedural justice approach) is further justified by current social-scientific studies. According to Boettcher and colleagues, there are many opportunities for both illegal and unethical acts in bankruptcy procedure and within the rules of the Bankruptcy Code, and the judge's misconduct or misjudgment is especially problematic because "the judge or trustee has great discretionary power during a bankruptcy petition."[79] Although it is a judge's responsibility to evaluate the feasibility of the proposed reorganization plan, since it demands much of the judge's time and resources, the judge tends to approve a bankruptcy proposal without careful analysis.[80]

We should also keep in our mind that the most important legal principle in corporate bankruptcy—the absolute priority rule—is not actually "absolute" as its name may imply. For example, legal scholars Mark J. Joe and Frederick Tung argue that it is often up for grabs because "the bankruptcy process is in fact rife with rent-seeking, as creditors and their professionals contest existing distribution rules and seek categorical changes to improve their private bankruptcy returns."[81] In a similar vein, Liliya Gritsenko also argues that although the APR was traditionally recognized to apply to both individual and corporate reorganizations, the 2005 amended code brings the applicability of rule into question in individual Chapter 11 bankruptcies.[82] The key issue is whether the absolute priority rule was effectively abrogated for individuals filing under Chapter 11. Depending on how to interpret the 2005 amendment, the courts are split between "broad view" and "narrow view." While the former holds that the 2005 BAPCPA intended to entirely eliminate the absolute priority rule, based on the revised sections of the code, the latter views that the absolute priority rule still applies to prepetition assets because of congressional intent to curb abuse of the code by effectuating stronger control over debtor behavior.[83] Jessica R. Ellis also joins these legal scholars in deconstructing the absolute priority rule: "Despite its name, the absolute priority rule has never been absolute, and courts have recognized exceptions throughout its existence."[84] Given that many corporations go bankrupt not necessarily because of their managerial fault and failure but because of other uncontrollable external factors, we should consider replacing the name and the status of the absolute priority rule with those of a "relative priority rule."

## Conclusion

Above I have attempted to do justice to various cases of debt default and subsequent bankruptcy. By critically engaging in the three categories of debt insolvency—individual, sovereign, and corporate—I develop an argument that, beyond fairness and retribution, what we need in order to do justice to various cases of debt insolvency is restorative and relational justice for victimized debtors and affected creditors. No debtors should be under a permanent indebted situation, and bankruptcy should be designed in a way to give defaulted debtors another chance to restart.[85] No debtors should violate their fundamental ethical duty, either, that they should pay off their debt when they have sufficient assets to meet their financial obligations. To do better justice to various cases of debt default, we must also consider that the problem of debt and its default are not merely a contractual issue between the creditor and the debtor. The ever-deepening financialization of the global economy has already changed the problem of debt as a major structural and social issue, which can be managed only by democratic rule of laws. In this sense, all affected stakeholders are to engage in continuous political discourse to renew the economy of debt according to just and humane moral ideas.

## CHAPTER FOUR

# Islamic Financial Ethics and the Case against Rentier Economy of Debt

## Introduction

The U.S. financial crisis of 2007–2008 was an important test case for Islamic scholars of finance and economics, whose main concern was the resilience of the Islamic financial service industries. Scholars such as M. Kabir Hassan and Rasem Kayed, for instance, argue, "The current global financial crisis is largely seen as a real test of the resilience of the Islamic financial services industry and its ability to present itself as a more reliable alternative to the conventional financial system."[1] In a similar vein, as Volker Nienhaus reports, "Proponents of Islamic finance and Islamic economics go one step further and assert that Islamic banks exhibited greater resilience in the recent crisis than conventional banks, and they claim that this is due to the observance of ethical standards and specific prohibitions."[2] He succinctly summarizes the main argument of these proponents of Islamic finance and economics as follows: "In short: the global financial crisis has proven that Islamic finance is more efficient, stable and just."[3]

The purpose of this chapter is not to verify this argument. Perhaps it will be too precipitous to make any conclusive judgment on that. We simply need more time to come to such a conclusive judgment because Islamic finance and banking industries are still in an "evolving" stage.[4] The purpose of this chapter is, rather, geared toward a critical investigation of the ethical foundations of Islamic finance and banking industries with the purpose of drawing on key moral insights in constructing a more holistic ethics of debt.

There is a compelling reason why Western society should seriously engage in an ethical exploration of the Islamic finance and banking industries beyond the business purpose of catering to the rising Islamic financial market in the West. Although Islamic finance and banking industries were not left unscathed by the aftermath of the global financial crisis, Islamic finance has demonstrated its relatively resilient financial strength and effectiveness despite the gloom and volatility of the prevailing global financial environment.[5] It has been strongly argued by some Islamic scholars that if global banking practices had adhered to the principles of Islamic finance such as "entrepreneurship" and "transparency," the global crisis might have been prevented or its impact significantly curtailed. Hassan and Kayed, for example, argue that since the financial crisis was largely caused by such factors as "subprime mortgage, inadequate assessment of risk, complex financial instruments to shift risk, speculation and short selling, excessive leverage, lax regulatory framework and excessive lending," it would be impossible for a financial crisis to occur in the Islamic capital markets.[6]

It is important to note that Islamic finance and banking industries are not just tied to religious regulations such as Shari'ah law; they are also deeply saturated by ethical principles and moral ideals that demand that financial transactions should be consistent with fairness, justice, and transparency. For example, Islamic ethical emphasis on close relationship and trust between financiers and investors has helped them attain a high level of transparency in business transactions. Thanks to such an ethical emphasis, Islamic financiers and investors have been greatly motivated not to engage in risky, excessive, and speculative financial transactions. This chapter is devoted to uncovering such Islamic ethical insights with a view to developing a more holistic ethics of debt for global financial and banking systems. As Hassan and Kayed note, these Islamic ethical insights are now gaining wide acceptance in Islamic as well as in non-Islamic financial landscapes, and even the Vatican has accredited Islamic ethical finance in 2009 through its official newspaper (*L'Osservatore Romano*) by urging conventional banks to consider the ethical rules of Islamic finance.[7]

## Islamic Banks, Shari'ah Law, and Economic Justice

As is well known, the Qur'an is the holy book for Muslims regardless of their nationalities. Islamic law or Shari'ah is based on the Qur'an and the words and teachings of the Prophet Mohammed (*Hadith* and *Sunnah*), and this means that more than 20 percent of the world's population is to live the principles of Shari'ah law, not just in their personal life but also in their business and professional lives. To understand Islamic ethics of banking and financing, we should first attempt to understand the essence of an Islamic worldview. According to Habib Ahmed, "The essence of Islamic worldview is *tawheed* which means oneness and sovereignty of God (Allah)."[8] The moral significance of the concept of *tawheed* is quite expansive because it has implications related to all aspects of Muslims' life, including finance and economics. Since God (Allah) is the only source of value and norms, all discussions on law and morality, including all types of financial transactions, ensue from this concept. Ahmed thus writes, "Islamic economics and finance will reflect the Islamic worldview and, as such, is driven by Islamic laws and morals related to economic transactions."[9]

Since Muslims believe that God (Allah) not only commands the good because it secures the welfare of the community but also forbids evil because it is against the public good, they believe that the main goal of Islamic law and morality is to contribute positively to public welfare and the common good (*maslahah*). Ahmed argues that the Islamic distinction between laws and morals is made possible through the exemplification of five types of any human act: "obligatory (*wajib* or *fard*), recommended (*mandub*), reprehensible (*makruh*), permissible (*mubah*) and forbidden (*haram*)."[10] Among these, the first and last types of activities—*wajib* and *haram*—have legal force, while the rest fall in the moral domains that may not be adjudicated in courts. What, then, does this distinction have to do with commercial or financial transactions? In general, the basic principle for commercial or financial transaction is that of permissibility, which signifies that unless there is some specific injunction of prohibition, all commercial or financial transactions are permissible. What, then, is the specific injunction of prohibition, especially with regard to financial transactions?

We find this prohibitive injunction in Shari'ah law. Jane Pollard and Michael Samers claim that there are two broad concerns of Shari'ah law regarding the structure of Islamic finance and banking industries. "First is the prohibition of *riba* (increase) as it is viewed as exploitative and unfair. . . . A second suite of concerns affecting IBF [Islamic banking and finance] is the prohibition of excessive risk or uncertainty (*gharar*)."[11] It is important to observe that there is no dissension among Muslims regarding the prohibition of *riba* (usury). As Muhammad Ayub states, "All Muslim sects consider indulgence in Riba-based transactions a severe sin."[12] Why is this so? The most obvious reason for this prohibition is that, as the primary sources of Shari'ah, the Qur'an and the Sunnah strongly condemn the practice of riba. Some of the key Qur'anic prohibitions of riba are as follows:

> You who believe, beware of God: give up any outstanding dues from usury, if you are true believers. (*Al-Baqara* 2:278)

> You who believe, do not consume usurious interest, doubled and redoubled. Be mindful of God so that you may prosper—beware of the Fire prepared for those who ignore [him]—and obey God and the Prophet so that you may be given mercy. (*Al-'Imran* 3:130-32)

> For taking usury when they had been forbidden to do so; and for wrongfully devouring other people's property. For those of them that reject the truth we have prepared an agonizing torment. (*Al-Nisa'* 4:161)[13]

Why, then, is the practice of riba prohibited in Islamic tradition? Why, in Islam, does God (Allah) permit trade yet forbids riba?[14] To answer this question, we need to take into consideration that loans may be drawn for two purposes: for consumption and for investment in a business venture. According to M. Siddieq Noorzoy, riba is unlawful on both cases. Noorzoy reasons that "the basis of the injunction against riba on consumption loans is that those who borrow are assumed to be in need of such loans for purposes of maintaining some minimum standard of living."[15] In other words, riba can cause the exploitation of the needy. Unfortunately, this type of exploitation of the needy still exists in modern times. For example, a 1992 Policy Studies Institute report concludes that "the poor pay more in absolute terms for their money, while seeking credit only for absolute necessities rather than to finance the acquisition of luxury goods which they cannot afford."[16] For this reason, making a loan to another person without riba becomes an act of charity. Making a loan to a needy one with riba, on the contrary, becomes a form of social evil because "it inculcates selfishness, miserliness, inhumanity and financial greed," resulting in sufferings of fellow citizens.[17] Noorzoy thus argues that, in Islamic tradition, "those with higher incomes and, therefore, higher savings (surplus funds) are asked to make loans to those with lower incomes who are in need without having to exact riba from them."[18]

Riba is also unacceptable to the case of loans for business investment. What, then, is the rationale for this? The fundamental reason for the prohibition of riba for business investment is that it can generate income without labor (work) on the part of the lender.[19] As is evident, while profits are the result of a definite value-creating process such as manufacturing industries and trading enterprises, usury is not so. "In the case of interest

[riba] you know your return and can be sure of it. In the case of profit you have to work to ensure it."[20] Since riba creates wealth without engaging any productive economic activity or increasing in commodity supply, Islam considers it to be "unfair, unjust, and morally unjustifiable."[21] As Noorzoy poignantly indicates, the prohibition of riba in business and industrial investment implies that "money has no productivity per se."[22] By prohibiting riba in both cases of making loans (consumption and investment), Islamic tradition stipulates that the time value of money should be conceived as nonexistent.

Regarding the prohibition of riba, there is an ideological contention among the Islamic scholars. The essence of this contention is about how to interpret riba. Does it mean more narrowly "usury" or more broadly "interest"? Noorzoy summarizes this contention as follows: "Thus, the fundamental aspect of the controversy about the doctrine of interest in Islam is whether the rate of interest is zero, in which case riba is interpreted to mean interest per se, or whether a positive rate of interest is permissible, in which case riba is interpreted to mean usury."[23] Noorzoy goes further by saying that the room for different interpretations of the Qur'anic injunctions against riba is traceable to the time of Hadhrat-i-Omar in the first century of the Islamic period.[24] He was quoted as saying, "The last to be revealed was the verse of usury and the Prophet expired without explaining it to us. Therefore, give up usury or anything resembling it."[25] Noorzoy then points out that the word "usury," rather than "interest," is used in this translation. So he raises a question: "Did Omar mean usury or interest by riba?"[26]

While most traditional Islamic scholars would interpret riba as interest, some scholars view it as usury. If Omar regarded riba as interest in his statement, then any interest above zero would become riba. Muhammad Ayub, for instance, argues that "conventional interest is Riba."[27] Ayub develops an argument that all income and earnings, salaries and wages, remuneration and profits, usury and interest, rent and hire, and so on can be categorized into two types:

- Profit from trade and business along with its liability—which is permitted.
- Return on cash or a converted form of cash without bearing liability in terms of the result of deployed cash or capital—which is prohibited.[28]

For Ayub, since riba would include all gains from loans and debts as well as anything over and above the principal of loans and debts, riba "covers all forms of 'interest' on commercial or personal loans."[29] Ayub's traditional position is then challenged by those who would oppose the zero rate of interest. Their major argumentation is that "such a loan [zero rate of interest on a business loan] involves an opportunity cost to the lender determined by the foregone profits that the lender would have earned had he invested the funds in a business investment."[30] Of course, there is no guarantee that the business investment will always bring higher profits. This argument, however, implies that, just like investment, there is also a degree of risk in the act of loaning money. Among these opponents, Yusuf Ali, an eminent translator of the Qur'an, is most conspicuous. In favor of a positive rate of interest within the structure of modern credit and banking systems, Ali translates riba as usury and states, "My definition [of usury] would include profiteering of all kinds, but exclude economic credit, the creature of modern banking and finance."[31] In a similar way, Mahmoud A. El-Gamal also argues that riba is not the same as interest. He states that "most contemporary jurists and scholars of Islamic finance wish to exclude discussions of this topic, precisely to continue the mistaken one-to-one rhetorical association of 'riba' with 'interest.' In fact, equivalence of the two terms is far from appropriate."[32]

Above, we have seen how riba has been conceived in Islamic financial tradition. What moral insights, then, can we draw on from Islamic injunctions on riba? The first key moral insight, I argue, is that the rate of interest on loans is an essential social justice issue, not merely a contractual matter between creditors and debtors. What does the rate of interest have to do with social justice? The rate of interest is not just a fairness issue between financiers and loaners because it can lead to the concentration of wealth in a few hands. Muhammad Farooq is right when he says, "It is the rate of interest due to which money is treated as a commodity leading to the concentration of wealth in a few hands; and as a consequence, the whole economy then suffers."[33] We should note that, since the 1980s, the concentration of wealth has been ever deepened to an alarming level. According to the Oxfam International Davos report *An Economy for the 1%*, the sixty-two richest people own the same as half the world population in 2015. What is more alarming to us is that the number of people whose wealth is equal to that of the poorest half of the world's population has been significantly reduced in recent years (for instance, it was 388 in 2010, and 92 in 2013).[34] Since extreme concentration of wealth, which we are witnessing today, is structurally interrelated with interest-based global financialization, which also entails various social injustices, especially the exploitation of the poor, the rate of interest on loans is an integral aspect of social justice. In this respect, Martin Lewison's following contention makes sense: "If it is important for society to alleviate the suffering of the poor and permit them to achieve economic self-sufficiency, then it is important to investigate inexpensive lending services as a possible policy tool."[35]

The second moral insight we can draw from Islamic injunctions on riba is that the quest for financial justice is a matter of the financial system as a whole, rather than an individual issue, and at the core of the financial system lies the rate of interest. Islamic injunctions on riba are based on a key anthropological insight that humanity is unfortunately not strong enough to withstand the lure of the capitalist mantra of the market economy that maximizing profit is good. Once colonized by the lure of this capitalist mantra, humanity can be easily swayed by what Farooq calls "selfishness, miserliness, inhumanity, and financial greed." The colonized people then "become careless about the needs of their fellow citizens. . . . The same happens to the international relations."[36] The social injustice of maximizing profit through the unjust charging of optimal interest rates is then structurally interlinked with the systemic problem of the global financialization: the growing dissension between the real growth of the economy and a sustainable development and more equitable distribution of wealth. Indeed, the potentially destructive and exploitative force of riba lies in its power to manipulate the supply of money through the creation of debt rather than through the real growth of economy. Since, as Hassan and Kayed hold, "Muslims are strictly prohibited from investing in or dealing in economic activities that involve interest, uncertainty, and speculation,"[37] they are better protected from the social evils of riba. From a non-Islamic financial perspective, it is certainly debatable whether interest on loans as such is a source of evil. Although it is unlikely that Islamic and non-Islamic scholars of finance and economics would agree on this issue, they might come to a certain consensus that it is unjustifiable to charge an excessive amount of interest, causing inhumane exploitation of the poor. For the sake of doing away with the financial exploitation of the poor, global society should seriously consider the Islamic moral injunction on riba.

Along with riba, the other broad injunction of Shari'ah law for Islamic finance and banking industries is the prohibition of excessive risk or uncertainly, known as gharar. Although the word gharar is not specifically mentioned in the Qur'an, two verses are known to refer to it:

> Do not eat up your property wrongfully, nor use it to bribe judges, intending sinfully and knowingly to eat up parts of other people's property. (*Al-Baqara* 2:188)

> You who believe, do not wrongfully consume each other's wealth but trade by mutual consent. (*Al-Nisa'* 4:29)

According to Russell Powell and Arthur DeLong, "The prohibition of gharar, an excessively uncertain transaction, forms the second central tenet of Islamic finance."[38] Commonly translated as "risk," "danger of loss," or "uncertainty," gharar is also defined as "the sale of probable items whose existence or characteristics are not certain, due to the risky nature which makes the trade similar to gambling."[39] Indeed, gambling (*qimār*) is strictly prohibited in Islam. The Qur'an delivers an injunction as follows: "They ask you about intoxicants and gambling: say, 'There is great sin in both . . . the sin is greater than the benefit'" (Al-Baqara 2:219). Qimār (gambling) is often described as *maisir*, which refers to "something attained without effort." Gambling is banned by Islam because it involves high risk. It can also result in the loss of one's property without legal or proper exchange, lacking in procedural justice and fairness. Powell and DeLong thus say, "Gharar, like riba, relates directly to the Islamic view of fairness in a transaction such that any ambiguity or uncertainty about the end result of a contract invalidates the contract."[40]

We should note that in a business contract, uncertainly is often caused not only by risky behavior such as gambling, but also by ignorance. This is why *jahāla*, which means ignorance, can invalidate a sale. For instance, "if the object of sale or its price were unknown to a buyer, due to ignorance, then it would be impossible to buy, sell or exchange money for the goods due to *jahāla*."[41] Given that the prohibition of gharar purports to eliminate such factors that could be left unidentified or unknown, along with *qimār* and *maisir*, *jahāla* can be considered a form of gharar. Kunhibava and Shanmugan thus write, "*Maisir* or gambling due to its high risk and uncertain outcome, as well as *jahāla* sales in which ignorance can lead to uncertainty, are *gharar* and therefore invalid. It follows that *maisir*, *qimār* and *jahāla* can be described as subsets of *gharar*."[42]

Mahmoud A. El-Gamal specifically introduces four necessary conditions for gharar to invalidate a contract as follows:

1.  It must be major.
2.  The potentially affected contract must be a commutative financial contract.
3.  The gharar must affect the principal components of the contract (e.g., the price and object of sale, language of the contract). Thus, the sale of a pregnant cow is valid, even though the status of the fetus calf may not be known.
4.  That there is no need met by the contract containing gharar that cannot be met otherwise.[43]

As such conditions imply, trading in certain amounts of risk can be allowed as an exception, particularly if the risk is minor, not major, or if the economic need for the contract embodying the risk is substantial. Of course, there are differences in opinion among Islamic jurists about which types of gharar are considered minor or major, but the key point lies in the implication that the protection of contractors from potential major risks is a key ethical ethos of gharar.[44]

Powell and DeLong also stipulate that gharar can also be conceived by two general principles: "(1) A ban on transactions involving items that do not currently exist; and (2) a prohibition on the existence of uncertain elements in the performance of a contract, such as duration, price, or delivery."[45] They also remark that since contractual parties' full awareness of any contractual conditions is essential to prevent gharar, "if the subject matter of the contract were intangible, if the quality of the subject could not be assessed, or if the parties did not know what they bought or sold, then the contract is gharar, and hence invalid under Shari'ah."[46]

One should note that although zero-sum exchanges are commonly forbidden on the basis of gharar, certain types of contracts are forbidden on the basis of gharar without having a zero-sum component. According to El-Gamal, for instance, the case of "two sales in one contract" belongs to this category. To be more specific, it refers to "the situation where a seller offers two prices (one cash-and-carry and one deferred; or two cash-and-carry prices, one price stated in barley and the other in wheat, etc.) for the same item."[47] In the case of "two sales in one," although it is possible that both the buyer and the seller would be better-off, such a sale is forbidden because the ambiguity of the offer may lead to uncertainty regarding the price in the contract. Other gharar sales forbidden in the *Hadith* include the sale of camel sperm, unfertilized camel eggs, and the unborn calf in its mother's womb, which demonstrate that "it is not zero-sumness which is being forbidden, but rather 'excessive risk' attached to the object of sale."[48]

What moral insights, then, can we draw on from Islamic injunctions on gharar? Regarding any financial transactions including a debt contract, the most important moral insight we could learn from Islamic injunctions on gharar is that any uncertain, irresponsible, and excessive financial transaction should be checked for the sake of more sustainable long-term financial management. A definite illustration of such financial transactions can be found in the derivatives market. At the end of 2011, the derivatives market stood at a nominal value of $648 trillion, but the entire goods and services produced by the world for the entire world were valued at just $70 trillion.[49] According to Kunhibava and Shanmugam, Islam objects to financial derivatives, and the main reasons for such an objection may be summarized as follows:

1. In futures transactions, because neither countervalue, that is, money or goods, is present at the contract, the sale is not genuine but merely an exchange of promises. A sale is valid under Shari'ah law as long as only the price or delivery, but not both, is postponed.
2. For a sale to be valid, ownership of the item sold must exchange hands. Therefore, a seller who does not own the item cannot transfer ownership. The rationale behind taking possession is to prevent gharar.
3. Futures and options trading that involve speculation verge on *maisir*, *qimār*, and gharar.
4. Options trading is merely the right to buy or sell, for which charging a fee is impermissible.
5. Futures trading, where both countervalues are deferred, is the illegal exchange of one debt for another.[50]

As is well known, the 2007–2008 U.S. financial crisis was a showcase that finance in the United States was largely driven by the "goal of generating the highest possible return" before that moment, and it often led to short-term investment decisions as well as to uncertain, irresponsible, and excessive speculation, creating financial bubbles. If U.S. financial institutions had adopted the underlying principle of gharar, they would have created a more sustainable long-term business strategy. Indeed, as Powell and DeLong claim, "Islam unequivocally condemns such practices, at least in theory."[51]

The documentary called "*The Warning*," aired by PBS's *Frontline* on October 20, 2009, provides us with a compelling reason why financial leaders and regulators should have seriously considered the Islamic injunctions on gharar. In the documentary, "veteran FRONTLINE producer/director Michael Kirk reveals an intense battle among high-ranking members of the Clinton administration, and uncovers a concerted effort not to regulate the emerging, highly complex, and lucrative derivatives markets, which would become the ticking time-bomb within the American economy."[52] What we should note is that in the late 1990s, Brooksley Born, the head of an obscure federal regulatory agency—the Commodity Futures Trading Commission—not only warned of the potential for economic meltdown but also tried to convince the country's key economic power brokers to take actions that could have helped avert the crisis. Unfortunately, despite Born's effort to regulate the secretive, multitrillion-dollar derivatives market whose crash helped trigger the financial meltdown in 2008, former Fed chairperson Alan Greenspan, former treasury secretary Robert Rubin, and former assistant treasury secretary Larry Summers blocked Born's attempt to regulate the risky derivatives market, ignoring her warnings. Later Greenspan acknowledged error on regulation in a congressional hearing.[53]

Above, we have seen not only two moral guidelines of Islamic finance, riba and gharar, but also their moral insights to financial transactions. Both injunctions on riba and gharar help us develop what Timur Kuran, a Turkish American economist and professor of Islamic studies, calls "two general principles: equality and fairness."[54] Equality is more concerned with the outcome of the economic process, fairness with the process itself. Kuran defines more specifically the principles equality and fairness as follows:

> The principle of equality forbids gross inequalities in the distribution of goods: "moderate" inequality is acceptable, but "extreme" inequality is ruled out. A society would not be considered properly Islamic if it allowed some of its members to live in luxury while others eked out an impoverished existence. The principle of fairness is that people's economic gains are to be "earned" and their losses "deserved." It requires the economic system to treat similar economic contributions similarly, and different contributions differently.[55]

We may say, then, while the Islamic injunction on riba generally helps promote equality between debtors and creditors, the Islamic injunction on gharar helps enhance fairness within the financial systems. How, then, do Islamic financial agencies (e.g., banks) implement such moral principles of equality and fairness? In Kuran's words, how would an Islamic economic system achieve a greater degree of economic justice than existing capitalist and socialist systems?[56] I attempt to find an answer to this question in the following section.

### The Islamic Finance Alternative: Risk Sharing in Islamic Banking and Finance

As seen above, Islamic injunctions on riba and gharar signify that Islamic finance is more based on equity capital than on debt (*dayn*). In Islamic finance, although debt is not necessarily considered bad per se, the word *dayn* (debt) in Arabic implies submission and humiliation.[57] The term *gharim* (debtor) is used to describe any indebted person failing to repay his or her debt. Such a debtor is considered to be poor and hence is entitled to *zakat* (alms giving). Islam, however, allows gratuitous loans for use while prohibiting a loan involving interest, be it from a bank or from other individuals. In a similar vein, it recognizes the possibility of organizations becoming indebted and allows for the transfer of debts. This process can be possible only in an atmosphere of cooperation between debtor and creditor.[58] One may wonder, though, how Islamic banking industries would be possible if Islamic finance is characterized by such restrictions as banning of riba and gharar in today's globalized financial world? In 1975, the first Islamic commercial bank, Dubai Islamic Bank, was established, heralding the arrival of a new age in Islamic finance. By the end of 1996, the number of Islamic banks rose to 166 with a total paid-up capital of $7.3 billion and total assets of $177 billion.[59] According to the 2015 World Bank report, Islamic finance has expanded rapidly since the 2000s, growing at 10–12 percent annually. Shari'ah-compliant financial assets have also grown up to $2 trillion by 2015, covering bank and nonbank financial institutions, capital markets, money markets, and insurance (*takafol*).[60]

The Islamic banking system differs from dominant conventional banking in some key aspects. For instance, while money is a commodity as well as a medium of exchange and store of value for the latter, money is not regarded as a commodity for the former. Time value is the basis for charging interest on capital in the conventional banking system, whereas profit on trade of goods or charging for providing a service is the basis for earning profit for Islamic banking. Besides, while interest is charged even in such cases where borrowers suffer financial losses in the conventional banking system, Islamic banking operates on the basis of profit and loss sharing, such as *mudarabah* or *musharakah*, which I will shortly explore. Zaman and Movassaghi summarize the key difference as follows: "The basic difference is that conventional banks provide long-term fixed interest-based deposits as well as loan accounts that do not necessarily have any close relationship with their overall costs of operation and desired level of profit. The alternative Islamic bank will not have any fixed rate of interest and the interest charged or paid must closely reflect the actual costs and returns of the bank."[61]

One should note before exploring Islamic finance that although Islamic finance is hailed and presented by its proponents as the superior system, as Volker Nienhaus points out, it is not necessarily so. He, however, acknowledges that "Islamic finance has a potential for development," arguing that "growing uneasiness with and critique of the conventionalization of Islamic finance today may lead to some new initiatives in the future."[62] What is the main critique brought to the growing Islamic banking industries? According to Zaman and Movassaghi, there is a discrepancy between what is written on paper and what actually happens in the Islamic financial world, and the main critique is focused on the financial instruments used by Islamic banks. They argue that although Islamic financial instruments used by Islamic banks should implement the objective of Islamic economics such as ensuring equitable and fair dealings for all participants in economic transactions, they "appear to be quite different on paper."[63] For example, they point out that the experience of the Faisal Islamic Bank of Egypt between 1979 and 1991 shows the contradiction between claims and reality. More than half of the assets of the Faisal Islamic Bank of Egypt were deposited at other banks that received interest, demonstrating that its actual business policy contradicts the Islamic injunction against riba.[64]

What are the financial instruments of Islamic financial institutions? The most common forms of Islamic financial instrument include (1) *murabaha*—a business finance contract in which the Islamic bank purchases goods, takes title, and then resells these to a member at an agreed markup or on deferred payment; (2) *mudarabah*—a business finance arrangement in which the Islamic bank provides capital for a business venture and receives a percentage of the profits later; (3) *musharakah*—a business project in which the bank enters into a partnership with a client, sharing the equity capital and management, including profit or loss sharing later; and (4) *ijara*—a leasing contract in which assets are purchased by the bank and leased to the client.[65] In addition to these, there are other financial instruments such as *takaful* (insurance), *muqarada* (Islamic bonds), and *salem* (forward-financing transaction).[66] According to Kazi and Halabi, many conventional banks in the West (including Citibank, ANZ, Dresdner, Deutsche Morgan Grenfell, and ABN Amro) have already started handling Shari'ah-compliant funds by not only setting up offices to deal with Islamic banking facilities but also designing products that meet the needs of Islamic investors.[67]

According to Zaman and Movassaghi, murabaha, ijara, or musharakah transactions are problematic. In the case of murabaha, the Islamic bank first buys a product with a purpose of reselling it to the borrower at a markup. Later the bank collects back the amount in installments. The markup is a predetermined profit to the bank, and Islamic banks do not regard this as interest. For example, in a car purchase, the Islamic bank purchases the car priced at $20,000 and then resells it to the borrower with a markup price of $25,000, as compared (for instance) to $22,418.59 charged by the conventional bank with 11.21 percent interest on a two-year loan ($934.10 × 24 months). In such a case, as Zaman and Movassaghi point out, even though no interest is said to have been added to the loan, this "profit" of $5,000 over a two-year period implies interest earned for the bank. In the latter case, in which the borrower loans money from the conventional bank, he or she actually saves $2,581.41 for the same car. In this respect they say, "For the privilege of not calling it 'interest' the customer of the Islamic banks is overcharged, which cannot be justified on any ground. No matter how we look at it, murabaha transactions . . . can only be called usurious by even Western standards."[68] In the same manner, Aggarwal and Yousef also remark that despite the popularity of markup instruments, their acceptability under Islamic law is disputed because they can imply a fixed return on investment for the bank.[69] For this reason, as Aggarwal and Yousef point out, many Islamic scholars have taken the position that markup techniques, while permissible, should still be avoided or restricted because they may open a "back door" to interest.[70]

For Zaman and Movassaghi, ijara (leasing) is not so different from the case of murabaha, because the ijara contracts also appear to have been fashioned in a similar manner to the leasing contracts in the conventional leasing business in the West. There are two types of Islamic ijara—one where the installment payments made by the lessee go toward the ultimate purchase of the property or equipment by the lessee, and one where the lessor maintains the ownership leasing the property or equipment for a contracted period of time. As DeBelder and Khan observe, however, "Current Pakistani business practice results in monthly lease rentals generally working out to be equal to installments of principal plus about an amount equivalent to interest of 22 percent per annum."[71] For this reason, Zaman and Movassaghi hold that ijara is "another example of Islamic banks imitating poorly Western business practices under the disguise of profit sharing."[72]

Another controversial Islamic financial instrument is musharakah. Zaman and Movassaghi argue that since the Islamic bank not only provides the capital but also joins the borrower in managing the financed venture, it is unrealistic for the Islamic bank to be an impartial partner while working as the banker to the depositor because of the inevitable "conflict of interest." They thus write, "Even the well-trained finance operatives in the West seldom perform such varied tasks under the umbrella of one single financial institution."[73]

Above I have reviewed the common financial instruments of Islamic banks and some of their problems raised by some Islamic scholars. In the following, I turn to a more progressive and conducive aspect of Islamic finance by discussing the profit-and-loss sharing (PLS) principle of Islamic finance. What is the profit-and-loss sharing principle or the principle of risk sharing in finance? Unanimously accepted in the Islamic legal and economic literatures as the cornerstone of financial transactions, the PLS principle stipulates that the bank may either earn a return on invested funds if the project prospers or bear a loss if the project fails.[74] Islamic financial instruments such as mudarabah and musharakah are based on this principle although the latter is potentially interlinked with the problem of conflict of interest. In the case of mudarabah financing, while the bank provides capital, the entrepreneur contributes effort and exercises complete control over the business venture. Hence, if a loss occurs, "the bank earns no return or a negative return on its investment and the entrepreneur receives no compensation for her effort"; in the same manner, if there is a gain, "returns are split according to a negotiated equity percentage."[75]

According to Hossein Askari and colleagues, "Islam has long endorsed risk sharing as the preferred organizational structure for all economic activities," and the Qur'an ratifies it affirming *al-bay'* (mutual exchange) while condemning *al-riba* (2:275). They also claim that "through its rules governing just exchange, distribution, and redistribution, the entire Qur'anic position on economic relations is oriented toward risk sharing."[76] Promoting maximum risk sharing is then not an option to consider in Islamic finance, because it is arguably the ultimate objective of Islamic finance.[77] Other Islamic scholars such as Aggarwal and Yousef emphasize that not just for the sake of Islamic theology but for the economic rationale, the appropriation of the profit-and-loss sharing principle is superior to the use of interest. They thus endorse the explanations of the International Association of Islamic Banks, which claim that if interest is replaced by profit sharing, then some economic imbalances are to be reduced. It is worth quoting the main economic rationales for Islamic banks to choose the profit-and-loss sharing principle over interest:

> First, the return on capital will depend on productivity. Allocation of investable funds will be guided by the soundness of the project. This will in effect improve the efficiency of capital allocation.

> Second, the creation of money by expanding credit will be created only when there is a strong likelihood of a corresponding increase in the supply of goods and services. In case the enterprise loses, repayment of capital to the bank is diminished by the amount of loss. Thus in the profit-sharing system, the supply of money is not allowed to overstep the supply of goods and services. This will eventually curb inflationary pressures in the economy.

> Third, the shift to profit sharing may increase the volume of investments that translates into job creation. This is because the interest mechanism makes feasible only those projects whose expected profits are sufficiently high to cover the interest rate plus added income. This filters out projects which otherwise would be accepted in the profit sharing system.

Fourth, the new system will also ensure more equitable distribution of wealth. Wealth would bring more wealth to its owners only when its use has actually resulted in the creation of additional wealth. This would in time reduce the unjust distribution of wealth which continued for decades during the interest regime.

Fifth, the abolition of interest, together with the restriction of forward transaction, as prescribed by Shari'ah, will curtail speculations measurably. But still, there will be a secondary market trading common stocks and investment certificates based on profit-sharing principles. This will bring sanity back to the market and allow raising of funds for enterprises and liquidity to equity holders.[78]

Despite the theological and economic rationales that we have discussed above, the actual implementation of the profit-and-loss sharing principle by Islamic banks is insignificant. Islamic banks heavily depend on markup financing rather than on PLS financing. As Pollard and Samers point out, in practice, PLS transactions such as mudarabah and musharakah represent only a small percentage of financing by Islamic banks (roughly 5 percent of all transactions in the early 2000s). The main reason for this low representation by Islamic banks lies in the uncertainty in calculating their returns.[79] Although the PLS principle of Islamic finance is minimally appropriated by Islamic banks, we should consider that the financial system on which it is based has a great potential to become an alternative model to the dominant form of Western finance based on debt and interest. Why is this so?

First, it offers greater financial stability across the entire financial system by reducing the chances of recurring debt crisis compared to the conventional banking system. This is basically the main argumentation of Islamic scholars who uphold the PLS principle. Aggarwal and Yousef, for instance, write, "The last two decades of the 20th century witnessed a number of global bouts with financial instability and debt crises, with devastating consequences for a large segment of humanity, thus raising consciousness regarding the vulnerability and fragility of the financial systems which are based, at their core, on fixed-price debt contracts."[80] It is true that Islamic finance based on risk sharing has a much shorter history than does conventional finance, but we need to remember that in the West before the rise of debt financing in the mid-sixteenth century, equity financing was preeminent.[81] Given that a growing number of specialists recognize debt as the essential source of financial instability, the reconstruction of risk-sharing finance, which is more "trust intensive," would bring a conducive financial stability and confidence to national and global financial markets.

Second, the PLS principle of Islamic finance would help establish debt in accordance with the criteria of just debt, which I discussed in chapter 2. In particular, the PLS principle has a lot affinity with the third principle of just debt—the principle of shareability, which stipulates that when the debt turns out to be unpayable due to unexpected events and thus insolvent, creditors should bear at least partial responsibility for the failed loans with debtors. The PLS principle may not guarantee the fast and voluminous financial gains for banks and financial institutions, but it not only ensures a greater financial stability but also grounds the entire financial system on a more humane and justifiable moral ground. As some Islamic scholars take note, "Modern Islamic finance has not been developed on a solid Islamic foundation with the necessary scaffolding to enable its adoption as a complete financial system."[82] In my view, to provide a truly alternative financial model to the Western conventional financial system, Islamic banks should be more proactive and cooperative in their representation of the PLS principle in the West as well as in Islamic world.

### Against Usurious Debt: The Case of Credit Cards

Above we have explored both the prospects and the delimitations of Islamic financing by investigating its major financial instruments; we have also explored the PLS principle of Islamic finance with a view to remedying the systemic weaknesses of the conventional financial system such as periodic financial crises, which we experienced most recently in 2007–2008. In this section, we lastly attempt to examine one of the most common forms of consumer debt—that is, credit card debt—with regard to the Islamic moral principles of finance.

According to the most recent *Quarterly Report on Household Debt and Credit*, published by the Federal Reserve Bank of New York, "As of March 31, 2016, total household indebtedness was $12.25 trillion, a $136 billion (1.1%) increase from the fourth quarter of 2015."[83] Overall household debt remains still 3.3 percent below its peak of $12.68 trillion in the third quarter of 2008. Out of this total household debt, credit card balances amount to $712 billion (about 6 percent). In 2007, before the financial meltdown, revolving credit card debt was close to $900 billion, and it had increased at an average annual rate of almost 9 percent over the previous ten years.[84] Ever since 1951, in which the Franklin National Bank in New York issued the first credit card, it became increasingly popular. MasterCard began in 1966, when a number of banks formed the Interbank Card Association, which later bought the rights to use "Master

Charge" from the California Bank Association in 1969. It was renamed MasterCard in 1979.[85] The first credit card that entered the Arab world was issued by the Arab African Bank of Egypt in 1982, the Bank of Egypt issued Visa card in the decade of 1990, and the Bank of Cairo also entered in this competition in 1996. In September 1990, one billion Visa cards were issued in the world.[86]

Regarding credit card debt, the most significant regulatory legal decision was made in 1978 by the U.S. Supreme Court in *Marquette National Bank of Minneapolis v. First Omaha Services Corp* (435 U.S. 299), which held that "states cannot regulate interest rates charged on credit card loans if the lender is an out-of-state bank."[87] Two banks were involved in the case: Marquette National Bank of Minneapolis, in which the state's usury law capped interest rates for loans at 12 percent, and the First National Bank of Omaha in Nebraska, where an interest rate of up to 18 percent was allowed. When the Omaha bank started marketing no-annual-fee credit cards to Minnesota residents, Marquette sued, charging that the Omaha bank was in violation of Minnesota's usury law. The Supreme Court's ruling—usury laws do not apply to nationally chartered banks based in other states—made a sweeping interpretation of the National Bank Act, a law passed by Congress in 1864. Before the establishment of the National Bank Act, banks were chartered only by states, but the National Bank Act created a new way for the federal government to charter its own banks with the right to issue bank notes backed by government bonds.

The Supreme Court's ruling had a dramatic impact on the credit card industry. After this decision, banks that issued credit cards quickly moved to such states as South Dakota and Delaware, which had abolished their usury laws to lure credit card companies to relocate within their borders. Suddenly, states that offered favorable legal sanctuary, such as freedom from usury regulations, could entice credit card companies, and South Dakota was the first to offer what amounted to unlimited interest rates. As Issacharoff and Delaney write, "Any state with a small population would likely serve as an attractive candidate for being importuned with the promise of tax revenues and jobs, with the burden primarily shouldered by voiceless consumers in other states."[88] As Pat Curry also points out, it was no accident that South Dakota became the home state for subprime card issuer First Premier Bank, which offered a card with an interest rate of 79.9 percent.[89]

The 1996 *Smiley v. Citibank* case was another landmark Supreme Court decision regarding the credit card industry, which expanded the *Marquette* exportation doctrine. In this case, a California woman, Barbara

Smiley, filed a class-action lawsuit against Citibank's South Dakota–based credit card division, charging that the fifteen-dollar late fee was in violation of California state law. Citibank argued that the late fee was, in effect, interest and legitimized by the National Bank Act, and the Supreme Court agreed. As a result of this ruling, states with permissive regimes continued to hold sway over the rest of the country regarding late fees as well as interest rates. As expected, after this decision was made, credit card companies changed their pricing strategies, incorporating a wider variety of fees and using variable interest rates.[90]

The impact of the Supreme Court's *Marquette* ruling was not restricted to the legal, business, and job areas. According to Michelle White, international comparison shows a connection between credit card debt and bankruptcy filings. For example, in Canada, both credit card debt and bankruptcy filings increased rapidly starting in 1969, a year after general credit cards were first issued. But in the United States, usury laws in a number of states limited the maximum interest rates on loans, and this helped U.S. bankruptcy filings to remain constant throughout the 1970s. In 1978, however, the *Marquette* ruling effectively abolished state usury laws, and both credit card debt and bankruptcy filings increased rapidly in the United States after the decision.[91]

The abuse of card holders by credit card companies is especially egregious in the market for "subprime credit cards" or "fee harvester cards." These cards target subprime consumers—those who have low credit scores. Not only do these cards offer very low credit limits, but they charge high upfront fees that in effect increase the interest rate by eating up available credit. According to National Consumer Law Center Report of 2007, several small banks such as South Dakota–based First Premier and First National of Pierre and Delaware-based First Bank of Delaware specialized in the issuance of fee-harvester cards. Some big banks such as Capital One and HSBC also have big stakes in the subprime cards market.[92] To be more specific, First Premier advertised cards "with no processing fee" but charged $178 in initial fees to open an account with a $300 credit limit.[93] Credit companies' potential abuse of consumers largely hinges on interest rates and exorbitant fees, and their tactics include providing favorable introductory terms, rewards programs, and the low minimum repayment requirements to potential consumers. For instance, the minimum monthly payment plan, which typically comprises the previous month's interest and fees plus 1 percent of the principle, would mean that debtors who pay only the minimum each month still owe nearly half of any amount borrowed after five years.[94]

There was a great need to restrain such financial abuses by credit card companies, and finally, in 2009, the Credit Card Accountability Responsibility and Disclosure Act, commonly known as the Card Act, was passed by Congress and signed by President Obama. Fortunately, the Card Act turned out to be effective in remedying credit abuses by some credit card companies. Neale Mahoney, an economist of the University of Chicago, and his colleagues discovered that the regulation worked. According to their estimation, "the law is saving American consumers $20.8 billion a year" by cutting down the costs of credit cards, particularly for borrowers with poor credit.[95] Numerous cases of credit card abuse prompt us indeed to reconsider Islamic injunctions on riba and gharar as well as the PLS principle of Islamic banking and financing. This becomes more imperative if we take into our consideration an important fact that most people use credit card for the sake of consumption rather than investment.

Regarding the consumptive aspect of many credit cards, we should perhaps remind ourselves of Noorzoy's poignant point that the basis of Islamic injunction against riba on consumption loans is that those who borrow are assumed to be in need of such loans for purposes of maintaining some minimum standard of living. In other words, interest rates on credit cards can directly or indirectly cause the exploitation of the needy. From an ethical perspective, subprime credit cards or fee harvester cards are problematic because those companies issuing such cards are intentionally targeting those financially vulnerable exactly to take advantage of their helplessness and susceptibility. From the perspective of the PLS principle of Islamic finance, the concept of the penalty interest rate, also known as the default rate, is problematic. The penalty rate is the rate you will pay on your credit card if you fail to make on-time payments. This penalty rate is often much higher than the initially offered rate. For example, while the average interest rate has fluctuated between 12 percent and 16 percent since 2005, the penalty interest rate of major companies was between 27 percent and 29.99 percent in 2016. This means that the penalty or default rates are at the minimum 7–8 percent higher than the worst rates one would normally receive, and almost 20 percent higher if one has an excellent credit profile.[96]

The case of the penalty or default rate shows an important fact that the U.S. credit card business is unfairly skewed toward the interest of lenders rather than being based on the PLS principle. For us to transform our financial system in a fairer and more justifiable way, credit card companies should also be ready to share financial burdens instead of letting the card holders take up all the financial burdens in such cases of defaulting or exceeding the limit. Addressing this financial unfairness and injustice, economists such as Michelle White develop an argument that "lenders [should] have a great chance of facing losses when they supply too much credit or charge excessively high interest rates and fees."[97]

What is the Islamic view on credit cards? Is there such a thing that can be considered as Shari'ah-compliant Islamic credit cards, given that credit cards are operated by interest? If yes, how is it possible for Islamic banks to issue credit cards to their clients against the religious injunctions against riba? One solution is that a bank offers a line of credit to cardholders charging a monthly or yearly usage fee tied to the outstanding balance of the credit line. According to Cokgezen and Kuran, the other solution is to treat credit card purchases as resale contracts akin to murabaha. To be more specific, the card issuers buy a good on the customer's behalf at the very moment and then sell it to the customer at a prespecified markup. Although this transaction does not technically involve interest, Cokgezen and Kuran view this transaction as equivalent to an "interest-based transaction." They thus write, "Although the Shari'ah boards of Turkey's Islamic banks have all endorsed the use or murabaha, various Shari'ah scholars view it as a veil for riba."[98]

Cokgezen and Kuran are critical of the increasingly popular Islamic credit card business because "Islamic credit cards contribute to the pathologies of the conventional credit card industry."[99] At the bottom of this trend lies Islamic banks' participating in "market competition." They diagnose, "To acquire and guard market share within the credit card industry and, more broadly, within the Turkish banking sector as a whole, they have shedded the 'Shari'ah-compliant' characteristics of their cards, or opted to leave them unenforced."[100] They quickly added their comment that, "in sum, completion on both the demand and supply sides of the labor market may erode an ethical norm when unethical behavior gives individual decision makers a competitive advantage."[101] It is true that competitive pressures can cause the spread of unethical behavior as Cokgezen and Kuran point out, but one should be careful in distinguishing the ethical codes of conduct in competitive market and religious injunctions. Most economists, including some Islamic economists, would agree that reasonable interest charges actually have a conducive effect on the overall economy while condemning usurious interest rates. In fact, Cokgezen and Kuran also admit that "nothing above implies that charging interest is intrinsically harmful or that the credit card is an intrinsically harmful instrument."[102]

## Conclusion

Above we have explored key ethical aspects of Islamic finance and banking with the purpose of constructing a more holistic ethics of debt in an increasingly interconnected and globalized world. Among many teachings of an Islamic ethics of debt, the most important insight lies in its emphasis that debt is intrinsically an ethical phenomenon. Debt is not an amoral phenomenon; it is supposed to be fundamentally a moral phenomenon. In this respect, it condemns riba and gharar because they have a formidable potential to disrupt the whole financial system beyond the exploitation of the vulnerable and poor borrowers. They can also defile lenders' moral character, rendering them greedy. This insight is very true in today's financial world. As Al-Azhari clearly lays out, "The objective of debt in the Islamic perspective is virtue and to fulfill the need of a needy person without wishing for a reward."[103] Indeed, the wealthy in early Islam were originally encouraged to offer not only alms but also benevolent loans to people in distress, expecting only the principal from the recipient.

From the perspective of an Islamic ethics of debt, debt is not simply a matter of contract between creditor and debtor. For a debt to be a just debt, it should meet another ethical criterion that it should be a form of gift to the needy, not an instrument to exploit them. What if, then, charging a reasonable amount of interest on debt or allowing a manageable amount of financial risk in financial transactions would actually bring a financial benefit to both creditors and debtors? Should Islamic finance allow and ratify such transactions? After all, as Cokgezen and Kuran point out, the most common general justification in terms of interpreting financial distress and benevolence is based on the Qur'an 2:185: "Allah desires your well-being, not your discomfort."[104] Answering this question is ultimately up to Islamic scholars and their interpretations. Despite potential interpretive differences and debates among Islamic scholars on the moral status of the reasonable amount of interest and manageable level of risk, they would all agree that charging excessive interest (usury) or engaging too risky financial transactions are unacceptable.

Paradoxically, capitalism is typically abused by capitalists, not by its opponents, and the tools most widely adopted by them are manipulative interest and unbridled risk. In this respect, Islamic injunctions against riba and gharar are invaluable moral guidelines not just for Muslims but for all people in the world. In this respect, as Powell and DeLong hold, "U.S. firms might be able to incorporate some of the risk management principle from the riba prohibition, specifically, the profit- and loss-sharing structure of loan transactions. By creating financial products that incorporate a profit- and loss-sharing agreement, financial institutions could reduce their risk exposure."[105] Given that the exponentially growing financial gap between the wealthy and the poor becomes a serious global justice issue while no one, no institutions, and no nations can resolve the growing problem of the extreme concentration of wealth, Islamic financial principles such as achieving equity among different levels of income and wealth is definitely a much-needed moral insight that should be fully adopted not just by the Islamic world but also by the non-Islamic world.

## CHAPTER FIVE

# Jewish Ethics of Jubilee and the Question of Debt Forgiveness

## Introduction

In 1996 the Heavily Indebted Poor Countries Initiative was launched at the G7 summit in Lyon, France, following a proposal from the International Monetary Fund and the World Bank. The HIPC Initiative was later revised and reinforced in 1999 following the G7 summit in Cologne, Germany, which approved faster, deeper, and broader debt relief, strengthening the links among debt relief, poverty reduction, and social policies. In 2005, the HIPC Initiative was supplemented by the Multilateral Debt Relief Initiative, which would allow for 100 percent relief on eligible debts by three multilateral institutions—the IMF, the World Bank, and the African Development Fund—for countries completing the HIPC Initiative process. According to the factsheet (as of March 15, 2016) published by the IMF, "To date, debt reduction packages under the HIPC Initiative have been approved for 36 countries, 30 of them in Africa, providing $76 billion in debt-service relief over time."[1] Three additional countries (Eritrea, Somalia, and Sudan), identified as potentially eligible for HIPC Initiative assistance, have not yet reached their decision points. The factsheet also reports that before the HIPC Initiative, eligible countries on average spent slightly more on debt service than on health and education combined, but they have since increased markedly their expenditures on health, education, and other social services, spending about five times the amount of debt-service payments.

The HIPC Initiative was politically as well as ideologically influenced by an international coalition campaign, known as Jubilee 2000, which started in the United Kingdom in the early 1990s. The idea of this movement was first articulated by William Peters, a retired diplomat, and Martin Dent, a retired lecturer in politics at the University of Keele. They founded the Jubilee 2000 campaign by linking the Jewish concept of Jubilee to a modern debt relief program. In 1998, tens of thousands of Jubilee 2000 campaign supporters demonstrated at the G8 meeting in Birmingham, England, and the protests caught the attention of influential political leaders such as Prime Minister Tony Blair and Chancellor of the Exchequer Gordon Brown. The prime minister expressed his personal support for debt forgiveness publicly, and the support of global celebrities such as Bono, Muhammad Ali, Quincy Jones, and others made the campaign known to global society.

The purpose of this chapter is to engage in Jewish religious traditions and thoughts, especially the concept of Sabbath and Jubilee, with regard to the construction of a more comprehensive and holistic ethics of debt. To be more specific, I argue in this chapter that as our world is getting more globalized and financialized, the global-political appropriation of periodic Sabbath or Jubilee is more inexorably called for against the popular conception that Jubilee is an ancient Jewish concept and thus outdated and irrelevant. As we have seen in chapter 4, religious traditions and ideas provide us with invaluable ethical insights regarding how we should organize, manage, and evaluate our financial system, particularly those rules and policies related to the overall economy of debt. The HIPC Initiative is indeed a telling illustration of how religious traditions and thoughts can still be important and relevant sources in reconstructing a more holistic and also realistic ethics of debt in today's global society. This chapter is composed of three sections, and each section will focus on specific subject matters. The first section will be devoted to the historical and ideological exploration of the Jewish concepts of Sabbath and Jubilee. Based on this exploration, I will engage in two urgent issues of our world: ethical issues related to the odious debt of Third World countries and the invisible and uncontracted, yet largely acknowledged, environmental debt owed to Third World countries by wealthy creditors such as First World countries and multinational industries.

## Jewish Concepts of Sabbath and Jubilee

There are several key passages in the Hebrew Scripture that directly refer to the Sabbath year or Jubilee—Exodus 21:1-7, 23:10-11; Deuteronomy 15:1-18; and Leviticus 25:1-55.

> These are the ordinances that you shall set before them: When you buy a male Hebrew slave, he shall serve six years, but in the seventh he shall go out a free person, without debt. (Exod 21:1-2)

> For six years you shall sow your land and gather in its yield; but the seventh year you shall let it rest and life fallow, so that the poor of your people may eat; and what they leave the wild animals may eat. You shall do the same with your vineyard, and with your olive orchard. (Exod 23:10-11)

> Every seventh year you shall grant a remission of debts. And this is the manner of the remission: every creditor shall remit the claim that is held against a neighbor, not exacting it of a neighbor who is a member of the community, because the LORD's remission has been proclaimed. Of a foreigner you may exact it, but you must remit your claim on whatever any member of your community owes you. (Deut 15:1-3)

> You shall count off seven weeks of years, seven times seven years, so that the period of seven weeks of years gives forty-nine years. Then you shall have the trumpet sounded loud; on the tenth day of the seventh month—on the day of atonement—you shall have the trumpet sounded throughout all your land. And you shall hallow the fiftieth year and you shall proclaim liberty throughout the land to all its inhabitants. It shall be a jubilee for you: you shall return, every one of you, to your property and every one of you to your family. That fiftieth year shall be a jubilee for you: you shall not sow, or reap the aftergrowth, or harvest the unpruned vines. For it is a jubilee; it shall be holy to you: you shall eat only what the field itself produces. (Lev 25:8-12)

While the English word "Sabbath" comes from the Hebrew noun *sabbat*, derived from the verb *sabat*, meaning "to stop, to cease, or to keep," the English word "Jubilee" comes through the Greek form of the Hebrew word *yobel*, meaning "horn or trumpet." The blowing of the yobel heralded the beginning of the Jubilee year, and these actions are supposed to be undertaken "on signal," not out of an emotional rush, in response to a regular communal expectation.[2] As Richard H. Lowery, a Hebrew Bible scholar, takes note, of these main Sabbath-year texts in the Hebrew Scriptures, only Leviticus 25 describes the seventh year as the "Sabbath" year. He also holds that Sabbath year in Leviticus offers a utopian vision closely related to Sabbath creation in Genesis 1 and Sabbath manna in Exodus 16.[3] Although Exodus 23 interlinks the seventh year to the seventh-day Sabbath, the passage stops short of calling it a Sabbath year in Exodus 23:9-12.

Deuteronomy 15:1-18 offers us "the most comprehensive seventh-year law," not only emphasizing a debt release for Yahweh but also setting a cap on the length of time for debt slavery.[4] According to Robert Gnuse, the Jubilee legislation found in Leviticus 25 presents a social and economic transformative vision "unsurpassed in the ancient Near East."[5] This comprehensive economic vision includes four major aspects: slave release, debt forgiveness, the restoration of land to the original owners, and the rejuvenation of the land (fallow).

One needs to note, though, that Leviticus lacks direct reference to the debt release stipulations of Deuteronomy 15:1-11 (Sabbath year) and the national and universal release of slaves on the seventh year in Deuteronomy 15:12-18, although Leviticus 25:10 ("You shall return, every one of you, to your property and every one of you to your family.") implies them. In this respect, Gnuse raises the following question: "Did the Levitical reformers respect these Deuteronomic Laws, view them as binding, and merely feel no need to repeat them? Or were the Levitical reformers unaware of Deuteronomic Laws and knowledgeable only of the Covenant Code stipulations in Exodus 21-23?"[6] He, however, seems to overlook the fact that Exodus 21:2 actually refers to the forgiveness of debt attached to slavery. Perhaps the most contested question regarding the institution of Jubilee is whether it was ever practiced. The main reason for this contention originates in the radical transformative vision of the Jubilee practice, which many scholars call "utopian."

While defenders of the historicity of Jubilee point out the parallel cases in the ancient Near East as evidence,[7] opponents argue that the existence of customs in the ancient Near East does not verify the same practice in Israel, emphasizing that the Mesopotamian and old Babylonian promulgations of *mishnarum* (a royal edict that would cancel debts, suspend taxes, or release debt slaves) were not made on a regular basis.[8] "Only Deuteronomy 15, however, seeks to establish a regular cycle of debt release."[9] In his *The Jubilee from Leviticus to Qumran*, John Sietze Bergsma concludes this debate by saying that what really matters is not so much its historicity as its meaning for the people of Israel. "The most frequently asked question is invariably whether the jubilee was actually observed in ancient Israel. Unfortunately, neither the biblical nor the archeological data enables us to give a definitive answer to that question. What the biblical data does indicate, however, is that the meaning of the jubilee for the people of Israel developed over time."[10] In fact, what I am trying to do in this chapter is to broaden its religious meaning and ethical implication beyond the narrow perimeter of the people of Israel.

In this chapter, I uncover key ethical meanings of Sabbath and Jubilee by focusing on the distinctive Jewish teachings on the periodic forgiveness of debt. We should first note that Deuteronomy 15:2-3 makes a distinction between loans offered to a "neighbor" and to a "foreigner." Why is this distinction important? First, as Lowery points out, this distinction is not "merely ethnic." While loans to neighbors are "subsistence loans" to households that fall within the creditor's zone of responsibility, loans to foreigners are by their very nature "commercial loans."[11] In other words, the issue is not the ethnicity of the borrower but the nature of the loan. Lowery calls attention to the fact that the word "foreigner" in verse 3 is *nokrî*, not *ger*, "resident alien." This means that the resident alien is considered to be part of the network of mutual support among village households. Lowery thus writes, "So subsistence loans to resident aliens are more likely included among the loans to 'your neighbor, your kin' in verse 2 than among the loans to 'foreigners' in verse 3."[12] Raphael Jospe also writes that foreigners "may be charged usury, and their debts are not released in the sabbatical year."[13] What then about women? Regarding Exodus 20:10 and Deuteronomy 5:14, in which the commandment is addressed to "you" (masculine singular), Jospe holds, although it would appear that the omission of any explicit reference to women implies exclusion from the benefits of the Sabbath, the omission of any reference to the woman actually manifests her equality before the law.[14]

What is the ethical significance of the distinction between subsistence loans, which are subject to the release law, and commercial loans, which are exempt from such a regulation? Simply put, the care of the poor among your kin and the equal treatment of the other (foreigners) are the core of Jewish economic justice. The Hebrew word "release" or "remit" in verse 2 (*shamôt*) is from the same root as the noun "release" or "remission" (*shemittah*). Given that the basic meaning of *shamôt* is "to loosen" or "to drop," the law of release, *shemittah*, is considered to "loosen his grip" (literally, "release his hand") on the debtor's obligation to pay, which is the exact opposite of being tightfisted toward needy neighbors—that is, the debtors. Indeed, as Lowery holds, *shemittah* is a "concrete gesture of opening the hand to the poor."[15] Given that an Israelite was not only prohibited from charging interest but also required to lend food and money to any poor person (subsistence loans), we can conjecture that the subsistence loans to unfortunate poor and needy neighbors were actually a form of gift to them in a largely self-sufficient agricultural society.

Todd G. Buchholz, a legal scholar and economist, concurs with Lowery that ancient Israel distinguished subsistence loans from commercial loans. Buchholz reasons that lending at interest to foreign merchants (commercial loans) makes sense "because the merchant would not borrow unless the rate was reasonable."[16] He also holds that it is right for the debt release to not apply to the foreign merchant because he could not be expected to release Israelites from debt. Buchholz thus writes, "The laws tried to establish an equal basis for trade between merchants and Israelites."[17] Buchholz, however, points out that the ancient Israeli distinction between subsistence loans and commercial loans was possible because of its dualistic division of people: the one who shares the fraternity of the covenant (the descendants of Abraham) versus the others who are excluded from such a lineage. Not explicitly, though, he then seems to develop an argument that the Jubilee law would make sense only to those who are within that exclusionary boundary. In other words, the Jubilee law is basically conditional, not universal, depending on the moral nature of membership or peoplehood.

He then goes further by saying that there had been a major transformation in the Western world with regard to the basic nature of its moral bond "from brotherhood to otherhood" since medieval times. Since he follows Benjamin Nelson in developing this argument, we need to go to Nelson. In his seminal book, *The Idea of Usury*, Nelson lays out a chronicle of the changing interpretations of Deuteronomy 23:19-20, a text that prohibits loans on usury to "another Israelite" but allows them to "a foreigner." This passage represents the tribal brotherhood morality of the ancient Israelites, which is later transcended by the medieval aspiration toward universal brotherhood. The Reformation movement abandoned it while it deconstructed the medieval consensus. Calvin especially played an important role because he "self-consciously and hesitantly charted the path to the world of Universal Otherhood, where all become 'brother' in being equally 'others.'"[18] According to Nelson, Calvin was the first religious leader to interpret the passage in such a way that it is permissible to take usury from one's brother. Nelson writes, "Calvin, it is true, appeals intensely for brotherhood; but there is a world of difference between a brotherhood in which interest is abominated and a brotherhood in which it is authorized. Neither the Hebrews nor the Christians of the Middle Ages would have been able to understand the latter kind of brotherhood."[19]

In his epilogue, Nelson states that we are not supposed to despair because of the transformation of the moral bond from "tribal brotherhood to universal otherhood." According to him, "A society which embodies recognizable norms for people in general is ethically superior to one in which there are privileges for the insiders, temporary concessions for good neighbors and strangers, and no obligations at all toward distant 'barbarians.'"[20]

He, however, laments that as a moral community expands its boundary while merging with another one into "one set of brothers," it generally comes along with a moral price. What is this price? He says that the price is an attenuation of the love that previously bonded them together. He thus writes, "It is a tragedy of moral history that the expansion of the area of the moral community has ordinarily been gained through the sacrifice of the intensity of the moral bond, or, to recall the refrain of this sketch, that all men have been becoming brothers by becoming equally others."[21]

Nelson's insightful book may pose a serious ideological challenge to the religious-ethical attempt to appropriate the Jubilee principle into our modern economic and financial world. Why is this so? It is because one may argue that the Jubilee law, which was originally designed for an ancient Jewish tribal community of brotherhood, is no longer relevant to our modern world in which "brother" has become merely "other." Is, then, the Jewish concept of Jubilee an outdated utopian idea that has no practical relevance to the modern world? Does it have only a religious meaning and totally lack any economic sense in a capitalist system? Buchholz epitomizes such a capitalist suspicion as follows: "From a theologian's point of view, the laws (on debt release) seem logical, given the precepts of the religion. From an economist's perspective, the laws would appear as grave obstacles."[22] In constructing a more holistic and realistic ethics of debt in an age of global financialization, then, how could we prove that the ancient idea of Sabbath or Jubilee actually has both ethical and practical relevance?

In the following, I answer this question by demonstrating that debt forgiveness is not only an ethical requirement because it is a matter of justice but also an ecological and economic necessity because debt destroys ecological sustainability, ultimately resulting in economic disruption. It is true, as Nelson says, that the West is no longer identified by the clan comradeship of the Hebrews or the medieval ideal of universal brotherhood. But it is too shortsighted to claim that the West is only led away on to the "atomized individualism" or "universal otherhood" of modern capitalism. Ironically, I argue, as our world is more capitalized and globalized, we are becoming more closely connected to each other, and the need to care for others, especially foreign strangers and the environment, is increasingly called for. In a similar manner, Lowery also writes, "As individual alienation increases and a sense of social solidarity declines, as the boundaries of time and place that once defined the world of work disappear into cyberspace, sabbath speaks a word of proportion, limits, social solidarity, and the need for rest, quiet reflection, and nonconsumptive recreation. In the emerging world, sabbath consciousness may be the key to human survival, prosperity, and sanity."[23] The rising migration crises in many parts of the world as well as the deepening ecological catastrophes on a global scale undeniably verify the fact that the changing moral landscape of our world is in much need of the political-economic appropriation of the Jubilee ideal.

What is the ethical principle or spirit of the Jewish law of Sabbath and Jubilee, which may transcend its distinctive religious, ethnic, or cultural boundaries? We may answer this question by uncovering two aspects of justice: preventive justice and restorative justice. Jewish Bible scholar Jacob Milgrom, for instance, argues that the Jubilee reflects preventive justice by delimiting the growing gaps between the haves and the have-nots. He writes, "The jubilee is a socio-economic mechanism to prevent latifundia and the ever-widening gap between the rich and the poor which Israel's prophets can only condemn, but which Israel's priests attempt to rectify in Leviticus 25."[24] Along with preventive justice, what we may also draw on from the Jewish law of Sabbath and Jubilee is what social theorists call "restorative justice": the restoration of such social ethical ideals as equality, liberty, reciprocity, and sustainability. The concept of restorative justice is relatively new, mainly developed in the field of criminal justice. Lorraine S. Amstutz, for instance, holds that "although the language of restorative justice is relatively recent, practices of restorative justice are not new" in that it was already practiced in indigenous cultures around the world until these traditions were stifled by Western colonialism.[25] It is important to note that although the primary locus for restorative justice has been the criminal justice arena, its principles and practices are now increasingly implemented outside that system, for example, in schools, workplaces, and churches.[26] What I attempt to do in this chapter is to apply its principles and practices to commercial, legal, or financial institutions.

Regarding the concept of restorative justice, Christo Thesnaar offers us an important insight. Focusing on healing and restoration, unlike retributive justice, restorative justice "attempts to reach a more complete understanding of justice" by "involving those who have a role to play in bringing healing to the offender and the survival."[27] If we consider that Jubilee legislation attempts to involve all related social members of society, including slaves, debtors, creditors, alien residents, and even land, we can say that the Jubilee legislation reveals the original ideal of restorative justice. Pope John Paul II's apostolic letter "Tertio Millennio Adveniente" (As the third millennium draws near) affirms the restorative nature of Jubilee justice as follows:

> The jubilee year was meant to restore equality among all the children of Israel, offering new possibilities to families which had lost their property and even their personal freedom. On the other hand, the jubilee year was a reminder

to the rich that a time would come when their Israelite slaves would once again become their equals and would be able to reclaim their rights. At the times prescribed by Law, a jubilee year had to be proclaimed, to assist those in need.[28]

Despite its "utopian," "radical," or "idealistic" nature, the restorative nature of Jubilee justice has continuously inspired not just religious communities but also those who aspired to transform society according to its ethical ideal. In his study of the concept of Jubilee in late eighteenth- and nineteenth-century England, for instance, Malcolm Chase uncovers that the Levitical concept of Jubilee was often appropriated by English radicals of the late eighteenth and early nineteenth centuries. According to Chase, "The appeal of Leviticus 25 to a politically aware Christian is obvious. . . . In short, the Levitical jubilee can be read as a time of social renewal upon principles of justice, communal ownership, liberty, and the rights of labor."[29] Given that the Jubilee law provides for the periodic redistribution of the land with the purpose of ensuring a stable and equable balance of state as well as preventing the alienation of property from the people and its concentration in too few hands, it caught the imagination of radical reformers.[30]

We should note here that not all revolutions are equal in their natures and actualizations. Revolutionary though, the radical nature of the Jubilee legislation is distinguished from other types such as Marxian proletarian revolution. As a result of the decades of global financialization and unbridled neoliberal capitalism, as Derrida correctly observes in his *Specters of Marx*, our world has been turned into a state in which the specter of communism begins to emerge. To deflect this haunting specter and to save the world from violent revolutions, the world needs a different kind of revolution whose paradigm, I contend, we discover in the model of Jubilee and its restorative justice. In this respect, the Jubilee legislation and its restorative justice will certainly have much to do with the moral vision of Derrida's "New International." In the following, by engaging two issues (Third World debt and environmental debt), I demonstrate how the concept of Jubilee and its restorative justice can actually transform our debt-stricken world and the environment into a more debt-free symbiotic global community.

## The Case of the Third World Debt Crisis and the Jubilee Legislation

Religious scholars such as Ton Veerkamp and Norman Solomon contend the ancient biblical text on debt can still illuminate the problem of the mounting debt burdens of many poor countries. Veerkamp, for instance, writes, "The consideration of debt in the ancient biblical texts, although it pertains to the debt of people or households, can help illuminate the question of the debt burden of the governments of poor countries. It sheds light on the ethical principles and political action that might be applied in seeking solutions to the debt problem."[31] He calls attention to the reforms of Nehemiah, which he summarizes as the "system of brotherhood." According to Veerkamp, debts were the main origin of serfdom in all ancient societies, and it was widespread. The historical narrative of Nehemiah 5, 8, and 9 illustrates that, as a Persian governor of Judea who had the main task of keeping or restoring the social and political stability of the province, Nehemiah envisioned a renewed political and social life that was based on an egalitarian economy by decreeing a debt release and redistribution of the land, which originates in the Jubilee legislation and its restorative justice.[32]

In his article "Economics of the Jubilee: Putting Third World Debt in Context," Norman Solomon explores the possibility of how we could apply the restorative justice of the Jubilee legislation to today's global economic situation. He diagnoses that the inequitable distribution of wealth results in social and economic injustice among and within nations, and the overexploitation and destruction of natural resources. Among these, as he emphasizes, the problem of Third World debt is one of the most worrisome symptoms of the disease.[33] In attempting to draw on more detailed ethical solutions to the problem of Third World debt, he suggests that we should be realistic rather than idealistic. For instance, we should take it into our consideration that even within the rabbinic tradition, where biblical commandments are normally taken in a practical, although not necessarily literal, sense, there is a reluctance to put the Jubilee principles into practice.[34] In this respect, he writes, "In other lands and times, we may derive inspiration and learn lessons from them but must attend carefully to the specific needs of our own situation."[35]

According to Solomon, in tackling the issues of Third World debt, what seems to be the most "frustrating aspects of the Third World debt problem is that the world could indeed afford to cancel debts if it would serve a lasting, useful purpose."[36] This argument makes sense if we look into a few statistics. In 1995 the top ten Japanese banks wrote off ¥6.2 trillion ($64 billion) of bad loans without going bankrupt, and, between 1985 and 1995, multilateral and bilateral banks lent $75–85 billion to African countries. He thus writes, "Evidently, if the sum written off by Japanese banks alone in 1995 is almost as much as the total loaned to African governments in the whole of the previous decade, we are dealing with sums that the 'rich' nations could relinquish without lasting harm."[37] It is worth noting some of the "pragmatic" and "heuristic" solutions that he develops based on the Levitical laws on economic matters:

• Aim at the fair distribution of wealth, work, and credit (numerous biblical laws on the care of those in need and the marginalized). Global extension: let rich nations assist poor ones. Provide credit for finance with favorable terms.
• Provide an opportunity for remission of excessive debt (sabbatical release). Global extension: reschedule and remit debt.
• Do not overexploit the land (let it "rest" every seven years). Global extension: conserve the environment.[38]

What are the distinctive features and conditions of the modern financial system that we should critically consider in appropriating and implementing the ethical principles and strategies drawn from the Jubilee legislation and sabbatical regulations? How does the Third World debt crisis of the modern capitalist system differ from the household debt crisis of the ancient Israeli agricultural economy? First of all, what is the Third World debt, and how should we understand it?

The Third World debt generally refers to the debt of developing countries of Africa, Asia, and Latin America, known as the Global South. According to *BBC News*, during the three decades from 1970 to 2002, total debts amassed by the world's poorest countries shot up from $25 billion to $523 billion. In 1970, Africa's proportion of the total was less than $11 billion, not even half the total owed by poor nations, but by 2002 that had risen to well above half, or $295 billion. And yet, although African countries had paid back $550 billion in principal and interest over the three decades on $540 billion of loans, "they still go on paying, sacrificing both the health and the education of their people, as well as any prospect of economic recovery and growth."[39] According to the report published by the Jubilee Debt Campaign in 2014—"Don't Turn the Clock Back: Analyzing the Risks of the Lending Boom to Impoverished Countries"—of the forty-three developing countries investigated (twenty-three have received debt relief under the HIPC Initiative and Multilateral Debt Relief Initiative between 2000 and 2012), twenty-nine countries (67 percent) will have significant increases in debt payment if economic growth is lower than IMF and World Bank predictions but still substantial.[40] According to the report, the median average for the forty-three countries shows a general trend of rising debt payments as a percentage of government revenue in all possible scenarios. "The average relative debt payment burden increases by between

85 percent and 250 percent, depending on growth rates and frequency and extent of any economic shocks."[41]

Jocelyne Sambira, a UN staff member and writer for *Africa Renewal Online* also reports that "the acquisition of new debt is an emerging pattern among beneficiaries of the world's most comprehensive debt reduction program to date."[42] According to the *Guardian*, total lending to the group of poor countries has increased by 60 percent, from $11.4 billion a year in 2009 to $18.5 billion in 2013.[43] The recent lending boom can be problematic. Sarah-Jayne Clifton, director of the Jubilee Debt Campaign, writes, "There is a real risk that today's lending boom is sowing the seeds of a new debt crisis in the developing world, threatening to reverse recent gains in the fight against poverty and inequality."[44] A significant portion of this debt is created in the form of government bonds. For instance, according to Amadou Sy, the director of the Africa Growth Initiative at the Brookings Institution, "From 2006 to 2014, at least 14 other countries have issued a total of $15 billion or more in international sovereign bonds."[45] Of course, when these bonds are issued, investors of the First World countries snatch up these bonds, seduced by the continent's favorable growth outlook and promise of high returns. It all makes sense, then, that some observers worry that African countries are borrowing "too much and too fast."[46]

Why, then, is the increasing sovereign debt of Third World countries problematic? Increasing debt is problematic because it can have a significant impact on global poverty. The typical scenario goes this way. Many Third World countries spend several times as much on servicing debt each year as they do on health care and education, which subsequently results in chronic health crises and a lack of public education for children in Third World countries. The debt also results in the transfer of the wealth of the South to the countries of the North, while the South is impoverished. Sovereign debt is typically contracted with compounded interest, and this brings a detrimental effect to the debtor countries, rendering a serviceable debt unsustainable, especially if this rate is variable. For instance, according to Sharma and Kumar:

> The debt has progressively increased, from $567 billion in 1980 to $1.4 trillion in 1992. In that same twelve-year period, total foreign debt payment from Third World countries amounted to $1.6 trillion. Thus, in spite of having already paid back three times over the $567 billion they had borrowed, by 1992, these countries, far from being less indebted, ended up owing 250 percent more than they did in 1980. So the debt continues to feed on itself in a vicious circle where money is borrowed to pay interest.[47]

Regarding Third World debt and the appropriation of the concept of Jubilee, one of the most challenging issues is to define the "sustainable" level of total debt and its service payments. Joseph Hanlon rephrases this question as follows: "How much debt would be cancelled, and how was the burden to be shared?"[48] According to him, the World Bank and IMF announced that debt would be considered sustainable "if it was likely to be repaid without defaulting, and that this level was considered [to] be a total NPV (net present value) debt between 200 and 250% of annual exports and annual debt service payments between 20 and 25% of export earnings (known as the 'debt service ratio')."[49] He, however, argues that no justification was provided to ratify this figure, and all other evidence shows that "these ratios are substantially too high."[50] Despite its announcement, Hanlon reveals, the World Bank actually wrote in 1994 that "debt-to-export ratios of over 200% have 'generally proved unsustainable in the medium term.'"[51]

The case of Europe's cancellation of Germany's debt in 1953 (the London Debt Accords) provides us with a different perspective in defining what a "sustainable" level of total debt and its service payments would be. According to the Jubilee Debt Campaign, the German debt consisted of two sources: Roughly half of German debt was from loans in the 1920s and early 1930s to meet payments ordered by the Treaty of Versailles in 1919, and the other half originated from reconstruction following the end of World War II. The 1920s reparations payments were only 13–15 percent of exports, and by 1952, Germany's foreign-owed debt was around 25 percent of national income.[52] In February 1953 the Allies agreed to a substantial cancellation of German debt. According to Hanlon, they initially asked for a debt-service ratio of 10 percent, but German negotiators successfully settled with their creditors, and the ratio was reduced to 3.5 percent.[53] The case of Germany's debt cancellation in 1953 is strikingly different from later cases in Latin America and Africa (1980s and 1990s), East Asia (late 1990s), Russia and Argentina (turn of the millennium).[54] Given that many Third World countries have paid their debts with the "debt service ratio" (20 and 25 percent of their export earnings), it seems difficult to explain why poor countries of the South should pay six times as much as Germany paid.

Several features of the London Debt Accords significantly benefited Germany in addition to the cancellation of debt. First, it was agreed that West Germany could pay the debt only out of trade surpluses. Second, all types of creditors were brought into the process, including foreign governments and companies. Third, the London Debt Accords addressed all debts, including debts of German individuals, companies, and the government. Fourth, the agreement also stipulated that, in case West Germany could not meet debt repayments, there would be consultations between the debtor and creditors. Of course, there was a distinctive historical background behind the 1953 London Debt Accords. The Cold War had started, and the cancellation of the Germany's debt was specifically calculated to allow enough money for West Germany's rapid reconstruction in contrast to the new socialist Germany (East Germany). Even though we acknowledge the unique historical factor behind the London Debt Accords, we cannot but come to an apparent conclusion that in today's world, "sustainability is only defined in terms of ability to repay, if squeezed hard enough."[55]

How could we legitimately determine the "sustainable" level of total debt and its service payments? What is the justifiable amount of cancellation in forgiving the debts of the Third World countries or any other countries burdened with onerous debt? I argue first that the sustainable level of total debt and its service payment should not be exclusively determined by the executive directors of the IMF and the World Bank. As consistently argued in this book, the matter of debt and its service payment is not merely a matter of money and economy; it is also a matter of life, dignity, prosperity, social cohesion, and human development. In this respect, determining the sustainable level of payable debt should be a matter of ethics, religion, and politics as well as of economy and finance. This means that various philosophical, religious, and political voices should be included into the process of determining the sustainable level of total debt and its service payments.

To be more specific, I suggest that Amartya Sen's and Martha Nussbaum's concept of "capabilities" should be seriously considered and critically appropriated once again in determining the sustainable level of total debt and its service payments. In his *The Idea of Justice*, Amartya Sen lays out the concept of capabilities by proposing a "serious departure from concentrating on the *means* of living to the *actual opportunities* of living."[56] By "means," Sen refers to John Rawls' "primary goods," which include such all-purpose means as income and wealth, powers and prerogatives of offices, the social bases of self-respect, and so on. According to Sen, the focus on "actual opportunities" should matter in conceiving the concept of justice because "the capability approach focuses on human life, not just on some detached objects of convenience, such as incomes or commodities that a person may possess, which are often taken, especially in economic analysis, to be the main criteria of human success."[57] Perhaps the most important aspect (and contribution) of the capabilities approach is that the key element of justice is not merely about the distribution of primary goods; rather, it should be about helping each individual to achieve combinations of valued functionings. He thus writes, "The capability that we are concerned with is our ability to achieve various combinations of functionings that we can compare and judge against each other in terms of what we have reason to value."[58] Although Nussbaum generally agrees with Sen, she develops the concept of capabilities in light of the idea of equal human dignity, emphasizing such aspects as the neediness, sociability, and practical activity of human beings. She writes, "The basic intuitive idea of my version of the capabilities approach is that we begin with a conception of the dignity of the human being, and of a life that is worthy of that dignity."[59] It is important to note that the capabilities approach promotes nonparochialism as a requirement of justice because "the encounter of public reasoning about justice should go beyond the boundaries of a state or a region."[60] How, then, does the capabilities approach to justice help us to determine the sustainable level of total debt? In short, the capabilities approach suggests that the sustainable level of total debt and its service payments should be determined in such a way as to not violate or compromise the basic human capabilities. In other words, the sustainable level of debt service payments should not go below the threshold level delineated by the capabilities approach.

The political appropriation of the concept of Jubilee to the case of the Third World debt becomes much more justified and called for if we consider the historical background and origin of its crisis. Paul Vallely, in his *Bad Samaritans: First World Ethics and Third World Debt*, offers us a detailed historical background of the Third World debt crisis. He argues that the Third World debt crisis is basically the continuation of the "colonial imbalance" to the "benefit of every man, woman and child living in the First World today."[61] According to Vallely, there are three distinctive methods by which rich countries maintain their advantage over the poor nations. What are these distinctive methods? The first is the mechanism of modern international trade, and the second is through multinational companies. The third and perhaps most powerful method is the whole international financial system.[62] As for the first mechanism, we can think of tariffs and government subsidies, which protect only the citizens of the First World countries while significantly compromising the interests of the Third World countries and their environment. The second mechanism is commonly interlinked with structural exploitations of human labor (sweatshops) as well as environmental destruction by multinational companies of First World countries in many Third World countries. In his article "The 147 Companies That Control Everything," Bruce Upbin of *Forbes* reports that out of 43,060 transnational corporations worldwide, 147 firms control 40 percent of the wealth in the network, and a total of 737 control 80 percent of it all.[63] The problem of the global dominance of multinational companies is that their operations are not equally beneficial to Third World countries. In this respect, Vallely writes, the "seventh structure of sin" is not the "operation of a First World company in a Third World economy, but a method of operation which is not rooted in mutual benefit and true partnership."[64]

As for the third mechanism of the imbalanced international financial system, we should investigate the historical background and the structural origin of the Third World debt crisis in the 1980s and 1990s. The origin of the debt crisis in the Third World countries is commonly attributed to two "oil shocks" in 1973 and 1979, which were influenced by such incidents as the U.S. termination of the Bretton Woods Accord (1971) and the Yom Kippur War (1973). The increase in oil prices led to a large amount of money in European banks deposited by members of OPEC (Organization of Petroleum Exporting Countries). To pay interest and make a profit on the deposited money, the banks actively sought out Third World borrowers for lending the money—the so-called petrodollars. According to Mokgethi Motlhabi, "They offered favorable loan terms, with low interest rates, without even concerning themselves much with how or for what purpose the money was to be used."[65] As is well known, the U.S. Federal Reserve increased interest rates as high as 20 percent in 1980, and this had a detrimental effect on Third World countries in terms of paying back their debts on petrodollars. The critical moral failure on the part of the lenders was that they did not alert Third World borrowers to the possible consequences of taking a loan whose interest rate was vulnerable to the fluctuating interest rates in the course of the debt repayment.[66]

If we seriously consider the historical background and the structural origin of the Third World countries' debt crisis, we may come to have a different perspective on approaching the problem. If the debt is defaulted on, of course the lender would lose money, being a financial victim. In the case of the Third World debt crisis, it is not actually clear who is the real victim. As much as the First World creditors, the Third World countries are also victimized by the unwanted debt crisis. If we would go further taking into consideration the long-lasting oppressive legacy of the colonialism on Third World countries, the First World countries' aid to Third World countries should be renamed reparation; also, what is needed in the case of the debt default is not oppressive structural adjustment in Third World countries while bailing out the First World banking industries, but a negotiation-based appropriation of the Jubilee legislation.

## The Case of Environmental Debt and a Jubilee Injunction on Sustainability

Above we have explored how the concept of Jubilee may apply to the case of the Third World debt crisis. It is important for us to see that there is a critical difference between our world, characterized by a neoliberal global economy, and ancient Israeli society, based on an agricultural local economy. Global structural mechanisms and agencies such as free trade agreements, multinational companies, IFIs, and the Paris Club were nonexistent at the time in which the original concept of Sabbath and Jubilee were born. This critical difference calls for a new and creative approach to rising global debt crises with different yet innovative economic strategies and enhanced moral responsibilities, instead of rendering them obsolete just because they are outdated.

Paradoxically enough, as our world is becoming more liberalized and globalized, our world and its people are getting closer to each other through such mechanisms as the movement of people (migration) and sharing of information and technology. This new phenomenon strangely reminds us of the time of ancient communal society, when debt was supposed to be a form of gift and everyone was called to be the keeper of their brothers and sisters. It is my contention that we are now called in a different way to be the keepers of near or remote strangers of this planetary community. Like ancient communal society, the new planetary community should also be the place where debt is supposed to be a form of gift to each other rather than an exploitative and oppressive mechanism. Since the Jubilee legislation is devised to restore equality, solidarity, and economic and environmental sustainability to the community of "brotherhood," its concept and practical measures have much to do with our global community of new brotherhood and sisterhood. In this section, we explore the further application of the concept of Jubilee by specifically focusing on the growing problem of ecological or environmental debt.

What is ecological or environmental debt? Let me answer this question by illustrating two cases. The first case is a story about the displacement of Pacific Islanders due to rising sea levels. In June 2014, the people of Kiribati, a group of islands in the Pacific Ocean with a population of about 110,000, finalized the purchase of twenty square kilometers on Vanua Levu, one of the Fiji Islands, about two thousand kilometers away. According to the *Guardian*, the Church of England sold the property, mainly covered by dense forest, for $8.77 million.[67] This purchase, however, was controversial because it was revealed that Kiribati paid four times more per acre than other buyers in the past few years. Tetawa Tatai, a former health minister and a member of Parliament said that he was shocked to know that the Church of England, which he called "one of the most trusted institutions in the world," would "gouge one of the poorest and most isolated countries in the world."[68] The *Guardian* raises an important issue by pointing out a key aspect that "the cost of protecting these places against rising sea levels, compared with national income, is among the highest in the world."[69] Considering that the problem of rising sea levels has been directly or indirectly caused by other countries (mostly developed countries), who should pay the cost of protecting these places and their people? Simply put, these kinds of environmental costs are what the concept of ecological debt refers to.

The case of Tanzania in Africa provides us with a different kind of ecological debt. Tanzania has vast mineral resources including gold, petroleum, gas, and huge tracts of forest. Mineral extraction comprises nearly half of Tanzania's exports. Despite its bountiful natural resources, it is still ranked one of the poorest countries in the region.[70] According to the *International Debt Statistics 2016*, published by the World Bank, Tanzania's external debt stocks have increased consistently since 2000. In 2000, its external debt was $7.2 billion, but this increased to nearly $10 billion in 2011 and $14.5 billion in 2014.[71] Researchers Demetrius Kweka and Shauna Accongiagio report that "despite the end of colonialism, the global economic system still facilitates the skewed extraction and exploitation of natural resources that has led to the excessive plunder and exploitation of mineral resources by Northern countries,"[72] which result in the drain of natural resources and raw materials, undermining the capacity of Southern countries. They especially point out that, in Tanzania, the exploitative practices of foreign companies "have been detrimental to economic development and have caused vast ecological damages"[73] instead of boosting its economic growth. The case of Tanzania illustrates that any excessive—that is, unsustainable—exploitation of natural resources should be regarded as ecological debt.

The concept of ecological debt was coined in the 1990s by a South American nongovernmental organization called Acción Ecológica, and it defines its concept as follows:

> The responsibility that the industrialized countries have for the gradual destruction of the planet caused by their production and consumption patterns. . . . Ecological Debt includes the illegitimate appropriation of the atmosphere and of the absorption capacity of the planet. It is the obligation and responsibility that the industrialized countries of the North have with the countries of the Third World, for the looting and use of natural goods: petroleum, minerals, forests,

biodiversity and marine resources; to the cost of human energy of their people and of the destruction, devastation and contamination of their natural heritage and sources of sustenance.[74]

According to this definition, Tanzania becomes the creditor of ecological debt, which is owed by the North "on account of resource plundering, environmental damages, and the free occupation of environmental space to deposit wastes, such as greenhouse gases."[75] The concept of ecological debt has consistently drawn attention on a global scale thanks to the works of nongovernmental organizations as well as scholarly publications, and it has become a widely circulated idea, at least in academia. This concept has also evolved since its first formulation, and religious ethicist Cynthia D. Moe-Lobeda develops it further by positing three kinds of ecological debt: "intragenerational, intergenerational, and interspecies."[76] Although the concept of ecological debt is now much more circulated than before in the public, "not only are those ecological debtors not held accountable, international institutions and governments have yet to acknowledge and measure the size of the ecological debt."[77]

In December 2015, at the UN Climate Change Conference, commonly known as COP21, Todd Stern, the U.S. special envoy for climate change, specifically rejected the concept of ecological debt, stating,

> There's one thing that we don't accept and won't accept in this agreement and that is the notion that there should be liability and compensation for loss and damage. That's a line that we can't cross. And I think in that regard we are in the exact same place my guess is with virtually all if not all developed countries. This is not a U.S.–centric position, but it is a position that is important for us.[78]

This statement can be translated as an official negation of the concept of ecological debt on the part of the U.S. government, even though Stern adds that "we are in favor of support, financial, technical support going to countries for loss and damage."[79] Such denial of the existence of ecological debt becomes the reason why those who represent the voice of Third World countries argue, "Many studies of ecological debt espouse the view that quantification of the debt is unimportant, what is important is the recognition of the existence of an ecological debt."[80]

What, then, does the concept of Sabbath and Jubilee have to do with the problem of ecological debt? To answer this question, we should first take note that concern for the land is a core tenet of Sabbath and Jubilee. For instance, the Levitical demand for the preservation and redemption of the land clearly demonstrates that Sabbath and Jubilee are deeply ecological as well as socioeconomic: "In the seventh year there shall be a Sabbath of complete rest for the land" (25:4); "Throughout the land that you hold, you shall provide for the redemption of the land" (25:24). We should also note that such concern for the land as a core tenet of Sabbath and Jubilee resurfaces in other parts of the Hebrew Bible, such as Isaiah 24:5,19.[81] We should also observe that there is a structural connection between the rising amount of debt and the deepening environmental exploitation and destruction in Third World countries. Hans Ucko succinctly captures this connection: "The depletion of the rain forest in the South for furniture in the North has effects on global warming throughout and is caused by the infinite debt of the South to the banks and nations of the North."[82]

In a nutshell, Jewish ideas of Sabbath and Jubilee have to do with ecological debt not only because of their demands to preserve and redeem the exploited and damaged land but also because of the structural connection between rising Third World debt and its environmental destruction. The Jubilee challenge to forgive the rising Third World debt requires that ecological debtors take up a special responsibility to preserve and redeem the damaged natural environment. The Jubilee challenge, however, should be contextualized in today's world, especially its new global economic system. As Moe-Lobeda points out, neoliberalism has two broad impacts on climate change and the accruement of ecological debt: "The increase in unregulated trade and investment—especially in extractive industries—results in increased greenhouse gas emissions. And the financial benefits of carbon-fat industry accrue disproportionately to large corporations and finance institutions whose beneficiaries are largely people of economic privilege."[83]

One, however, may raise a question that since the concept of Jubilee is about cancelling outstanding debt, how can we apply it to the case of ecological debt? Does it mean that creditors of ecological debt are supposed to cancel it per the demand of ecological debtors? This confusion is caused by two factors: (1) the misunderstanding of what it means to pay off ecological debt and (2) the lack of a critical perspective to see the interconnectedness between the Third World debt crisis and its ecological crisis. What does it mean to pay off or cancel ecological debt? Unlike financial debt based on contract and paper, whose cancellation is completed by the forgiveness of the creditor, the cancellation of ecological debt is not simply done by the creditor's will to forgive. In the latter case, the cancellation is completed only by restoring the ecological sustainability to the affected environment. This is the reason why ecological debt cannot be simply monetized, unlike financial debt. We should note that, whereas the purpose of the cancellation of financial debt is to restore economic sustainability on the part of debtors, the purpose of the cancellation of ecological debt is to restore ecological sustainability to the environment. In this respect, the distinction between ecological creditors and ecological debtors is not always as clear as in the case of financial debt. In many cases, both ecological creditors and ecological debtors are to work together to restore ecological sustainability in the affected environment. Given that many ecological creditors are not financially or technologically capable of restoring the damaged ecological sustainability, ecological debtors (First World countries and their companies) are required to assist them to restore the damaged ecological sustainability. This requirement becomes even more evident from a structuralist perspective.

The structuralist perspective demands that we see that the debt crisis of the Third World is deeply intertwined with its ecological crisis.[84] During the global economic turbulence of the 1970s, when "debt was good" on the international economic scene because interest rates were effectively negative, the corresponding mantra ("ecological debt is good") was also spawned in the minds of its creditors and debtors because there did not seem to be any obvious interest rate to pay. As Andrew Simms poignantly points out, however, "The reckless environmental credit boom is over and a huge ecological deficit has opened up. Recrimination is inevitable and the books have to be put straight for the planetary budget."[85] This is the reason why it is mistaken to say that the debt crisis of the Third World is one thing and its ecological crisis is another. To the contrary, they are deeply intertwined on a global scale. The contextualized Sabbath or Jubilee principle, thus, requires that the First World countries' cancellation of Third World debt be accompanied by the provision of the financial and technological resources to restore the damaged ecological sustainability in the Third World countries.

Is it politically and economically feasible for our world to realize this contextualized Jubilee principle? Is this approach too utopian? How could we materialize this seemingly too idealistic moral provision? Fortunately, or maybe unfortunately, we are all living in a world where we are connected to each other financially as well as ecologically. Out of this context, something unprecedented is created, and the idea of "debt-for-nature swaps" has been developed to address both financial and ecological debt. Although not perfect, I hold, debt-for-nature swaps offer us an effective illustration of how the contextualized Jubilee principle can actually be realized in today's debt-stricken world.

Debt-for-nature swaps were initiated in 1984 by the World Wildlife Fund as a mechanism for enhancing conservation efforts in developing countries. James Resor, director of World Wildlife Fund–United States in the 1990s, writes that "the idea arose from the observation that much of the world's biological diversity is harbored in the same countries that face the greatest financial strain from foreign debt burdens."[86] Debt-for-nature swaps are either bilateral or three-party agreements. In the case of bilateral swaps, creditors such as developed countries agree to forgive a developing country's debt on the condition that the developing county fund and implement a domestic conservation program. In the case of three-party agreement among a creditor, a nongovernmental conservation organization, and a developing country debtor, the nongovernmental organization, such as the World Wildlife Fund or Conservation International, plays the role of broker in hammering out the swaps. There is also a commercial swap, and, in that case, creditors sell a developing country's debt to a conservation organization at a reduced rate, and the conservation organization agrees to forgive part or all of the debt with the proviso that the developing country funds and implements a domestic conservation program.[87] Since the first agreement in 1987 between the government of Bolivia and Conservation International, in which Conservation International was able to acquire U.S.$650,000 of Bolivian external debt at a discounted price of $100,000, more than thirty countries have participated in debt-for-nature swaps.[88]

Of course, this program is not perfect. Dal Didia, for instance, argues that "neither debt-for nature swaps nor outright debt cancellation is capable of curtailing the rapid depletion of tropical forests, because the inhabitants of these forests depend on them for their livelihood."[89] He then suggests that debt cancellation should be "preceded, or at the minimum, accompanied by, democracy and democratic institutions, property rights, and an effective market system."[90] Others, such as Nicole Hassoun, point out the problem of debt-for-nature swaps by suggesting a scenario according to which debt-for-nature swaps may compromise the rights of the debtor country's subjects with the required environmental programs. "It is possible, for instance, for a swap to lighten the country's debt burden, increase its ability to protect some of its subjects' rights, and *still* prevent the country from protecting other rights (even those very same) subjects possess. Such a swap is *prima facie* impermissible."[91] It is not my intention to defend debt-for-nature swaps in this section, but it seems too precipitous to do away with this program for such criticism. Instead of terminating it, global society should work together to make it better by fixing its potential problems.[92]

## Conclusion

We have seen above how Jewish concepts of Sabbath and Jubilee have become an indispensable ethical framework in tackling some of the most critical and urgent issues of today's global society: the Third World debt crisis and its ecological crisis. These two issues are not separate from each other from a structuralist point of view, and the contextualized Jubilee principle demands that the wealthy creditors of the First World should consider forgiving onerous debts of Third World countries for the sake of restoring economic sustainability to Third World debtors. The HIPC Initiative was indeed an unprecedented realization of the spirit of Sabbath and Jubilee on a global scale. At the summit meeting in Toronto in 1987, French president François Mitterrand proposed an across-the-board forgiveness of one-third of governmental and government-guaranteed debts of the poorest sub-Saharan African states, which Morris Miller calls the "most dramatic official gestures."[93] In 2013 Norway surprised the world by announcing the cancellation of Myanmar's debt, whose total amount was NOK 3.2 billion. These cases demonstrate how relevant and practical the moral vision of Sabbath and Jubilee can be in today's world. The growing number of debt-for-nature swaps also demonstrates how creatively the Jubilee principle can be implemented in the environment as well. Where there is an outcry for the restoration of economic or ecological sustainability, there also is a need for the implementation of the moral vision of Sabbath and Jubilee.

CHAPTER SIX

# CHRISTIANITY AND A VIRTUE ETHICS OF DEBT

## Introduction

In January 2011 the Financial Crisis Inquiry Commission[1] chaired by Phil Angelides submitted the 663-page *The Financial Crisis Inquiry Report* to the president, the Congress, and the American people. The commission was created to examine the causes of the current financial and economic crisis in the United States. The report concludes that the financial crisis was avoidable, by identifying essential factors as the causes of the financial crisis. These factors include such causes as credit and housing bubbles, nontraditional mortgages, credit ratings and securitization, financial institutions' concentrated and correlated risk, leverage and liquidity risk, contagion risk, and shock and panic. Interestingly enough, The report also points out that failure in virtue was very patent in the crisis. As Aliza D. Racelis, among others, correctly notes, "Excessive leverage and imprudent risk-taking, failure in fiduciary duties and in stewardship, as well as greed, lack of moderation, and fraud" are particularly conspicuous.[2]

The report summarizes its critical investigation by judging that although the soundness and the sustained prosperity of the financial system and our economy depend on such key moral virtues as fairness, integrity, and transparency, "we witnessed an erosion of standards of responsibility and ethics that exacerbated the financial crisis."[3] Regarding the failure in virtue and ethics, the report particularly emphasizes that while a crisis of this magnitude cannot be the work of a few bad actors, the lack of expected virtues among those in financial and public leadership positions significantly contributes to the financial crisis. For instance, it reports, "The captains of finance and the public stewards of our financial system ignored warnings and failed to question, understand, and manage evolving risks."[4] One, however, needs to take note that pointing out failures in virtue among those who run the financial system does not necessarily mean that we can reduce all financial crises to individual moral failures. As social scientists Laura Hansen and Siamak Movahedi argue, identifying the root cause of the contemporary financial crisis, say, with "personal greed" is a lack of "sociological imagination."[5] Personal troubles and structural or public issues should be distinguished, and, according to their analysis, the financial crisis of 2007–2008 should be understood as a structural issue rather than as a matter of individual virtue.

Although I greatly sympathize with Hansen and Movahedi, I am not necessarily in agreement with their implied "either-or" reasoning. Instead, as the report seems to employ, I adopt the "both-and" approach in analyzing the root causes of the financial crisis and also developing a more holistic ethics of debt. In previous chapters, I have investigated and analyzed various structural and historical aspects of the financial crisis by developing an argument that the needed ethics of debt in an age of financialization is a social ethics. In this chapter I continue to maintain this thesis while constructively embracing key ethical insights of virtue ethics. A careful analysis of the financial crisis clearly demonstrates that it was caused by both structural and agential failures. To develop a more holistic ethics of debt, thus, we should integrate both structural and agential aspects of an ethical reconstruction.

With that said, in this chapter I attempt to devise a new virtue ethics that is designed specifically for agents who are related to the world of finance either as its managers and service providers or as its users and regulators. With this new type of virtue ethics, I hope to develop a more comprehensive and holistic ethics of debt. In doing so, I particularly engage in Christian religious thoughts and discourses. As I have done in the two previous chapters, the religious engagement is specifically focused on the further development of critical ethical insights into a more holistic ethics of debt rather than on indoctrinating religious ideals to the world of banking and finance.

## Uncoupling between Morals and Debt: The Amoral Genealogy of Greed

Above all, with regard to the conclusive judgment of *The Financial Crisis Inquiry Report* that there was a pervasive failure in virtue and ethics among those who run the financial system, we should ask why those persons failed to incorporate and demonstrate virtues in managing the financial system. Answering this question is an initial step toward the development of Christian virtue ethics. We should first realize that the lack of virtue in the financial sector is as much the *effect* of an ideological and philosophical invention of the late eighteenth century as the *cause* of the financial crisis in the early twenty-first century. This ideological and philosophical invention was enabled by English philosopher, jurist, and the founder of modern utilitarianism, Jeremy Bentham.

In his 1787 *Defence of Usury*, concerning the "liberty of making one's own terms in money-bargains," Jeremy Bentham makes a central proposition as follows:

> No man of ripe years and of sound mind, acting freely, and with his eyes open, ought to be hindered, with a view to his advantage, from making such bargain, in the way of obtaining money, as he thinks fit: nor, (what is a necessary consequence) anybody hindered from supplying him, upon any terms he thinks proper to accede to.[6]

For Bentham, the really important question regarding usury is the political or legal one,[7] and he develops his genealogical argumentation against the prohibition of usury by saying that there was no such thing as usury prior to "custom growing from convention." Usury law, for him, is nothing but a customary matter, which has nothing to do with any naturalistic moral grounding. He skillfully obliterates the naturalistic or intrinsic moral grounding of usury law by raising the following questions: "For what rate of interest is there that can naturally be more proper than another? What natural fixed price can there be for the use of money more than for the use of any other thing? Were it not then for custom, usury, considered in a moral view, would not then so much as admit of a definition."[8]

According to Bentham, since usury law is divested of its naturalistic or intrinsic moral basis, any usury laws cannot be regarded as having an inherent moral justification. All usury laws are reduced to a matter of "custom resulting from free choice."[9] For instance, he illustrates how the legal rate of usury law varied depending on its historical context (12 percent for Romans until the time of Justinian, 5 percent for Bentham's contemporary England, 8 percent for the West Indies, 30 percent for certain cases in

Constantinople, etc.). He then argues, "Now, of all these widely different rates, what one is there, that is intrinsically more proper than another?"[10] For him, the legal rate of usury law is nothing but a customary convention that can be reduced to a matter of "convenience." He thus writes, "What can there then be in custom, to make it a better guide than the convenience which gave it birth? And what is there in convenience, that should make it a worse guide in one case than in another?"[11] From the perspective of convenience, Bentham holds, usury law turns out to be "absurd" because the law resulting from peoples' choice of convenience prohibits them from choosing their own convenience. He illustrates, "It would be convenient to me to give 6 percent for money: I wish to do so. 'No,' (says the law) 'you can't'—why so? 'Because it is not convenient to your neighbor to give above 5 for it.' Can anything be more absurd than such a reason?"[12]

What is the significance of Bentham's argument against any usury laws with regard to the establishment of an ethics of debt? Above all, Bentham's *Defence of Usury* plays a major role in altering the traditional moral concept of debt and its phenomena into an amoral or morally neutral customary matter, which should be ruled by convenience, not by any natural or intrinsic moral values. Whether he intended it, his book became a key ideological basis in transforming the matter of debt into an amoral issue, not a moral one. As a result of this important ideological sea change, the entire field of finance, even the realm of economy as such, has been separated from the realm of morals and ethics, at least on an ideological basis. Christian ethicist D. Stephen Long, for instance, writes, "The difference between the secular rise of modern ethics after Bentham, and Christian reflection on economics prior to Bentham, involves a complete break in how one thinks about money."[13] Paul B. Rasor also judges that, despite the increasing acceptance of interest, it was not until the end of the eighteenth century, when Bentham published his *Defence of Usury*, that economic analysis began to push aside moral and theological analysis in the usury debate. He goes further, saying, "Bentham's utilitarian arguments eventually carried the day and, together with the church's declining influence, resulted in the gradual decline of restrictive laws during the nineteenth century. All English usury laws were repealed in 1854, and most of Europe followed shortly thereafter."[14]

The significance of this ideological sea change, which transforms the problem of debt into a morally neutral issue, is that it has resulted in peoples' behavioral change. Unfortunately, from a critical-moral perspective, at the heart of this behavioral change lies an overall degradation of virtues and ethics. John Dobson, a professor of finance at California Polytechnic State University, acknowledges that the behavioral assumption in finance is grounded in an amoral stance. He writes, "In addition, the behavioral assumptions of finance have been presented as prescriptively *(i.e., morally) neutral*, thus failing to recognize that this narrow and rigid invocation of self-interest has moral implications. Not only do these assumptions have an implicit moral agenda, but they also tend to promote this agenda through the modern business school."[15]

We should note that Bentham never attempts to demoralize the problem of debt. He just tries to amoralize it. Indeed, he does not endorse fraud, cheating, embezzlement, and the like in financial matters. He, however, affirms that convenience, self-interest, and unregulated contract should be the rule of the game. His position is, then, widely endorsed by and resonates with modern contemporary economists. For instance, Walter E. Block, an economist at Loyola University New Orleans, summarizes the core amoral view on the matter of interest rate as follows in his cowritten article "Money Does Not Grow on Trees: An Argument for Usury": "Therefore, the just price must be, and can only be, the mutually agreed upon price, or interest rate."[16] In a typical Benthamite fashion, he defends payday loans because the state's usury law only "adds another element of arbitrariness." He goes on further, arguing, "Each state in the U.S. is allowed to limit the annual interest rate collected by the company or even outlaw this practice. How can this practice, which is based on a voluntary exchange, be considered economically exploitative?"[17] In a 1970 *Newsweek* article, "Defense of Usury," Milton Friedman also defends usury by evoking the name of Jeremy Bentham. Friedman argues that while Bentham's pamphlet has been widely accepted by economists, it was widely neglected by politicians. He then adds, "Bentham's explanation of the 'grounds of the prejudices against usury' is as valid today as when he wrote."[18]

Bentham's defense of usury and his followers' endorsement entail several hermeneutic-ethical problems. First, by defending usury, Bentham and his followers are not able to differentiate a legitimate level of interest from a usurious rate. They are not able to agree either that an interest rate is one thing and a usurious rate is another. The fact that each different society establishes its different interest rate actually reflects an important fact that humanity shares a certain common sense to call certain interest rates usurious. Of course the exact rate can be variable depending on the socioeconomic context of each different society, but this does not mean that the concept of usury is a merely arbitrary notion. From a phenomenological perspective, the different rates show that they are determined by the shared notion of justice, not by mere convenience. By neutralizing debt and its economy, Bentham and his followers are not able to see more critically that the economy of debt can be subject to an immoral exploitation of its system by those who are willing to abuse it for their own sake.

Second, Bentham and his followers fail to see that the economy, including the economy of debt, is in fact deeply anchored in society rather than freestanding on its own. By uprooting the realm of debt and its economy from its social foundation of political community, they in fact open the backdoor through which immoral behaviors can enter the realm, cloaking themselves as amoral acts. The result of the amoralization of debt and its economy is not the prolongation of the amoral economy of debt but its devolvement into an increasing immoralization. We should also note that the uprooting also comes along with another significant moral payment— that is, the reduction of credit to the mere obverse of debt. Philip Goodchild correctly perceives that once credit has been reconceived as the mere obverse of debt, then "the temporal reality of people's changing lives and expectations is replaced by the collective fiction of an unchanging debt."[19] What does he mean by "collective fiction"? It is none other than the single-minded logic of the economy of debt; that is, one should always pay back one's debt.

Goodchild argues that credit, confidence, and faith always have been essential to economic life by pointing out anthropological evidence that "most societies have operated on the basis of generosity, hospitality, mutual favors, sharing, patronage, and tribute, without reciprocity, barter, exchange, or money, except perhaps between strangers and enemies."[20] He goes on further by drawing on David Graeber's anthropological discovery that "credit, in its original sense, precedes money."[21] The reduction of credit to the mere obverse of debt violates an important anthropological truth that credit also precedes the birth of monetary debt. Goodchild is right to say, "Credit is a fact of life for temporal creatures who make promises, enter contracts, and place trust in others."[22] By uprooting the economy of debt from its social foundation of political community, Bentham and his followers fail to see the real picture of *Homo economicus*, whose existence is grounded in moral credit in social interactions. As Goodchild indicates, "The normal principle of social interaction is mutual credit rather than reciprocity [which reduces credit to the obverse of debt] and this remains true at an interpersonal level even today."[23]

Third, Bentham and his followers mislead people, especially those in finance, to believe that moral virtue does not matter in their professional world. By amoralizing the economy of debt, they desensitize the moral sensibility of those who run the system as its leaders and agencies. As a result of this desensitization, these people do not apply moral judgment to such moral vices as greed from a critical-ethical perspective. Many Wall Street scandals caused by such high-profile individuals as Dennis Levin, Ivan Boesky, Michael Milken, Bernard Madoff, and Robert Stanford demonstrate that the moral vacuum created by the amoralization of the financial world is much more likely filled by immoral desires and moral vices. The desensitization of moral sensibility was epitomized by the character Gordon Gekko of the 1987 movie[24] *Wall Street*, who claimed unabashedly that "greed is good, greed is right!" How should we then understand the problem of the lack of virtue among many financial leaders and their agencies?

Surendra Arjoon suggests an interesting argument that the lack of moral virtues among financial leaders and executives is the result of the narcissistic personality disorder: "The current global financial crisis was caused, in part, by the narcissistic personality disorder (NPD) of corporate leaders who substituted robust risk management for greed and personal gains by promoting self-serving and grandiose aims."[25] Arjoon justifies his argument by drawing on extensive empirical research and cultural analysis of psychologists such as Jean Twenge, Keith Campbell, Roy Baumeister, and others. He also defines narcissistic personality disorder as "an extravagant sense of self-importance, a sense of superiority, self-centered and self-referential behavior, exaggeration of talents, boastful and pretentious behavior, grandiose fantasies of unlimited success, . . . a willingness to exploit others, lack of empathy, . . . and arrogant behavior."[26]

Although Arjoon's psychological analysis offers us an intriguing critical perspective, I think it is a little too much to reduce entire immoral behaviors of financial leaders and agencies to some kind of psychological disorder. We should note that behind such narcissistic behaviors lies a more fundamental structural or systemic aspect. It is my contention that such a structural and systemic background has been set as a result of the ideological transformation we have seen above. The seeming lack of moral virtue among many financial leaders and corporate executives may then be considered as an unintended outcome of the Benthamite amoralization of the economy of debt. I am not arguing, though, that there is no moral accountability to be held on the part of these individual agencies. Indeed, they are responsible for their immoral behaviors as individuals, but we should not overlook an important aspect that there is an ideological background that has shaped their behaviors. The pervasive moral deficiencies such as greed in the financial sector is not the only culprit in financial crises. As Aliza Racelis notes, "Greed played a role but the bigger problem was incompetence."[27] Why, then, have all related parties become so incompetent, including managers who made dangerous and foolish decisions, consumers and investors who engaged in risky behavior, and regulators who were ineffective?[28] There is a deeper and larger reason that goes beyond the level of narcissistic personality disorder. How could we, then, cope with the Benthamite amoralization of the financial world?

We should first note that the Benthamite amoralizing project is hinged on a taken-for-granted assumption, which Bentham lays out clearly as follows: "One thing then is plain; that, antecendently to custom growing from convention, there can be no such thing as usury."[29] Bentham's remark strangely smacks of Hobbesian "state of nature." Of course he does not literally evoke Hobbesian state of nature, but Bentham certainly imagines that there is a precustomary state in human history in which no usury is existent. While Hobbes imagines a state of nature where no debt is existent, Bentham imagines Hobbesian state of nature where no usury is conceived. Interestingly enough, according to James Crimmins, "Historians of political thought commonly assume that the similarities in the thought of Thomas Hobbes (1588–1679) and Jeremy Bentham (1748–1832) are the product of Bentham's reading of Hobbes and infer that Bentham was in a certain sense a disciple of Hobbes."[30]

Despite the seeming commonality of Bentham's precustomary society and Hobbes' state of nature, anthropologists oppose the existence of such ahistorical states, as Graeber and others have already uncovered. This means that Hobbesian philosophical justification of a political dictatorship and Benthamite ideological justification of an amoralized financial market are both based on their philosophical imaginations. Bentham and Hobbes also inadvertently share the same philosophical position that there is no such thing as moral credit in earliest human society, which is again directly refuted by anthropologists such as Mauss. By failing to see the significance of the moral credit in developing their political and economic thought, they eventually come to justify different types of dictatorship: political dictatorship of the absolute sovereign (Hobbes) and the material god of wealth—Mammon (Bentham). For Hobbes, dictatorship by Leviathan in political life is justified because it appears to provide political stability and social security; for Bentham, dictatorship by Mammon in amoralized economic life is justified because it seems to offer wealth and prosperity. In a world dictated by Mammon, such moral vices as greed and avarice are converted into economic virtue, while, in a world dictated by Leviathan, such moral vices as brutality and ruthlessness are turned into political virtue. By plucking out the political and economic realms from the social foundation of communal life based on mutual trust, respect, and honor, they construct an ideological road map for a political and economic imagination that is not grounded on moral ideals and virtues.

## Reconstructing a Theological Foundation for the Moral Economy of Debt

We have seen above how the pervasive lack of virtue among the agencies of the financial and corporate world can be traced back to the ideological invention of amoral economy of debt by Bentham and subsequent economists. From the vantage of this genealogical perspective, the lack of moral virtue in the financial and corporate world cannot be simply explained away as individual moral failures. It is to be seen, rather, as an inevitable outcome of Benthamite ideological invention. In the amoral financial world, economic good (money and wealth) substitutes for moral good, and greed takes on a quasi-moral quality to be pursued. The concept of credit has been radically reduced to the state of a mere obverse of debt as well. Interestingly enough, Bentham completely ignores religion when he attempts to tackle usury law despite the fact that religion plays a key role in its establishment in Western history.

Such a lack of religious consideration in Bentham's defense of usury does not seem to be accidental if we recall that Bentham actually carried out an exhaustive examination of religion with the declared intention to extirpate religious beliefs, even the idea of religion itself, from the minds of people between 1809 and 1823.[31] According to James Crimmins, "Applying the utilitarian test at every turn, his analysis was squarely focused upon the supposed perniciousness of man's reverence for otherworldly beings, for the authority of 'holy books' and the sanctity of churches and their clerical officiates."[32] As Crimmins holds, his religious works, such as *Swear Not at All* (1817), *Church-of-Englandism and Its Catechism Examined* (1818), *Analysis of the Influence of Natural Religion on the Temporal Happiness of Mankind* (1822), and *Not Paul, but Jesus* (1823), "constitute the negative side of his plans for the construction of an entirely secular and rigorously utilitarian society."[33] I am not proposing here that his ideological project to amoralize the economic world has directly to do with his antireligious stance; however, it seems evident that for him there is no place for religion and its ethics in his amoral world of money and debt.

How could we imbue a moral ethos into the amoralized economy of debt? How could we reanchor the amoral economy of debt back into the social world of moral and symbolic credits? More specifically, how could Christian theology and its moral thoughts contribute to the moral reconstruction of an ethics of debt in today's neoliberal world? I attempt to answer these questions by exploring the possibility of establishing a Christian virtue ethics of debt. How, then, is a Christian virtue ethics of debt possible? First of all, I hold, a Christian virtue ethics of debt becomes possible when we begin to realize that debt is composed of two key elements: logic and story. By logic, I mean the economic logic of reciprocity such as exchange, barter, give-and-take, credit and debt, gain and loss, and so on. The quasi-moral force of this logic is best exemplified as "you should pay back your debt." Although this logic is indispensable in the establishment of debt, unless checked by some justifiable qualifications, it can subject defaulted debtors to various forms of dehumanization.

In his *Making of the Indebted Man*, Italian sociologist and philosopher Maurizio Lazzarato calls the dehumanized debtor the "indebted man." He concludes that the neoliberal creditor-debtor relationship makes up the subjective paradigm of modern-day capitalism as debt "breeds, subdues, manufactures, adapts, and shapes subjectivity."[34] According to Lazzarato, the birth of the indebted man becomes a key moral issue in an increasingly neoliberalized society. In a similar manner, Hollis Phelps also says, "Debt under neoliberalism, in other words, is not just a financial instrument; it also functions ideologically to infiltrate the very being of the subject, and in this sense can be said to encompass all aspects of life."[35] What is, then, the fundamental factor that causes the making of the indebted man and the infiltration of debt into the very being of the subject? It is none other than the quasi-moral force of the logic of debt. The economic logic of debt lies at the core of neoliberal dehumanization. How could we then liberate the indebted man from the dehumanizing logic of neoliberal debt?

It is extremely important for us to see that there is another key element that comprises debt—that is, story. What story? What does it mean that debt has a story aspect? Margaret Atwood provides us with the answer to this question in her 2008 *Payback: Debt and the Shadow Side of Wealth*. She first claims, "Without memory, there is no debt. Put another way: without story, there is no debt."[36] She then lays out her understanding of story as follows:

> A story is a string of actions occurring over time—one damn thing after another, as we glibly say in creative writing classes—and debt happens as a result of actions occurring over time. Therefore, any debt involves a plot line: how you got into debt, what you did, said, and thought while you were in there, and then—depending on whether the ending is to be happy or sad—how you got out of debt, or else how you got further and further into it until you became overwhelmed by it, and sank from view.[37]

According to Atwood, debt is conceived not only in terms of social obligations, guilt, sin, and revenge but also as a *plot* that structures the story of human life. She illustrates this aspect by introducing various stories such as the story of Shylock in *The Merchant of Venice*, the story of Scrooge in *A*

*Christmas Carol*, the story of the divine Furies pursuing Orestes in Aeschylus' *Eumenides*, and the like. For instance, Atwood warns us as Scrooge of *A Christmas Carol* that humanity will face "payback" unless we pay up our unacknowledged and unpaid debt to our environment. According to her, the ultimate payback is the ecological one. Unless we pay up our ecological debt, our reckless borrowing from the earth beyond its sustainable level will eventually lead us to the inevitable moment of reckoning with our creditor, Mother Earth.

In *Payback* Atwood challenges us to look at all debts as storied debts, which have their unique plots, and this proposal will look as if it is a revolutionary thesis to many who are deeply immersed in the neoliberal economy of debt, which is profiled by the law-like logic of reciprocity. Atwood's idea of storied debt helps us see the matter of debt in a new perspective. The economic logic of debt is no longer detached from the real-life story of debtors and creditors, and as a result we begin to see that the problem of debt is not a mere neutral logic of "give and take" but an actual and concrete matter of people whose different characters and dispositions do matter. Indeed, all debts have their unique stories, and since all stories have their distinctive plots and characters involved, we begin to see the methodological possibility of constructing a Christian virtue ethics of debt. In order to develop it, then, we must answer this more specific question: What does Christian theology have to do with the moral significance of the story aspect of debt?

Relying on two Christian theologians, Kathryn Tanner and Stephen H. Webb, I propose an idea that a Christian virtue ethics of debt can be possible by radicalizing the anthropological insight I discussed in chapter 1. Recall the key ethical insight of anthropologists such as Marcel Mauss, according to whom debt was originally conceived as a form of gift to the debtor in archaic societies. The economy of debt was conceived as a secondary or derivative kind to the moral economy of gift. In other words, the key moral plot of a storied debt has originally to do with the moral ideal of gift exchange. We should also remember an important anthropological discovery that, in earliest kinship society, gift exchange played an important role of keeping and building up social cohesion and solidarity. By almost completely ignoring the story aspect of debt as well as by separating the realm of debt from the moral domain of gift-giving, neoliberalism and its economy of debt have turned a blind eye to the original plot of humanity's storied debt: to help each other, keeping social cohesion and solidarity.

How does Christian theology radicalize such an anthropological insight? What does this radicalization have to do with the establishment of the Christian virtue ethics of debt? In a nutshell, by Christian radicalization of the anthropological insight, I mean that Christian theology discovers the original moral paradigm of gift giving in God's "giftfulness" (Tanner) or "gifting" (Webb) instead of originating it in archaic society. Christian theology radicalizes the anthropological insight to provide a deeper theological meaning of what it means to be in debt or to provide a credit as well as to be a debtor or to be a creditor. In doing so, Christian theologian Kathryn Tanner's theological imagination is critical because she helps us see how Christian theology deepens the anthropological insight on the moral economy of debt with her theological idea of "economy of grace." It is worth exploring her theological idea of the economy of grace rather at length in the following.

She begins her theological thesis on the economy of grace by asserting that Christian theology has an ability to "expand the Western social imaginary." She argues that Christian views of economy are not limited to explicit Christian commentary on property and possession; they are not restricted either to familiar debates surrounding Christian norms like agape and their implications for social relations. She is imagining a much greater role of Christian theology in the social world, particularly the economy. What, then, does Christian theology have to do with the world of economy? To answer this question, she insists, we should see that "basic Christian notions of God and God's relations to the world are themselves viewed as economic in nature."[38] As she illustrates, such fundamental economic activities as relations of exchange and the circulation of goods are at issue throughout the biblical stories through which Christians narrate about God, creation, providence, covenant, and salvation in Christ. Acknowledging the variability of Christian theology in terms of reading such stories, she proposes her own creative way of "reworking" them with the purpose of formulating a Christian perspective on the market economy.

She first engages John Locke as a starting point of her Christian theological construction of an alternative economic model. According to Tanner, although Locke's famous proponent of property is sufficiently similar to the modern understanding of property, his position represents a genuine second logic of property. What is this second logic? For Locke, unlike the modern case, the property one owns is inalienable. Tanner writes, "Because this property is inalienable, Locke denies that one can freely contract to be subject to a ruler with absolute power or freely contract to become a slave."[39] Despite its conceptual progression, Tanner finds that Locke's property right is problematic. For instance, Locke's notion that "work as a requirement for private or exclusive rights undercuts the force of common right."[40] According to Tanner, Locke's implied theology is questionable because according to him God only owns substance and thus has the right to limit the use of such substance of what one is (including one's capability) and all the materials, but not the actual exercise of one's powers through acts of one's own will. For this reason, Tanner judges, "In short, the theology underpinning Locke's logic of property and exchange exhibits a rather deflated understanding of God's grace."[41]

After engaging Locke, she then moves to anthropological discussions of noncommodity exchanges (the phenomenon of gift) that have become quite influential in the field of contemporary Christian theologies. We have already covered anthropological discussions in chapter 1 on this topic, and Tanner discovers a new possibility that anthropological discussions on the "category of gift" provide a better alternative to both a Lockean and a modern logic of property in developing a new model of economy. She affirms, "With such a category, theology and economy could be correlated in much the way they are for Locke."[42] Tanner, however, comes to the conclusion that the anthropological breakthrough with the category of gift ultimately turns out to be "worse than anything we saw in Locke."[43] Why is this so? According to her, "All that the features distinguishing a gift economy from an explicit debt economy like Locke's produce is a world of infinite debt."[44] The embedded logic of debt in the gift economy (gift exchanges turn into explicit loans) ultimately spoils everything, including the category of gift, as such creating a new category of "infinite debt." She thus writes, "Debts can never be completely paid off; they simply multiply without end. For similar reasons, once it starts up, competition for prestige, disconnected from the meeting of needs, presses on to absurd lengths; nothing curbs it."[45] As Tanner points out, if this logic of creating infinite debt is located in unequal relations such as between superiors and subordinates, it would only promote the ideal of an unpayable debt rendering "ineradicable domination" possible.[46]

What, then, is Tanner's alternative solution to overcome the conceptual limitations of Locke's and anthropologists' models? Distinctively from a theological perspective, she begins to outline her economy of grace by first formulating the idea of God's own giftfulness. She writes, "Every stage of this history represents a greater effort to communicate God's own giftfulness as that is made possible by different but analogously structured relations between God and the world, relations differentiated in theological discussion by such terms as creation, covenant, redemption, and consummation in Christ."[47] Given that God's giftfulness encompasses all relations, if human relations would reflect God's giftfulness, they should be marked by unconditional giving that is not obligated by prior gift giving. She then claims that this unconditional giving is the first principle of the economy of grace that "might cover both God's relations to us, in their diversity, and our relations with each other, within the same overall theological structure of things."[48] This first principle of unconditional giving, however, clearly separates its logic from the conditional logic of gift. She states, "This principle marks all these relations off from *do ut des* giving—'I give so that you will give,' the alternative principle of conditional giving that covers barter, commodity exchanges, and *debtor/creditor relations.*"[49]

Tanner's unconditional gift, then, may be renamed "gift without gift" in the Derridean sense, as Derrida lays out in his *Gift of Death* (Tanner says, "Derrida would like"). God's giftfulness, however, is not visible despite its ubiquity. For instance, she holds that God's gifts efface themselves in their very occurrence.[50] Her concept of the unconditional gift, however, is different from Bourdieusian "genuine gift," which is not still entirely free from the conditional economy. According to Tanner, recalling Nietzsche, the fact that God cannot be repaid in principle and never by us sinners does not establish an infinite, unpayable debt. As she emphasizes, the cross of Jesus does not save us from our debts to God by paying them, but instead "the cross saves us from the consequences of a debt economy in conflict with God's own economy of grace by canceling it."[51] Reminiscing John Howard Yoder's *Politics of Jesus*, Tanner continues to argue, "In Christ, we see the manner of divine action that the Jubilee traditions of the Hebrew Bible aimed to reflect: debts are forgiven rather than paid, debtors freed from the enslavement that accrues through nonpayment."[52] She, however, does not clearly illustrate how we should correlate the theology of God's unconditional giftfulness and the ethics of humanity's conditional giving in a way that the latter reflects the former. We may find a clearer illustration in Stephen Webb.

Stephen Webb's "gifting God" resonates with Tanner's concept of God's giftfulness. For example, Webb writes, "The Christian God squanders, but not as an exercise of blind self-affirmation or sovereign freedom; instead, God gives abundantly, in order to create more giving, the goal of which is a mutuality born of excess but directed toward equality and justice."[53] In a more emphatic and explicit way, Webb focuses on demonstrating how God's excessive gifting (grace) is "neither utterly irrelevant to human actions nor tied too closely to them."[54] Webb's theological concern lies in overcoming two theological misconceptions. One is the isolation and compartmentalization of God's grace from the practical realm of material culture, and the other is the reduction of God's grace to a mere form of the economics of exchange that pervades the modern spirit. Against these two options, he attempts to formulate an alternative theological paradigm. He claims, "God's giving must be correlated to our own practices of exchange and reciprocity, yet this correlation cannot be strict or exact."[55] For him, God is always both "excessive and reciprocal," and he calls this theological model of generosity "gifting."[56]

From the vantage point of God's gifting, Webb discovers the conceptual limitedness of modern anthropologists' works, including Marcel Mauss, Marshall Sahlins, Pierre Bourdieu, and others. For example, he writes that although Mauss argues for the priority of giving over exchange, "he does so in such a way as to leave the relationship between excess and reciprocity unclear."[57] As for Sahlins, Webb points out the theoretical limitedness in terms of its application to the modern world. Webb writes that Sahlins "locates excess in certain primordial cultures as a state of abundance prior to economic development; by doing so, he does not aid in the development of a theory of abundance and giving appropriate to the modern world."[58] Regarding Bourdieu, Webb holds that in many ways his position is the opposite of both Mauss and Sahlins. "His critique of the possibilities of giving is the most extreme instance of the exchangist mentality itself. Bourdieu raises the question of whether gift giving can ever be anything more than another form of economics proper."[59]

How does Webb correlate excess and reciprocity with his theology of gifting? He answers this question, saying, "My governing insight, then, is the following: *divine excess begets reciprocity*. Without excess, reciprocity becomes calculation, bartering, exchange; without reciprocity, excess becomes irrelevant, anarchic, and wasteful."[60] The trinitarian understanding of God is essential for Webb in correlating excess and reciprocity because the Christian model of giving follows a triadic pattern that holds together both excess and reciprocity throughout the whole process. He outlines more specifically this pattern by saying that in accordance with the trinitarian nature, God is understood as "the Giver, the Given, and the Giving." He summarizes this theological idea as follows: "What God gives is both God's self and the givenness of things that allows us to recognize, multiply, and return God's gifts."[61] For Webb, the correlation of excess and reciprocity is possible because what is given by God is the power of giving itself. He thus writes, "In the end, what God gives is the power of giving itself, the possibility that we can all participate in the movement of giving with the hope that such generosity will be enhanced, organized, and consummated in God's very own becoming."[62]

From Tanner's and Webb's theological perspectives, the amoralization of the economy of debt is a serious theological threat because it effectively delimits God's expectation that God's giftfulness or gifting will be reflected in all that the creature is and does.[63] The hidden (anti)theological message of the amoralization of the economy of debt is that God's giftfulness or gifting has nothing to do with the world of finance. Against this (anti) theological stance, Tanner counters, "Oriented around God's gift-giving relationship with us, our affections, cognitive faculties, volitions, and deeds should all become a register of that relationship."[64] Tanner's economy of grace and Webb's theoeconomics call for the deconstruction of the amoral economy of debt. It is critical, though, to see that our efforts to reflect God's giftfulness in all human relations, including the debtor-creditor relation, is not our way to pay our debt to God. "It is simply the only way of life appropriate to the way things are; it is simply our effort, as Karl Barth would say, to be what we already are."[65] In this perspective, Tanner states almost in a confessional way, "I don't think either a principle of unconditional giving or this principle of noncompetitive relations in a community of mutual fulfillment is unrealistic for implementation in the present."[66]

What practical ethical guidelines does Christian theology offer to us in developing a more holistic ethics of debt? First, the Christian theology of God's giftfulness or gifting helps us see that there is a common plot that should be embedded in all storied debts. What is this common plot? As a derivative type of the moral economy of gift, the economy of debt should be played out in such a way that God's giftfulness or gifting may be reflected in its own logic. Tanner illustrates the reflection of this common plot with the concept of a "win/win spiral" as opposed to the neoliberal "win/loss" mind-set. She correctly points out that "the unregulated international markets of today are indeed major forces blocking the development of a win/win spiral in the real economy."[67] The Christian theology of God's giftfulness or gifting calls for the restructuring of the global financial order, which would better serve the ethical goal of a global win/win spiral rather than the dehumanizing win/loss scheme. In the win/win structure of economy of grace, we should note, debt becomes a form of gift.

Christian theology of God's giftfulness or gifting also inspires the development of a Christian virtue ethics of debt in such a way that all related parties of the economy of debt including debtors, creditors, and regulators are to reflect God's giftfulness or gifting. This reflection is the virtue of labor. Virtue is thus necessary in developing a more holistic ethics of debt. We should note that this virtue is not attained automatically; it should be attained through our labor. Lewis Hyde critically distinguishes between work and labor: "Work is what we do by the hour. It begins and ends at a specific time and, if possible, we do it for money."[68] In contrast with work, Hyde holds, labor "sets its own pace. We may get paid for it, but it's harder to quantify. . . . Writing a poem, raising a child, developing a new calculus, resolving a neurosis, invention in all forms— these are labors."[69] Of course, neoliberalism also promotes its own kind of quasi-moral virtue (a virtuous debtor pays back his or her debt in full), but this virtue is formulated as "work" in Hydean terms. It serves only the logic of debt. In contrast, by Christian virtue, it means the virtue of "labor," which Hyde illustrates as something "wholly different from the obligation."[70] The Hydean idea of labor is necessary for the establishment of a Christian virtue ethics of storied debt.

## Christian Virtue Ethics for the Moral Economy of Debt: Moderation, Liberality, Fortitude, and Gratitude

For several reasons, virtue is indispensable in developing a more holistic ethics of debt. Without the proper formation of virtues among financial leaders, agents, and regulators as well as among ordinary citizens and residents, with only systemic and regulatory changes, we cannot fully realize the moral economy of debt. For the realization of a more holistic ethics of debt, the attainment of virtue is indispensable. Indeed, as Ronald Colombo holds, virtue "is capable of exerting its influence beyond regulation's outer limits. Virtue is capable of restraining the individual from exploiting a loophole which he or she discovers in the law—a loophole that would cause the individual's misconduct to evade detection and/or punishment. In short, virtue protects society where law cannot."[71] The amount and scope of virtue ethics is immense, and covering even a small part requires a book-length work. My critical engagement is thus specifically focused on this question: What moral virtues do we need for the life of living the economy of grace? In other words, how could we live a life of reflecting God's giftfulness? In this respect, this is a further Christian ethical radicalization of Tanner's and Webb's theological visions. In doing so, I will specifically focus on four financial virtues, which I call four cardinal virtues for the life of the economy of grace: moderation, liberality, fortitude, and gratitude. As one shall see shortly, these virtues are developed as a set of relational virtues: moderation regarding our relation to human nature (greed); liberality regarding our relation to others; fortitude regarding our relation to economic structure and system; gratitude regarding our relation to God.

The first virtue to explore is moderation or temperance, which is necessary to live a life of reflecting God's giftfulness. In his article "Corporate Finance and Original Sin," William J. Bernstein introduces a story of
Michael Smirlock:

> Michael excelled academically and acquired a Ph.D. in finance. Six years later, he
> was awarded a tenured chair at the Wharton School at the University of Pennsyl-
> vania, where he mentored a large number of future practitioners and academics.
> Drawn by the lure of bigger money, he found himself in 1990 at Goldman Sachs;
> by 1992, he had made partner. The very next year, he garnered a $50,000 fine
> and a three-month suspension by the U.S. SEC for suspicious late-trade allo-
> cations and was forced to resign. He then set up a real estate investment trust
> and a series of hedge funds. On 24 May 2002, Judge Gerald E. Lynch of the
> Federal District Court for the Southern District of New York sentenced him to
> four years incarceration and fined him $12.6 million for fraudulently concealing
> losses from his investors.[72]

This all-too-familiar story of Michael Smirlock allows us to raise a question:
"If this highly respected academic, who should not have had any problem
with the legal and ethical concepts involved, could not keep his hands
out of the cookie jar, what chance does the average broker or B-school
grad have?"[73] We should be reminded that one of the principal causes of
the financial crisis of 2007–2008 was such unethical behaviors as reckless
and predatory lending by banks, the selling of toxic financial products, the
failure to avoid conflicts of interest, massive fraud, and the negligence or
complicity of legislators.[74] These behaviors reflect the same commonality
in character: the lack of virtue among those who run the financial system
as its leaders, agents, and regulators. As many commentators have already
pointed out, "The credit crisis was caused by moral deficiencies on the part
of market parties in the financial sector."[75]

How can we address the problem of moral deficiency? St. Thomas
Aquinas offers us an important insight into how the vice of covetousness
(greed or avarice) becomes the root of the ills in financial capitalism even
in today's neoliberal world. As he observes, covetousness (defined as "excessive love of possessing riches") can tempt people to engage in "treachery,
fraud, falsehood, perjury, restlessness, violence, and insensibility to mercy"
in pursuit of the goods they excessively desire.[76] The vice of covetousness
is a powerful hindrance to the life of reflecting God's giftfulness; covetousness prevents us from living a life of giving. Following Aristotle (*Politics*,
book 1), Aquinas divides the concept of wealth into two types: "natural
wealth" and "artificial wealth." While natural wealth serves as a remedy for
people's natural wants such as food, drink, clothing, and the like, artificial

wealth, as money, serves as a medium of exchange, a store of value, and a unit of account. As Mary Hirschfeld interprets, "Artificial wealth, then, is an instrumental good to an instrumental good."[77] Artificial wealth plays an important role for people to pursue their infinite desire for artificial wealth itself. Aquinas writes, "The desire for natural riches is not infinite. . . . But the desire for artificial wealth is infinite, for it is the servant of disordered concupiscence, which is not curbed."[78] According to William Schweiker, covetousness or greed is not one form of vice, because it becomes the source of other vices. "Greed is a capital vice because it gathers around it other forms of viciousness that undercut the possibility of sustainable social existence."[79]

The virtue of moderation (temperance) is contrasted with the vice of covetousness. According to Aquinas, moderation "is chiefly concerned with those passions that tend towards sensible goods, viz. desire and pleasure, and consequently with the sorrows that arise from the absence of those pleasures."[80] Neoliberal capitalism sets no limits to what Aristotle calls the money-making art by amoralizing the economy of debt, which subsequently entails a huge socioeconomic gap among people on a global scale. At the heart of the neoliberal movement lies an unleashed passion for money and wealth. Moderation is indispensable in this respect because it is the only internal force that can check our tendency to pursue our infinite desire for artificial wealth. Regarding moral virtue of moderation, Jean Porter argues that the standard for moderation can never be completely conventional.[81] According to her, "The person who simply apes the conventions of courage and temperance has not really attained these virtues, because s/he has not adapted them to his or her own particular needs and temperament."[82] Although I am very much in agreement with her on the need to uphold unconventional moderation, I would like to suggest a small change to her idea. Instead of binding unconventional moderation with the individual's particular needs and temperament, I would argue, rather, that unconventional moderation should be linked to God's giftfulness. The purpose of moderation is not just for curbing one's passion toward artificial wealth; it is, rather, for helping us reflect God's giftfulness in all relations, including those in the world of finance.

We may find a good illustration of the unconventional moderation in Mark 10:17-22, in which we discover a story of a rich man. In this story, the rich man "ran up and knelt before him, and asked him, 'Good Teacher, what must I do to inherit eternal life?'" (v. 17). To this man, Jesus commanded, "Go, sell what you own, and give the money to the poor" (v. 21). Richard Hicks, a New Testament scholar, interprets the passage in light of a broader intertextual relationship with Malachi 3, and concludes that Jesus' insight about the rich man "lacking one thing" (v. 21) reveals that "the rich man is guilty of depriving and defrauding God and the poor."[83] From this insightful perspective, what Jesus commands to the rich man is not the work of "mercy" but the work of "justice." Jesus accordingly points out the rare revelation of the virtue of moderation among those who have wealth. He says, "How hard it will be for those who have wealth to enter the kingdom of God" (v. 23). In Jesus' short remarks, we can conjecture that the kingdom of God is like a state in which God's giftfulness is fully realized by all who reflect it through their labors. Without nurturing and embodying the virtue of moderation (temperance), then the kingdom of God is still far away from us.

The second virtue indispensable for the life of reflecting God's giftfulness is liberality. Liberality is demonstrated through giving and forgiving. According to Aquinas, liberality is praiseworthy in regard to riches. A person of liberality does not esteem wealth to the extent of wishing to retain it, so as to forgo what ought to be done.[84] A person of liberality is not hindered by the love and desire of money, which are passions of the concupiscible, from giving and spending. He thus writes, "This virtue is in the concupiscible."[85] Aquinas argues that Christ showed the highest kind of liberality by distributing what was given to him to the poor.[86] Aquinas' understanding of liberality resonates with Aristotle's classical view that liberality (generosity) is the mean between the excess of prodigality (extravagance) and the deficiency of illiberality (stinginess). The virtue of liberality also resides in the state of character of the giver, not in the amount of wealth one possesses.[87] One of Aristotle's most important moral insights regarding liberality is that "doing noble acts" is qualitatively different from "abstaining from base acts." He says, "We show gratitude to him who gives, not to him who does not take. . . . Also, it is easier not to take than to give, for people are less liable to give away what belongs to them than not to take what is another's."[88] Aristotle judges that only those who give are to be called liberal.

In his article "Liberality vs. Liberalism," John Milbank argues that liberality is not derived from liberalism. In fact, he holds, liberalism "tends to cancel those values of liberality," which include "fair trial, right to a defense, assumed innocence, habeas corpus, a measure of free speech and free inquiry, good treatment of the convicted."[89] According to him, these values of liberality are derived "from Roman and Germanic law transformed by the infusion of the Christian notion of charity."[90] Criticizing (neo)liberalism for its amoralization of the market, Milbank suggests that we should choose "a different sort of market: a resubordination of money transaction to a new mode of universal gift exchange."[91] He seems to support the Christian radicalization of the anthropological insight, which I lay out in this chapter, by affirming that liberality is a key moral virtue for the life of a "different sort of market." It is important to note that, for Milbank, the virtue of liberality stems from St. Paul, who "proposes a new sort of polis that can counteract and even eventually subsume the Roman empire."[92] There is a reason why the virtue of liberality is essential, especially for the Christian community. If we attempt to live by the passive moral principle of "abstaining from taking," we will never become a giver. Such a passive attitude ultimately keeps us from living a life of reflecting God's giftfulness. It reduces us to a mere state of consumers, users, buyers, and borrowers.

We encounter a remarkable illustration of liberality in the New Testament (Matt 18:23-35), known as the Parable of the Unforgiving Servant. According to the story, there was a king who wished to settle accounts with his slaves, and there was a slave who owed him an astronomical ten thousand talents. While the king decides to forgive the slave's ten thousand talents as he pleads, "Have patience with me, and I will pay you everything" (v. 26), the slave later refuses to forgive one hundred denarii (almost nothing compared to his own debt) owed to him by his fellow slave, who pleads with the same phrase, "Have patience with me, and I will pay you everything" (v. 29). What is ironic about this story is that the indebted debtor himself was also a creditor! According to the passage, when his fellow slaves saw what had happened, they were greatly distressed, and they went and reported to their lord all that had taken place. The unforgiving slave was summoned by the king and tortured until he payed his entire debt. This narrative illustrates an important message to us that the passive moral principle of "abstaining from taking" is not good enough. Liberality is an essential moral virtue for us to live a life of reflecting God's giftfulness in the world of credit and debt. In the parable, the slave debtor's critical problem was not his incapacity to pay back his own debt but his failure to imitate the king's liberality after he experienced it in such an unforgettable way. Instead of following the king's moral example, he has just kept to his old principle of "abstaining from taking."

The third virtue indispensable for the life of reflecting God's giftfulness is fortitude, which can be also identified as moral strength, insubordination, or even defiance. While the first two virtues (moderation and liberality) are more likely related to our tendencies and dispositions in regard to money and riches, the virtue of fortitude is related to structural injustice and its intimidation. What if cultural norms or the political-economic structure would prevent us from living a life of reflecting God's giftfulness? In her article "Why Support the Occupy Movement?," Tanner argues that the Christian "should be supportive of the Occupy Movement and not simply for the obvious religious reasons."[93] Tanner first points out that there is a legitimate worry about democracy because "our democracy is not really of the people anymore." She goes on to say, "Our chosen representatives are not working for us; we have little ability to influence policy in our own best interests through them."[94] She also points out the structural injustice of our economic system, which deepens the concentration of wealth, favoring the wealthiest 1 percent by way of current tax policy ("we are the 99 percent"). On top of that, finance-dominated capitalism increasingly exacerbates the financial plight of ordinary Americans, particularly students, as the government bails out powerful banks but not ordinary people ("banks got bailed out, we got sold out.")[95] The Occupy Movement demonstrates people's collective will to resist the structural injustices of our current economic and democratic systems, and at the heart of this movement lies a moral strength not to conform to unjust conventionality.

Aquinas defines fortitude as a strength of mind against any passions, especially fear and daring, which reside in the irascible part rather than in the concupiscible part.[96] He also divides fortitude into two kinds: "general fortitude," which denotes a certain firmness of mind as a condition for every virtue, and "special fortitude," which denotes firmness only in certain grave and imminent dangers.[97] Regarding the moral virtue of fortitude, we should consider the following question: How could we be morally strong? What makes us become a person of moral fortitude? The Aristotelian answer to this question is our love of nobility or honor. According to him, it is courageous to endure pain or suffering in cases when "it is noble to do so" or "base to refuse."[98] For Aristotle, the love of nobility or honor becomes the key motivating factor for the attainment of moral virtue of fortitude.[99] In contrast to Aristotle, St. Augustine offers us a different perspective on the moral origin of fortitude. In his *On the Morals of the Catholic Church*, he writes that "fortitude is love readily bearing all things for the sake of the loved object."[100] He then quickly adds that the object of this love is not anything but only God. As Elizabeth Agnew Cochran points out, "In a radical sense, this view of fortitude requires that we renounce earthly power for the sake of goodness and righteousness."[101] It is important for us to see that while the Aristotelian moral agent takes no pleasure in his or her suffering, Augustine affirms that fortitude involves joy.[102] Why is this so? It is because fortitude is not merely a will to resist; it is a *principled* resistance to the amoral injunction *you shall not give*. More proactively, it is a *wholehearted* determination to stick to the life of giving following after the model of God's giftfulness. The need for the moral virtue of fortitude in the financial world is especially noted because, without this virtue, one can be easily pressured to conform to the amoralized rule of the game by the fear of losing the game, which, unless checked by a proper virtue, would only serve Mammon, as Jesus warns in Matthew 6:24 and Luke 16:13: "You cannot serve God and wealth (Mammon)."

The last but not the least virtue for the life of reflecting God's giftfulness is gratitude, whose different names are thankfulness, appreciation, or gratefulness. Could we imagine a situation in which both the creditor and the debtor make their debt contract with gratitude and finish it with gratitude with the debtor's full payoff of the debt? It is rare for a debtor to send off a payment check to the creditor with gratitude; it is equally rare for a creditor to give a loan to a debtor with gratitude. What seems to be largely missing in the debtor-creditor relation is the virtue of gratitude on both sides. Gratitude is indeed a lost virtue in today's neoliberal world of debt economy.

According to Aquinas, gratitude is a "special virtue" that is owed a benefactor.[103] He reasons that the nature of the debt to be paid varies according to various causes giving rise to the debt. For example, first we have our debt to God, who is "the first principle of our goods"; second, we have our debt to our parents, who are the "proximate principle of our begetting and upbringing"; third, we have our debt to the person who excels in dignity, "from whom general favors proceed."[104] Since what we owe God, or our parents, or a person excelling in dignity is not the same, it follows that we pay God due worship, we pay our parents with piety, and we pay the person excelling in dignity with observance. By the same logic, but in a different way, we are to pay gratitude to our benefactors.[105] What is missing, though, in Aquinas' deliberation of the moral virtue of gratitude is a different kind of gratitude that is to be demonstrated by the giver (not the receiver). With regard to the giver, he narrowly considers only two things: the affection of the heart and the gift.[106] Gratitude does not seem to have to do with the giver.

There is a reason why the virtue of gratitude is expected to be displayed only on the part of the receiver, not the giver, in Aquinas' moral thought. It is because he sees gratitude as the "work" of the receiver, not as the "labor" of the soul. In this respect, in Lewis Hyde, we may find a better paradigm of conceiving gratitude as a key moral virtue for the life of reflecting God's giftfulness. Hyde first speaks of gratitude as a "labor," not a "work." According to Hyde, gratitude is regarded as "a labor undertaken by the soul to effect the transformation after a gift has been received."[107] What transformation? According to Hyde, the transformation is the transformation of the receiver's soul into the giver's. He thus writes, "The transformation is not accomplished until we have the power to give the gift on our own terms."[108] For Hyde, gift giving should never die, and gifts are to be "agents of change." If the act of gift giving lacks in gratitude, it is a sign that it has become a work of economy rather than a labor of the soul.

We may find an illustration of this type of gratitude in Luke 19:1-10 (the story of Zacchaeus). According to the passage, when Jesus visited his place, "Zacchaeus stood there and said to the Lord, 'Look, half of my possessions, Lord, I will give to the poor; and if I have defrauded anyone of anything, I will pay back four times as much'" (v. 8). We should note here that his promise of restitution goes beyond the requirement of Pharisaic law, which required fourfold or fivefold restitution only for stolen oxen and sheep (Exod 22:1). As argued above, if we begin to regard debt as a form of gift in the economy of grace of God's giftfulness, then we also begin to consider that gratitude is not a due payment ("work") always owed by a debtor but an effect of the transformation ("labor") of the indebted soul, which as such is also the reflection of God's giftfulness.

## Conclusion

In this final chapter, I have explored the possibility of developing a Christian virtue ethics of debt as an essential aspect of developing a more holistic ethics of debt. In doing so, I outline the "four cardinal virtues for the life of the economy of grace": moderation, liberality, fortitude, and gratitude. I develop these virtues as a set of relational virtues: moderation in regard to the internal relation to our nature (greed); liberality in regard to our relation to others; fortitude in regard to our relation to economic structure and system; gratitude in regard to God. These virtues, of course, are not complete or conclusive; they are only a minimal illustration of what is expected of us in developing a more holistic ethics of debt. Overall, Christian religious traditions and theologies contribute to the establishment of a more holistic ethics of debt by radicalizing the anthropologists' moral insight that debt was originally conceived as a derivative of gift. In this radical vision, debt is reconceived to serve humanity rather than to subjugate it. Also, according to this vision, a debtor is no longer reductively regarded as a potential culprit; instead he or she is now reconsidered as a prospective giver even while he or she is still in debt. A creditor is also reconceived as a giver or even as a potential liberator to the debtor, not as a mere collector.

# CONCLUSION

In this book, I have established a more holistic ethics of debt by engaging several different disciplinary traditions including anthropology, philosophy, economics, law, and religion (Abrahamic religions). While I have been exploring these areas, I have seen different faces of debt; some were good and even great, and others inhumane and ugly. The purpose of this book is then to help people see these different faces of debt with some in-depth understanding so that they can make a right arrangement in employing the economy of debt in their society and political economy. Given that every society needs to build up its basic social cohesion and solidarity for its sustainment and flourishing, one of my original questions was, What maintains basic social cohesion and solidarity in today's neoliberal world? In answering this question, I develop an argument that debt and its economy should be reconstructed in such a way to create and preserve social cohesion and solidarity rather than to disorient and disrupt them through the abuse of the economy of debt. We should recall that the earliest people in archaic society created and developed social cohesion and solidarity through gift giving. If we take into our consideration that debt is a key socioeconomic mechanism in today's neoliberal world, which interconnects so many people beyond any kind of social divisions, we begin to see more clearly why the problem of debt becomes such a foundational social issue we should care about.

In his *Theology of Money*, Philip Goodchild succinctly captures the core phenomenon of neoliberalism as follows: "The global economy is driven by a spiral of debt, constrained to seek further profits and always dependent on future expansion. The spectral power of money lies ultimately in its nature as debt."[1] He also writes, "A market based on debt money is an immanent system of credits and liabilities, of debts and obligations, and it is capable of unlimited growth."[2] We should note that among all things created by humanity, nothing can grow infinitely except debt and its obligations. This pseudo-infinity has always been a formidable threat to humanity as it has continuously unleashed its demonic power on many vulnerable people, especially debtors, emulating God with its own blind logic. Although hollow, this formidable logic of infinity has been a daunting ethical challenge, defying any single moral and ethical system. In this book, thus, I tried to integrate as much human wisdom as possible through a critical engagement in humanities and social sciences. What I have realized in this integrating process is that it indeed takes the whole of humanity and its concerted effort to tackle effectively the formidable threat of debt and its economic logic.

In this volume, by rediscovering and reconceiving the original meaning of debt as a form of gift, I have attempted to reconstruct a new moral economy of debt in which debt is reprogrammed to serve humanity, not vice versa. According to this new moral economy of debt, debt is no longer conceived as an amoral problem to be resolved solely by the economic logic of reciprocity. The new moral economy of debt acknowledges that all debts have their unique stories, and they should matter in doing justice to the problem of debt. According to this new moral economy of debt, the financial world is not separated from human societies any longer, and its agents and customers are not insulated from them either. For a debt to be morally established, its story should be free from any type of exploitation, abuse, or manipulation. In a more positive sense, its story should be life affirming, life saving, or life enhancing. The debt is then reconceived as a form of gift to the debtor, and, for the sake of its realization, society should not only regulate the financial market to prevent it from potential abuses but also cultivate proper moral virtues among its members through public education and social recognition. Unfortunately, we seem to have more negative cases than positive ones since neoliberalism has been globally introduced.

As Hans Jonas correctly argues in his *Imperative of Responsibility*, we have a great moral task that we should take up for our next generations—those who would soon occupy our world and its landscapes. The moral task of taking future generations into consideration should not be confined to the environment and ecology. The financial world is also an important and vast environment without which we may not sustain our lives. Just as humanity may not survive in a contaminated natural environment, it cannot subsist in a toxic financial environment. It is the moral task of our generation to clean up and detoxify our intoxicated financial world. As is the case of our natural environment, it takes the whole of humanity and its concerted effort to rebuild and reform our derailed financial environment. The purpose of the ongoing reconstruction of our financial world is not to create a debtless society. The society must defend just debt from its possible abuse and exploitation, but it should also defend just debt from its abolition and annihilation. Whether we like it or not, we all eventually end up an indebted being at the end of the day. No one can survive without being indebted to others, including the natural and the human. If humanity would finally realize that debt can indeed become a form of gift, it may redeem itself from many of its follies and miseries. I hope that this book will become a meaningful road map toward humanity's full critical appropriation of the moral economy of debt.

# Notes

## Introduction

1 Bob Sullivan, "Like a Drug: Payday Loan Users Hooked on Quick-Cash Cycle," *NBC News*, May 11, 2013.

2 Sullivan, "Like a Drug."

3 Sullivan, "Like a Drug." According to Bob Sullivan, although payday loan costs appear deceptively simple, on an annual basis, the rate is actually 391 percent. Since the loan is due in full after fourteen days (not fifteen days), borrowers typically do not change their financial situation in that two-week period, being forced to renew the loan multiple times. He also writes that an average payday lender pays $458 in fees to borrow $350 for about five months. The situation gets even worse if one borrows more money with a longer period ("An average title borrower pays $2,140 to borrow $950 for 10 months").

4 Manash Pratim Gohain, "New Evidence of Suicide Epidemic among India's 'Marginalized' Farmers," *Times of India*, April 17, 2014.

5 Gohain, "New Evidence of Suicide Epidemic." Rs 300 amounts to only $5, and the Indian government defines a mere Rs 25 as an adequate daily income in rural India.

6 Andrew Malone, "The GM Genocide: Thousands of Indian Farmers Are Committing Suicide after Using Genetically Modified Crops," *Daily Mail*, November 2, 2008.

7 Malone, "GM Genocide."

8 Karl Beitel, "The Subprime Debacle," *Monthly Review* 60, no. 1 (2008): 33.

9 Barry Ritholtz, "What Caused the Financial Crisis? The Big Lie Goes Viral," *Washington Post*, November 5, 2011.

10 Ritholtz, "What Caused the Financial Crisis?"

11   Michael Allen Gillespie, "On Debt," in *Debt: Ethics, the Environment, and the Economy*, ed. Peter Y. Paik and Merry Wiesner-Hanks (Bloomington: Indiana University Press, 2013), 68.

12   Aihwa Ong, "Neoliberalism as a Mobile Technology," *Transactions of the Institute of British Geographers*, n.s. 32, no. 1 (2007): 3.

13   History actually shows that "certain sorts of debt, and certain sorts of debtor," are actually treated differently than others. David Graeber, for example, writes,

> In the 1720s, one of the things that most scandalized the British public when conditions at debtors' prisons were exposed in the popular press was the fact that these prisons were regularly divided into two sections. Aristocratic inmates, who often thought of a brief stay in Fleet or Marshalsea as something of a fashion statement, were wined and dined by liveried servants and allowed to receive regular visits from prostitutes. On the 'common side,' impoverished debtors were shackled together in tiny cells, "covered with filth and vermin," as one report put it, "and suffered to die, without pity, or hunger and jail fever."

The British public's indignation to the discriminatory treatment of two groups of debtors shows that how to treat debtors is an important justice issue with regard to the social construction of the ethics of debt. See David Graeber, *Debt: The First 5,000 Years* (Brooklyn, N.Y.: Melville House, 2012), 7.

## Chapter 1

1   Thomas Hobbes, *Leviathan* (London: Penguin Books, 1985), 183.

2   Hobbes, *Leviathan*, 188.

3   Hobbes, *Leviathan*, 188.

4   Hobbes, *Leviathan*, 185.

5   Hobbes, *Leviathan*, 186.

6   John Rawls refers to Locke's *Second Treatise of Government*, Rousseau's *The Social Contract*, and Kant's *The Foundations of the Metaphysics of Morals* as definitive of the contract tradition. He is ambivalent to Hobbes' *Leviathan* because it raises "special problems" without specific exemplifications. See John Rawls, *A Theory of Justice* (Cambridge, Mass.: Harvard University Press, 1971), 11.

7   Rawls, *Theory of Justice*, 144–45.

8   Graeber, *Debt*, 8.

9   Graeber, *Debt*, 25.

10  Graeber, *Debt*, 23.

11  Adam Smith, *The Wealth of Nations* (New York: Modern Library, 2000), 24.

12  Smith, *Wealth of Nations*, 31.

13  Smith, *Wealth of Nations*, 485.

14  Graeber, *Debt*, 25.

15  David Graeber, "Debt, the Whole History," *Green European Journal* 7 (2014): 25.

16  Kennedy writes, "If Samuelson had read *Moral Sentiments* and *Wealth of Nations* for himself through its many editions and translations well into the 1970s, instead of recalling what he was taught at Chicago by his tutors and then passing on the same error to hundreds of thousands of readers of *Economics*, many of whom became tutors themselves, the current epidemic of misleading ideas about invisible hands may have become containable." See Gavin Kennedy, "Adam Smith and the Invisible Hand: From Metaphor to Myth," *Econ Journal Watch* 6, no. 2 (2009): 251.

17    Graeber, *Debt*, 40.
18    Graeber, "Debt, the Whole History," 25.
19    Graeber, "Debt, the Whole History," 26.
20    Cited in Gillespie, "On Debt," 57.
21    Gillespie, "On Debt," 57.
22    Gillespie, "On Debt," 57.
23    Kennedy, "Adam Smith and the Invisible Hand," 251.
24    Lee F. Monaghan and Micheal O'Flynn, "The Madoffization of Society: A Corrosive Process in an Age of Fictitious Capital," *Critical Sociology* 39, no. 6 (2012): 870.
25    Monaghan and O'Flynn, "Madoffization of Society," 872.
26    Matthew Sherman, *A Short History of Financial Deregulation in the United States* (Washington, D.C.: Center for Economic and Policy Research, 2009), 1–2.
27    Monaghan and O'Flynn, "Madoffization of Society," 870.
28    Graeber, "Debt, the Whole History," 26.
29    Graeber, "Debt, the Whole History."
30    "For the kingdom of heaven is like a landowner who went out early in the morning to hire laborers for his vineyard. After agreeing with the laborers for the usual daily wage, he sent them into his vineyard. When he went out about nine o'clock, he saw others standing idle in the marketplace; and he said to them, 'You also go into the vineyard, and I will pay you whatever is right.' So they went. When he went out again about noon and about three o'clock, he did the same. And about five o'clock he went out and found others standing around; and he said to them, 'Why are you standing here idle all day?' They said to him, 'Because no one has hired us.' He said to them, 'You also go into the vineyard.' When evening came, the owner of the vineyard said to his manager, 'Call the laborers and give them their pay, beginning with the last and then going to the first.' When those hired about five o'clock came, each of them received the usual daily wage. Now when the first came, they thought they would receive more; but each of them also received the usual daily wage. And when they received it, they grumbled against the landowner, saying, 'These last worked only one hour, and you have made them equal to us who have borne the burden of the day and the scorching heat.' But he replied to one of them, 'Friend, I am doing you no wrong; did you not agree with me for the usual daily wage? Take what belongs to you and go; I choose to give to this last the same as I give to you. Am I not allowed to do what I choose with what belongs to me? Or are you envious because I am generous?' So the last will be first, and the first will be last."
31    Friedrich Nietzsche, *On the Genealogy of Morals*, trans. Walter Kaufmann and R. J. Hollingdale (New York: Vintage Books, 1989), 85.
32    Nietzsche, *On the Genealogy of Morals*, 89.
33    Mathias Risse, "The Second Treatise in *On the Genealogy of Morality*: Nietzsche on the Origin of the Bad Conscience," *European Journal of Philosophy* 9, no. 1 (2001): 64.
34    Ilsup Ahn, "The Genealogy of Debt and the Phenomenology of Forgiveness: Nietzsche, Marion, and Derrida on the Meaning of the Peculiar Phenomenon," *Heythrop Journal* 51, no. 3 (2010): 454–70.
35    Kurt Raaflaub, *The Discovery of Freedom in Ancient Greece*, trans. Renate Franciscono, rev. and updated ed. (Chicago: University of Chicago Press, 2004), 47.
36    Alessandro Stanziani and Gwyn Campbell, "Introduction: Debt and Slavery in the Mediterranean and the Atlantic Worlds," in *Debt and Slavery in the Mediterranean*

*and Atlantic Worlds*, ed. Gwyn Campbell and Alessando Stanziani (London: Pickering & Chatto, 2013), 7.

37   Stanziani and Campbell, "Introduction," 26.

38   Stanziani and Campbell, "Introduction," 12.

39   See their website at http://www.globalslaveryindex.org/.

40   Kevin Bales, *Disposable People: New Slavery in the Global Economy* (San Francisco: University of California Press, 2004), 19.

41   The document is available at http://www.ohchr.org/EN/ProfessionalInterest/Pages /SupplementaryConventionAbolitionOfSlavery.aspx.

42   Kevin Bales, *Understanding Global Slavery: A Reader* (San Francisco: University of California Press, 2005), 61.

43   See Gwyn Campbell and Alessando Stanziani's coedited *Bonded Labour and Debt in the Indian Ocean World* (London: Pickering & Chatto, 2013) and *Debt and Slavery in the Mediterranean and Atlantic Worlds* (London: Pickering & Chatto, 2013).

44   Ei Murakami, "Two Bonded Labour Emigration Patterns in Mid-Nineteenth-Century Southern China: The Coolie Trade and Emigration to Southeast Asia," in Campbell and Stanziani, *Bonded Labour and Debt in the Indian Ocean World*, 154.

45   See Bok-rea Kim, "Debt Slaves in Old Korea"; Yoko Matsui, "The Debt-Servitude or Prostitutes in Japan during the Edo Period, 1600–1868"; and Matthew S. Hopper, "Debt and Slavery among Arabian Gulf Pearl Divers," in Campbell and Stanziani, *Bonded Labour and Debt in the Indian Ocean World*, 154.

46   Michael Northcott, *Life after Debt* (London: SPCK, 1999), vii.

47   Rafael Reuveny and William R. Thompson, "World Economics Growth, Systemic Leadership, and Southern Debt Crises," *Journal of Peace Research* 31, no. 1 (2004): 20.

48   Graeber, *Debt*, 91.

49   Graeber, *Debt*, 91.

50   Graeber, *Debt*, 94.

51   Marcel Mauss, *The Gift: Forms and Functions of Exchange in Archaic Societies*, trans. Ian Cunnison (Glencoe, Ill.: Free Press, 1954), 1.

52   Mauss, *Gift*, 2.

53   Mauss, *Gift*, 5.

54   Mauss, *Gift*, 45.

55   Mauss, *Gift*, 74.

56   Mauss, *Gift*, 75.

57   Mauss, *Gift*, 67.

58   Mauss, *Gift*, 67.

59   Mauss, *Gift*, 67.

60   Mauss, *Gift*, 69.

61   Yonatan Sagiv, "The Gift of Debt: Agnon's Economics of Money, God and the Human Other," *PROOFTEXTS* 34, no. 2 (2014): 430.

62   Mauss, *Gift*, 41.

63   Mauss, *Gift*, 41.

64   Marshall Sahlins, "The Spirit of the Gift," in *The Logic of Gift: Toward an Ethic of Generosity*, ed. Alan D. Schrift (New York: Routledge, 1997), 83.

65   Sahlins, "Spirit of the Gift," 84.

66   Sahlins, "Spirit of the Gift," 84.

67    Sahlins, "Spirit of the Gift," 84. According to Sahlins, Mauss' anthropological study of the gift in archaic society has historic merit in that "it corrected just this simplified progression from chaos to commonwealth, savagery to civilization, that had been the work of classical contract theory" (93).

68    Sahlins, "Spirit of the Gift," 95.

69    Lewis Hyde, *The Gift: Imagination and the Erotic Life of Property* (New York: Vintage Books, 1983), 74.

70    Pierre Bourdieu, "Marginalia—Some Additional Notes on the Gift," in Schrift, *Logic of Gift*, 231.

71    Bourdieu, "Marginalia," 231.

72    Bourdieu, "Marginalia," 232.

73    Bourdieu, "Marginalia," 232.

74    Bourdieu, "Marginalia," 232.

75    Bourdieu, "Marginalia," 233.

76    Bourdieu, "Marginalia," 232.

77    Bourdieu, "Marginalia," 232.

78    Pierre Bourdieu, *The Logic of Practice*, trans. Richard Nice (Stanford, Calif.: Stanford University Press, 1990), 113.

79    Mauss, *Gift*, 6.

80    Mauss, *Gift*.

81    Mauss, *Gift*, 6–7, emphasis in original.

82    Georges Bataille, *The Accursed Share: An Essay on General Economy*, vol. 1, trans. Robert Hurley (New York: Zone Books, 1988), 68, emphasis in original.

83    Bataille, *Accursed Share*, 70.

Chapter 2

1    Nick Dearden, "Jamaica's Decades of Debt Are Damaging Its Future," *Guardian*, April 16, 2013.

2    "Jamaica in Crisis Debt-Swap Plan," *BBC News*, February 12, 2013.

3    Dearden, "Jamaica's Decades of Debt."

4    Dearden, "Jamaica's Decades of Debt."

5    Dearden, "Jamaica's Decades of Debt."

6    Robert F. Drinan, "Jamaica, Entire Third World in Bondage to American Banks," *National Catholic Reporter* 30, no. 8 (1993): 18.

7    Dearden, "Jamaica's Decades of Debt."

8    Dearden, "Jamaica's Decades of Debt."

9    Jake Johnston, "Partners in Austerity: Jamaica, the United States and the International Monetary Fund." Center for Economic and Policy Research (CEPR). The primary surplus is what is left to service debt after such expenditures of governmental maintenance (wages, social and general spending) are taken out of revenues.

10    Johnston, "Partners in Austerity."

11    Greta Krippner, "The Financialization of the American Economy," *Socio-Economic Review* 3 (2005): 174–75.

12    Donald Tomaskovic-Devey and Ken-Hou Lin, "Income Dynamics, Economic Rents, and the Financialization of the U.S. Economy," *American Sociological Review* 76, no. 4 (2011): 539.

13   Gerald A. Epstein, "Introduction: Financialization and the World Economy," in
     *Financialization and the World Economy*, ed. Gerald A. Epstein (Cheltenham, UK:
     Edward Elgar, 2005), 3.

14   Epstein, "Introduction," 3.

15   Krippner, "Financialization of the American Economy," 174.

16   John Maynard Keynes, *General Theory of Employment, Interest and Money* (London:
     Macmillan, 1936), chap. 24. Keynes thought, though, that the rentier capitalism
     would disappear when "it has done its work" as a transitional phase. In much harsher
     terms, Marx criticizes the rentier class by calling them "class of parasites," "gang," and
     "bandits." *Capital*, vol. 3 (New York: International Publishers, 1967), chap. 33.

17   For example, financial market payments rose from relatively low levels in the 1950s
     to average about 30 percent of cash flow from the mid-1960s through the late 1970s.
     From 1984 to 2000, however, NFCs paid out well over half their cash flow to finan-
     cial agents except three years in the early 1990s. NFCs payment to financial market
     peaked at 76 percent in 1989 and again at 74 percent in 1998. See James Crotty,
     "The Neoliberal Paradox: The Impact of Destructive Product Market Competition
     and 'Modern' Financial Markets on Nonfinancial Corporation Performance in the
     Neoliberal Era," in Epstein, *Financialization and the World Economy*, 99.

18   Crotty, "Neoliberal Paradox," 78.

19   Epstein, "Introduction," 7.

20   Crotty, "Neoliberal Paradox," 107.

21   Randall Dodd, "Derivatives Markets: Sources of Vulnerability in US Financial Mar-
     kets," in Epstein, *Financialization and the World Economy*, 149.

22   Dodd, "Derivatives Markets."

23   Rex A. McKenzie, "Casino Capitalism with Derivatives: Fragility and Instability in
     Contemporary Finance," *Review of Radical Political Economics* 43, no. 2 (2011): 201.

24   "Table 19: Amounts Outstanding of Over-the-Counter (OTC) Derivatives," http://
     www.bis.org/statistics/dt1920a.pdf.

25   Beitel, "Subprime Debacle," 28.

26   "Elliott Has 'Vulture Picnic' in Korea Inc.," *Korea Times*, June 12, 2015.

27   McKenzie, "Casino Capitalism," 205.

28   McKenzie, "Casino Capitalism," 207.

29   McKenzie, "Casino Capitalism," 207.

30   Shu-Sen Chang, David Gunnell, Jonathan A. C. Sterne, Tsung-Hsueh Lu, and
     Andrew T. A. Cheng, "Was the Economic Crisis 1997–1998 Responsible for Rising
     Suicide Rates in East/Southeast Asia? A Time-Trend Analysis for Japan, Hong Kong,
     South Korea, Taiwan, Singapore and Thailand," *Social Science & Medicine* 68, no. 7
     (2009): 1322.

31   Chang et al., "Was the Economic Crisis 1997–1998 Responsible for Rising Suicide
     Rates?" 1322.

32   Oxfam, "Working for the Few: Political Capture and Economic Inequality," briefing
     paper, January 20, 2014, 1.

33   Oxfam, "Working for the Few," 2.

34   Thomas Piketty, *Capital in the Twenty-First Century*, trans. Arthur Goldhammer
     (Cambridge, Mass.: Belknap Press of Harvard University Press, 2014), 25. Based on
     more than a decade of research with a handful of other economists, Piketty uncov-
     ers an important historical financial geography that wealth has been increasingly

reasserting itself since the late 1970s after the shocks of the early twentieth century (Great Depression and two world wars), reminiscing about an eighteenth- and nineteenth-century western European society that was highly unequal. According to Piketty, "The top decile of the wealth hierarchy already owned between 80 and 85 percent of all wealth at the beginning of the nineteenth century; by the turn of the twentieth, it owned nearly 90 percent. The top centile alone owned 45–50 percent of the nation's wealth in 1800–1810; its share surpassed 50 percent in 1850–1860 and reached 60 percent in 1900–1910" (339).

35  Piketty, *Capital in the Twenty-First Century*, 295–96.

36  Piketty, *Capital in the Twenty-First Century*, 297.

37  According to Piketty, "from 1977 to 2007, we find that the richest 10 percent appropriated three-quarters of the growth. The richest 1 percent alone absorbed nearly 60 percent of the total increase of US national income in this period. Hence for the bottom 90 percent, the rate of income growth was less than 0.5 percent per year." Piketty, *Capital in the Twenty-First Century*, 297.

38  Marina Azzimonti, Eva de Francisco, and Vincenzo Quadrini, "Financial Globalization, Inequality, and the Rising Public Debt," *American Economic Review* 104, no. 8 (2014): 2300.

39  Joseph Stiglitz, *The Price of Inequality: How Today's Divided Society Endangers Our Future* (New York: Norton, 2013), 48.

40  Stiglitz, *Price of Inequality*, 402.

41  Marx, *Capital*, vol. 3, 478.

42  Marx, *Capital*, vol. 3, 232.

43  Marx, *Capital*, vol. 3, 250, emphasis in original.

44  John Bellamy Foster and Fred Magdoff, *The Great Financial Crisis: Causes and Consequences* (New York: Monthly Review Press, 2009), 80.

45  Although the rising rate has been lowered since 2008, the total private debt in the U.S. economy was still more than 250 percent in 2013. Thom Hartmann, "Private Debt—Not Government Debt—Will Destroy America," *Truthout*.

46  John Bellamy Foster, "The Age of Monopoly-Finance Capital," *Monthly Review* 61, no. 9 (2010): 4.

47  Foster and Magdoff, *Great Financial Crisis*, 133.

48  Foster, "Age of Monopoly-Finance Capital," 12.

49  Fred Moseley, "Marx's Economic Theory and Contemporary Capitalism."

50  Marx, *Capital*, 3:484–85.

51  Samantha Sparks, "Financing East-West Trade," *Multinational Monitor* 8 (1987): 54–55, 54.

52  Locke writes, "That labor put a distinction between them and common. That added something to them more than Nature, the common Mother of all, had done; and so they became his private right." John Locke, *Two Treatises of Government*, ed. Peter Laslett (Cambridge: Cambridge University Press, 1988), 288.

53  David Harvey, "The Future of the Commons," *Radical History Review* 109 (2011): 104.

54  In this sense, I follow Joseph Stiglitz who says, "Because derivatives can be a useful tool for risk management, they shouldn't be banned, but they should be regulated to make sure that they are used appropriately." *Free Fall: America, Free Markets, and the Sinking of the World Economy* (New York: Norton, 2010), 174.

55    Karen Frefield, "NY Court Lets Lawsuit against Goldman over Timberwolf CDO Proceed," Reuters, January 30, 2014.

56    Tomaskovic-Devey and Lin, "Income Dynamics," 549.

57    Tomaskovic-Devey and Lin, "Income Dynamics," 553.

58    Stiglitz, *Price of Inequality*, 60.

59    Stiglitz, *Price of Inequality*, xxxi.

60    Tomaskovic-Devey and Lin, "Income Dynamics," 553.

61    Tim Jones, "A Legacy of Dodgy Deals: Auditing the Debts Owed to the UK," Jubilee Debt Campaign, June 2015.

62    M. Suchitra, "Crop of Debt," *Down to Earth* (August 1, 2015): 18–21.

63    Elaine Sternberg, "Ethical Misconduct and the Global Financial Crisis," *Economic Affairs* 33, no. 1 (2013): 22.

64    Jason N. Houle and Michael T. Light, "The Home Foreclosure Crisis and Rising Suicide Rates, 2005 to 2010," *American Journal of Public Health* 104, no. 6 (2014): 1073.

65    Houle and Light, "Home Foreclosure Crisis," 1073.

66    Kunibert Raffer, "Risks of Lending and Liability of Lenders," *Ethics & International Affairs* 21, no. 1 (2007): 85.

67    Raffer, "Risks of Lending," 86.

68    Raffer, "Risks of Lending," 89.

69    Ronald Dworkin, *Taking Rights Seriously* (Cambridge, Mass.: Harvard University Press, 1978), 90, emphasis added.

70    Dworkin, *Taking Rights Seriously*, 91.

71    Dworkin, *Taking Rights Seriously*, 91.

72    Bob Davis, "What's a Global Recession?" *Wall Street Journal*, October 16, 2015.

73    Onora O'Neill, "Agents of Justice," *Metaphilosophy* 32, nos. 1–2 (2001): 184.

74    O'Neill, "Agents of Justice," 185.

75    Onora O'Neill, *Towards Justice and Virtue: A Constructive Account of Practical Reasoning* (Cambridge: Cambridge University Press, 1996), 147.

76    O'Neill, *Towards Justice and Virtue*, 148.

## Chapter 3

1    Bankrupt is different from "broke." Bankrupt means a filing in a federal court to request protection from the creditor through the bankruptcy laws.

2    Jukka Kilpi, *The Ethics of Bankruptcy* (London: Routledge, 1998), 10.

3    Kilpi, *Ethics of Bankruptcy*, 11.

4    Immanuel Kant, *Groundwork of the Metaphysic of Morals*, trans. H. J. Paton (New York: Harper & Row, 1964), 90.

5    Kilpi, *Ethics of Bankruptcy*, 76–77.

6    Kilpi, *Ethics of Bankruptcy*, 108.

7    Kilpi, *Ethics of Bankruptcy*, 113.

8    Kilpi, *Ethics of Bankruptcy*, 114.

9    Kilpi, *Ethics of Bankruptcy*, 124.

10   Kilpi, *Ethics of Bankruptcy*, 162.

11   Bill Bigelow and Bob Peterson, eds., *Rethinking Globalization: Teaching for Justice in an Unjust World* (Milwaukee, Wis.: Rethinking Schools Press, 2002), 84–85.

12  Martha Nussbaum, *Frontiers of Justice: Disability, Nationality, Species Membership* (Cambridge, Mass.: Belknap Press, 2006), 77–78.

13  Nussbaum, *Frontiers of Justice*, 78.

14  Nussbaum, *Frontiers of Justice*, 78.

15  Karen Gross, *Failure and Forgiveness: Rebalancing the Bankruptcy System* (New Haven, Conn.: Yale University Press, 1997), 21.

16  Gross, *Failure and Forgiveness*, 20.

17  Student loan debt is not dischargeable by the judge's discretion unless the debtor can prove undue hardship determined by the "Brunner Test." The test, however, is more focused on "a minimal standard of living" than on rehabilitating or restoring the debtor's dignified life.

18  "College Debt: More Is Less," *Economist*, August 15, 2015. As of October 2016, the total outstanding student debt has increased to $1.35 trillion.

19  Josh Mitchell, "School-Loan Reckoning: 7 Million Are in Default," *Wall Street Journal*, August 21, 2015.

20  Janet Lorin, "Who's Profiting from $1.2 Trillion of Federal Student Loans?" *Bloomberg Business*, December 11, 2015.

21  Andrew Haugwout, Donghoon Lee, Joelle Scally, and Wilbert van der Kalauw, "Student Loan Borrowing and Repayment Trends, 2015," *Federal Reserve Bank of New York*, April 16, 2015, 5–8.

22  Michael Greenstone and Adam Looney, "Rising Student Debt Burdens: Factors behind the Phenomenon," *Brookings*, July 5, 2013.

23  Kelley Holland, "The High Economic and Social Costs of Student Loan Debt," *CNBC*, June 15, 2015.

24  U.S. Senate Committee on Health, Education, Labor and Pensions, "Harkin: Report Reveals Troubling Realities of For-Profit Schools," http://www.help.senate.gov/ranking/newsroom/press/harkin-report-reveals-troubling-realities-of-for-profit-schools.

25  Greenstone and Looney, "Rising Student Debt Burdens."

26  Lorin, "Who's Profiting?"

27  Wenli Li, "The Economics of Student Loan Borrowing and Repayment," *Business Review* Q3 (2013): 1.

28  Chris Jochnick, "The Legal Case for Debt Repudiation," in *Sovereign Debt at the Crossroads*, ed. Chris Jochnick and Fraser A. Preston (London: Oxford University Press, 2006), 132.

29  Kunibert Raffer, "The IMF's SDRM—Simply Disastrous Rescheduling Management?" in Jochnick and Preston, *Sovereign Debt at the Crossroads*, 260.

30  Jochnick, "Legal Case for Debt Repudiation," 141.

31  Fantu Cheru, "Playing Games with African Lives: The G7 Debt Relief Strategy and the Politics of Indifference," in Jochnick and Preston, *Sovereign Debt at the Crossroads*, 41.

32  Christian Barry, "Sovereign Debt, Human Rights, and Policy Conditionality," *Journal of Political Philosophy* 19, no. 3 (2011): 284.

33  Jack Boorman, "Dealing Comprehensively, and Justly, with Sovereign Debt," in Jochnick and Preston, *Sovereign Debt at the Crossroads*, 229.

34    James M. Buchanan, "The Ethics of Debt Default," in *Deficits*, ed. James M. Buchanan, Charles K. Rowley, and Robert D. Tollison (Oxford: Basil Blackwell, 1987), 364.

35    Buchanan, "Ethics of Debt Default," 368.

36    Buchanan, "Ethics of Debt Default," 370.

37    Buchanan, "Ethics of Debt Default," 372.

38    Helena Smith, "Greece Erupts in Violent Protest as Citizens Face a Future of Harsh Austerity," *Guardian*, May 1, 2010.

39    Mohamed el-Erian, "Who Is to Blame for Greece's Crisis?" *Guardian*, May 18, 2012.

40    Nussbaum, *Frontiers of Justice*, 90–91.

41    Rawls, *Theory of Justice*, 302.

42    Brad Plumer, "How Greek Tax Evasion Helped Sink the Global Economy," *Washington Post*, July 9, 2012.

43    Adéa Guillot, "Greece Struggles to Address Its Tax Evasion Problem," *Guardian*, February 24, 2015.

44    Guillot, "Greece Struggles."

45    Kunibert Raffer, "Preferred or Not Preferred: Thoughts on Priority Structures of Creditors," paper presented at the 2nd meeting of the ILA Sovereign Insolvency Study Group, October 16, 2009, Washington, D.C.

46    Raffer, "Preferred or Not Preferred," 7.

47    Raffer, "Preferred or Not Preferred," 7.

48    Raffer, "Preferred or Not Preferred," 15.

49    Raffer, "Preferred or Not Preferred," 16.

50    James B. Stewart, "If Greece Defaults, Imagine Argentina, but Much Worse," *New York Times*, June 25, 2015.

51    Mariana Marcaletti, "Three Things to Know about the Supreme Court's Ruling on Argentine Debt—and Why It Matters to Argentina and the World," *Washington Post*, June 26, 2014.

52    Manuel Jordan Basso and Juan Pablo Hugues Arthur, "Argentina, Vulture Funds and a Sovereign Debt Convention," *Transnational Notes* (blog), July 20, 2015.

53    Basso and Arthur, "Argentina, Vulture Funds."

54    Julie A. Nelson, "Ethics, Evidence and International Debt," *Journal of Economic Methodology* 16, no. 2 (2009): 182.

55    Nelson, "Ethics, Evidence and International Debt," 182.

56    Matt Peterson and Christian Barry, "Who Must Pay for the Damage of the Global Financial Crisis?" in *Global Financial Crisis: The Ethical Issues*, ed. Ned Dobos, Christian Barry, and Thomas Pogge (New York: Palgrave-Macmillan, 2011), 164.

57    Peter Singer, "Famine, Affluence, and Morality," *Philosophy & Public Affairs* 1, no. 3 (1973): 231.

58    Peterson Christian Barry, "Who Must Pay?" 163.

59    Iris Marion Young, *Responsibility for Justice* (Oxford: Oxford University Press, 2011), 96.

60    Peterson and Barry, "Who Must Pay?" 170.

61    Anne O. Krueger, "A New Approach to Sovereign Debt Restructuring," *International Monetary Fund 2002*.

62    Raffer, "IMF's SDRM," 251.

63    U.S. Securities and Exchange Commission (SEC), "What Every Investor Should Know . . . Corporate Bankruptcy," http://www.sec.gov/investor/pubs/bankrupt.htm.

64    SEC, "What Every Investor Should Know . . . Corporate Bankruptcy."

65    SEC, "What Every Investor Should Know . . . Corporate Bankruptcy."

66    SEC, "What Every Investor Should Know . . . Corporate Bankruptcy."

67    Jacques Boettcher, Gerald Cavanagh, S.J., and Min Xu, "Ethical Issues That Arise in Bankruptcy," *Business and Society Review* 119, no. 4 (2014): 479, emphasis added.

68    Boettcher, Cavanagh, and Xu, "Ethical Issues That Arise in Bankruptcy," 478, emphasis added.

69    Edward R. Freeman, "Stakeholder Theory of the Modern Corporation," in *Ethical Theory and Business*, ed. Tom L. Beauchamp and Norman E. Bowie, 7th ed. (Englewood Cliffs, N.J.: Prentice Hall, 2003), 39.

70    Boettcher, Cavanagh, and Xu, "Ethical Issues That Arise in Bankruptcy," 476.

71    Boettcher, Cavanagh, and Xu, "Ethical Issues That Arise in Bankruptcy," 492.

72    William M. Fitzpatrick and Samuel A. DiLullo, "Bankruptcy: A Stakeholder Analysis," *Advances in Competitiveness Research* 20, nos. 1–2 (2012): 24.

73    Dinah Payne and Michael Hogg, "Three Perspectives of Chapter 11 Bankruptcy: Legal, Managerial and Moral," *Journal of Business Ethics* 13, no. 1 (1994): 27. In her book *Failure and Forgiveness: Rebalancing the Bankruptcy System*, Karen Gross also refers to the stakeholder theory of corporate bankruptcies. She writes, "Bankruptcy also touches broader communities: the community in which a business is located, the community into which the debtor's assets can be relocated if they are sold in the bankruptcy case, the community within an industry, or the communities affected by decreased or increased tax revenues." See Gross, *Failure and Forgiveness*, 197.

74    Jürgen Habermas, *Moral Consciousness and Communicative Action*, trans. Christian Lenhardt and Shierry Weber Nicholsen (Cambridge, Mass.: MIT Press, 1990), 66.

75    Jürgen Habermas, *Between Facts and Norms: Contributions to a Discourse Theory of Law and Democracy*, trans. William Rehg (Cambridge, Mass.: MIT Press, 1996), 166–67.

76    Ilsup Ahn, "Deconstructing the Economy of Debt: Karl Marx, Jürgen Habermas, and an Ethics of Debt," *Trans-Humanities* 6, no. 1 (2013): 20.

77    Boettcher, Cavanagh, and Xu, "Ethical Issues That Arise in Bankruptcy," 483, emphasis added.

78    U.S. Department of Justice, *Handbook For Chapter 7 Trustees*, October 1, 2012, http://www.justice.gov/ust/file/handbook_for_chapter_7_trustees.pdf/download, emphasis added.

79    Boettcher, Cavanagh, and Xu, "Ethical Issues That Arise in Bankruptcy," 484.

80    Boettcher, Cavanagh, and Xu, "Ethical Issues That Arise in Bankruptcy."

81    Mark J. Roe and Frederick Tung, "Breaking Bankruptcy Priority: How Rent-Seeking Upends the Creditor's Bargain," *Virginia Law Review* 99, no. 6 (2013): 1237.

82    Liliya Gritsenko, "Everybody Wins! Elimination of the Absolute Priority Rule for Individuals under BAPCPA: A Middle Ground," *Cardozo Law Review* 35, no. 3 (2014): 1257.

83    Gritsenko, "Everybody Wins!" 1257.

84    Jessica R. Ellis, "The Absolute Priority Rule for Individuals after *Maharaj*, *Lively*, and *Stephens*: Negotiations or Game Over?" *Arizona Law Review* 55, no. 4 (2013): 1148.

85    Boettcher, Cavanagh, and Xu, "Ethical Issues That Arise in Bankruptcy," 473.

CHAPTER 4

1    M. Kabir Hassan and Rasem Kayed, "The Global Financial Crisis and Islamic Finance," *Thunderbird International Business Review* 53, no. 5 (2011): 551.

2    Volker Nienhaus, "Islamic Finance Ethics and Shari'ah Law in the Aftermath of the Crisis: Concept and Practice of Shari'ah Compliant Finance," *Ethical Perspectives* 18, no. 4 (2011): 592.

3    Nienhaus, "Islamic Finance Ethics," 592.

4    Hassan and Kayed, "Global Financial Crisis and Islamic Finance," 551.

5    Hassan and Kayed, "Global Financial Crisis and Islamic Finance," 558.

6    Hassan and Kayed, "Global Financial Crisis and Islamic Finance," 558.

7    Hassan and Kayed, "Global Financial Crisis and Islamic Finance," 559. The *World Bulletin* says that "the ethical principles on which Islamic finance is based may bring banks closer to their clients and to the true spirit which should mark every financial service." "Vatican Offers Islamic Finance System to Western Banks," *World Bulletin*, http://www.worldbulletin.net/index.php?aType=haber&ArticleID=37814.

8    Habib Ahmed, "Defining Ethics in Islamic Finance: Looking Beyond Legality," *New Horizon: Global Perspective on Islamic Banking & Insurance* 184 (2012): 21.

9    Ahmed, "Defining Ethics in Islamic Finance," 21.

10    Ahmed, "Defining Ethics in Islamic Finance," 21.

11    Jane Polland and Michael Samers, "Islamic Banking and Finance: Postcolonial Political Economy and the Decentring of Economic Geography," *Transactions of the Institute of British Geographers*, n.s. 32, no. 3 (2007): 314.

12    Muhammad Ayub, *Understanding Islamic Finance* (West Sussex: John Wiley & Sons, 2007), 44.

13    These verses of the Qur'an are cited from the Oxford World's Classics (2010) version translated by M. A. S. Abdel Haleem.

14    We should note that all major religions including Judaism, Christianity, Islam, Buddhism, and Hinduism are united in denouncing usury.

15    M. Siddieq Noorzoy, "Islamic Laws on Riba (Interest) and Their Economic Implications," *International Journal of Middle East Studies* 14, no. 1 (1982): 6. Noorzoy continues to point out that "the prohibition of riba on consumption loans is clearly also aimed at the redistribution of purchasing power from the rich to the poor" (6).

16    Wayne A. M. Visser and Alastair McIntosh, "A Short Review of the Historical Critique of Usury," *Accounting, Business and Financial History* 8, no. 2 (1998): 183.

17    Muhammad Farooq, "Interest, Usury and Its Impact on the Economy," *Dialogue* 7, no. 3 (2012): 274.

18    Noorzoy, "Islamic Laws on Riba (Interest) and Their Economic Implications," 6.

19    Noorzoy, "Islamic Laws on Riba (Interest) and Their Economic Implications," 6.

20    Cited from Visser and McIntosh, "Short Review," 181.

21    Hassan and Kayed, "Global Financial Crisis and Islamic Finance," 557.

22    Noorzoy, "Islamic Laws on Riba (Interest) and Their Economic Implications," 6.

23    Noorzoy, "Islamic Laws on Riba (Interest) and Their Economic Implications," 3.

24    Noorzoy, "Islamic Laws on Riba (Interest) and Their Economic Implications," 4.

25    Noorzoy, "Islamic Laws on Riba (Interest) and Their Economic Implications," 4.

26    Noorzoy, "Islamic Laws on Riba (Interest) and Their Economic Implications," 4.

27    Ayub, *Understanding Islamic Finance*, 47.

28    Ayub, *Understanding Islamic Finance*, 47.

29   Ayub, *Understanding Islamic Finance*, 47.

30   Noorzoy, "Islamic Laws on Riba (Interest) and Their Economic Implications," 4.

31   Cited in Noorzoy, "Islamic Laws on Riba (Interest) and Their Economic Implications," 5.

32   Mahmoud A. El-Gamal, *Islamic Finance: Law, Economics, and Practice* (New York: Cambridge University Press, 2006), 51.

33   Farooq, "Interest, Usury and Its Impact on the Economy," 265.

34   Oxfam, "62 People Own the Same as Half the World, Reveals Oxfam Davos Report," press release, January 18, 2016.

35   Martin Lewison, "Conflicts of Interest? The Ethics of Usury," *Journal of Business Ethics* 22, no. 4 (1999): 336.

36   Farooq, "Interest, Usury and Its Impact on the Economy," 274.

37   Hassan and Kayed, "Global Financial Crisis and Islamic Finance," 557.

38   Russell Powell and Arthur DeLong, "The Possible Advantages of Islamic Financial Jurisprudence: An Empirical Study of the Dow Jones Islamic Market Index," *Fordham Journal of Corporate and Financial Law* 19 (2014): 401.

39   Powell and DeLong, "Possible Advantages of Islamic Financial Jurisprudence," 401.

40   Powell and DeLong, "Possible Advantages of Islamic Financial Jurisprudence," 401–2.

41   Sherin Kunhibava and Balachandran Shanmugam, "Shari'ah and Conventional Law Objections to Derivatives: A Comparison," *Arab Law Quarterly* 24, no. 4 (2010): 324.

42   Kunhibava and Shanmugam, "Shari'ah and Conventional Law Objections," 325.

43   Mahmoud Amin El-Gamal, "An Economic Explication of the Prohibition of Gharar in Classical Islamic Jurisprudence," paper prepared for the 4th International Conference on Islamic Economics, Leicester, August 13–15, 2000.

44   El-Gamal, "Economic Explication of the Prohibition of Gharar in Classical Islamic Jurisprudence," 3.

45   Powell and DeLong, "Possible Advantages of Islamic Financial Jurisprudence," 402.

46   Powell and DeLong, "Possible Advantages of Islamic Financial Jurisprudence," 402.

47   El-Gamal, "Economic Explication of the Prohibition of Gharar in Classical Islamic Jurisprudence," 7.

48   El-Gamal, "Economic Explication of the Prohibition of Gharar in Classical Islamic Jurisprudence," 7.

49   Powell and DeLong, "Possible Advantages of Islamic Financial Jurisprudence," 419.

50   Kunhibava and Shanmugam, "Shari'ah and Conventional Law Objections," 326.

51   Powell and DeLong, "Possible Advantages of Islamic Financial Jurisprudence," 419–20.

52   "The Warning," *Frontline*, October 20, 2009, http://www.pbs.org/wgbh/frontline/film/warning/.

53   Edmund L. Andrews, "Greenspan Concedes Error on Regulation," *New York Times*, October 23, 2008.

54   Timur Kuran, "On the Notion of Economic Justice in Contemporary Islamic Thought," *International Journal of Middle East Studies* 21, no. 2 (1989): 172.

55   Kuran, "On the Notion of Economic Justice," 172.

56   Kuran, "On the Notion of Economic Justice," 171.

57   Benaouda Bensaid et al., "Enduring Financial Debt: An Islamic Perspective," *Middle-East Journal of Scientific Research* 13, no. 2 (2013): 162.

58   M. T. Talib and Jamiu A. Oluwatoko, "Islam and the Debt Question in Nigeria," in *The Church and the External Debt: Report on a Conference Held in Jos, Nigeria, November 26–30, 1990*, ed. Jan H. Boer (Jos, Nigeria: 1992).

59   M. Raquibuz Zaman and Hormoz Movassaghi, "Interest-Free Islamic Banking: Ideals and Reality," *International Journal of Banking* 14, no. 4 (2002): 2428.

60   World Bank, "Islamic Finance," brief, March 31, 2015, http://www.worldbank.org/en/topic/financialsector/brief/islamic-finance.

61   Zaman and Movassaghi, "Interest-Free Islamic Banking," 2438.

62   Nienhaus, "Islamic Finance Ethics," 593.

63   Zaman and Movassaghi, "Interest-Free Islamic Banking," 2434.

64   Zaman and Movassaghi, "Interest-Free Islamic Banking," 2438.

65   Ashraf U. Kazi and Abdel K. Halabi, "The Influence of Qur'an and Islamic Transactions and Banking," *Arab Law Quarterly* 20, no. 3 (2006): 324.

66   Kazi and Halabi, "Influence of Qur'an and Islamic Transactions," 324. *Takaful* is Islamic insurance based on a policy of mutual cooperation, solidarity, and brotherhood against unpredicted risk or catastrophes. *Muqarada* is an Islamic financial instrument in which a bank floats Islamic bonds to finance a project and members take a share of the profits or losses of the project. *Salem* is a forward-financing transaction in which a buyer pays, in advance, a specified quantity of a commodity at an agreed price.

67   Kazi and Halabi, "Influence of Qur'an and Islamic Transactions," 324.

68   Zaman and Movassaghi, "Interest-Free Islamic Banking," 2436.

69   Rajesh K. Aggarwal and Tarik Yousef, "Islamic Banks and Investment Financing," *Journal of Money, Credit and Banking* 32, no. 1 (2000): 96.

70   Aggarwal and Yousef, "Islamic Banks and Investment Financing," 97.

71   Zaman and Movassaghi, "Interest-Free Islamic Banking," 2436. Cited from R. T. DeBelder and M. H. Khan, "The Changing Face of Islamic Banking," *International Financial Law Review* 12, no. 11 (1993): 28.

72   Zaman and Movassaghi, "Interest-Free Islamic Banking," 2437.

73   Zaman and Movassaghi, "Interest-Free Islamic Banking," 2437.

74   Aggarwal and Yousef, "Islamic Banks and Investment Financing," 96.

75   Aggarwal and Yousef, "Islamic Banks and Investment Financing," 96.

76   Hossein Askari, Zamir Iqbal, Noureddine Krichene, and Abbas Mirakhor, *Risk Sharing in Finance: The Islamic Finance Alternative* (Singapore: John Wiley & Sons, 2012), 51.

77   Askari et al., *Risk Sharing in Finance*, 52.

78   Cited in Aggarwal and Yousef, "Islamic Banks and Investment Financing," 97–98.

79   Polland and Samers, "Islamic Banking and Finance," 315.

80   Askari et al., *Risk Sharing in Finance*, 66.

81   Askari et al., *Risk Sharing in Finance*, 67.

82   Askari et al., *Risk Sharing in Finance*, 68.

83   Federal Reserve Bank of New York, *Quarterly Report on Household Debt and Credit*, May 2016, https://www.newyorkfed.org/medialibrary/interactives/householdcredit/data/pdf/HHDC_2016Q1.pdf.

84 Robert H. Scott III, "Credit Card Use and Abuse: A Veblenian Analysis," *Journal of Economic Issues* 41, no. 2 (2007): 567.

85 Yasmin Ghahremani, "Credit Card Statistics," Creditcards.com.

86 Manzoor Ahmad Al-Azhari, "Credit Cards and Their Juristic Appraisal," *Homdard Islamicus* 34, no. 2 (2011): 32.

87 Michelle J. White, "Bankruptcy Reform and Credit Cards," *Journal of Economic Perspectives* 21, no. 4 (2007): 179.

88 Samuel Issacharoff and Erin F. Delaney, "Credit Card Accountability," *University of Chicago Law Review* 73, no. 1 (2006): 160.

89 Pat Curry, "How a Supreme Court Ruling Killed Off Usury Laws for Credit Card Rates," Creditcards.com, November 12, 2010.

90 Issacharoff and Delaney, "Credit Card Accountability," 161.

91 White, "Bankruptcy Reform and Credit Cards," 179.

92 Rick Jurgens and Chi Chi Wu, "Fee-Harvesters: Low-Credit, High-Cost Cards Bleed Consumers," *National Consumer Law Center Report.*

93 Jurgens and Wu, "Fee-Harvesters," 25.

94 White, "Bankruptcy Reform and Credit Cards," 181.

95 Floyd Norris, "Card Act Cleared Up Credit Cards' Hidden Costs," *New York Times,* November 7, 2013.

96 Jonathan Wu, "Average Credit Card Interest Rates (APR)—2017," Value Penguin.

97 White, "Bankruptcy Reform and Credit Cards," 176.

98 Murat Cokgezen and Timur Kuran, "Between Consumer Demand and Islamic Law: The Evolution of Islamic Credit Cards in Turkey," *Journal of Comparative Economics* 43, no. 4 (2015): 870.

99 Cokgezen and Kuran, "Between Consumer Demand and Islamic Law," 872.

100 Cokgezen and Kuran, "Between Consumer Demand and Islamic Law," 872.

101 Cokgezen and Kuran, "Between Consumer Demand and Islamic Law," 872.

102 Cokgezen and Kuran, "Between Consumer Demand and Islamic Law," 880.

103 Al-Azhari, "Credit Cards and Their Juristic Appraisal," 45.

104 Cokgezen and Kuran, "Between Consumer Demand and Islamic Law," 871.

105 Powell and DeLong, "Possible Advantages of Islamic Financial Jurisprudence," 419.

## Chapter 5

1 International Monetary Fund (IMF), "The IMF Factsheet." March 2016, https://www.imf.org/external/np/exr/facts/pdf/hipc.pdf.

2 Walter Brueggemann, "Living with a Different Set of Signals," *Living Pulpit* 10, no. 2 (2001): 20.

3 Richard H. Lowery, *Sabbath and Jubilee* (St. Louis, Mo.: Chalice Press, 2000), 23.

4 Lowery, *Sabbath and Jubilee,* 24.

5 Robert Gnuse, "Jubilee Legislation in Leviticus: Israel's Vision of Social Reform," *Biblical Theology Bulletin* 15, no. 2 (1985): 43.

6 Gnuse, "Jubilee Legislation in Leviticus," 45.

7 Moshe Weinfeld collects several examples. For example, Enmetena of Lagash (ca. 2430 B.C.E.) restored household property and instituted debt relief; Manishtushu released thirty-eight cities from state labor and military draft obligations about three centuries later; Ishme-Dagan if Isin (1953–1935 B.C.E.) released the temple city Nippur from taxes and military draft. Debts were also canceled by local princes in

the Assyrian colonies of Cappadocia (twentieth and nineteenth centuries) and in Assyria itself by Ilushuma and Erishum I. Hebrew Bible scholar Richard H. Lowery points out that similar royal decrees were recorded in Egypt and in the reform of Solon in Greece (594–593 B.C.E.) See Lowery, *Sabbath and Jubilee*, 38–39.

8   Gnuse, "Jubilee Legislation in Leviticus," 46.

9   Lowery, *Sabbath and Jubilee*, 41.

10  John Sietze Bergsma, *The Jubilee from Leviticus to Qumran: A History of Interpretation* (Leiden: Brill, 2007), 1.

11  Lowery, *Sabbath and Jubilee*, 40.

12  Lowery, *Sabbath and Jubilee*, 40.

13  Raphael Jospe, "Sabbath, Sabbatical and Jubilee: Jewish Ethical Perspectives, in *The Jubilee Challenge: Utopia or Possibility?*" ed. Hans Ucko (Geneva: WCC, 1997), 89.

14  Jospe, "Sabbath, Sabbatical and Jubilee," 90.

15  Lowery, *Sabbath and Jubilee*, 41.

16  Todd G. Buchholz, "Biblical Laws and the Economic Growth of Ancient Israel," *Journal of Law and Religion* 6, no. 2 (1988): 413.

17  Buchholz, "Biblical Laws," 414.

18  Benjamin Nelson, *The Idea of Usury* (Chicago: University of Chicago Press, 1969), 73.

19  Nelson, *Idea of Usury*, 81–82.

20  Nelson, *Idea of Usury*, 137.

21  Nelson, *Idea of Usury*, 136.

22  Buchholz, "Biblical Laws," 414.

23  Lowery, *Sabbath and Jubilee*, 3–4.

24  Jacob Milgrom, "Leviticus 25 and Some Postulates of the Jubilee," in Ucko, *Jubilee Challenge*, 31–32.

25  Lorraine Stutzman Amstutz, "Restorative Justice: The Promise and the Challenges," *Vision: A Journal for Church and Theology* 14, no. 2 (2013): 24.

26  Amstutz, "Restorative Justice," 24.

27  Christo Thesnaar, "Restorative Justice as a Key for Healing Communities," *Religion & Theology* 15, nos. 1–2 (2008): 58.

28  John Paul II, "Tertio Millennio Adveniente."

29  Malcolm Chase, "From Millennium to Anniversary: The Concept of Jubilee in Late Eighteenth- and Nineteenth-Century England," *Past & Present* 129 (1990): 133.

30  Chase, "From Millennium to Anniversary," 133.

31  Ton Veerkamp, "Judeo-Christian Tradition on Debt: Political, Not Just Ethical," *Ethics & International Affairs* 21, no. 1 (2007): 167.

32  Veerkamp, "Judeo-Christian Tradition on Debt," 171.

33  Norman Solomon, "Economics of the Jubilee: Putting Third World Debt in Context," *Church and Society*, September–October 1998, 59.

34  Solomon, "Economics of the Jubilee," 59.

35  Solomon, "Economics of the Jubilee," 59.

36  Solomon, "Economics of the Jubilee," 61.

37  Solomon, "Economics of the Jubilee," 62.

38  Solomon, "Economics of the Jubilee," 67.

39  John Madslien, "Debt Relief Hopes Bring Out the Critics," *BBC News*, June 29, 2005.

40 "Don't Turn the Clock Back: Analyzing the Risks of the Lending Boom to Impoverished Countries," Jubilee Debt Campaign, October 2014.

41 "Don't Turn the Clock Back."

42 Jocelyne Sambira, "Borrowing Responsibly: Africa's Debt Challenge," *Africa Renewal Online*, August 2015.

43 Katie Allen, "Poor Nations Pushed into New Debt Crisis," *Guardian*, October 10, 2014.

44 Allen, "Poor Nations Pushed."

45 Amadou Sy, "Trends and Developments in African Frontier Bond Markets," *Brookings Institution*, March 2015.

46 Sambira, "Borrowing Responsibly."

47 Sohan Sharma and Surinder Kumar, "Debt Relief—Indentured Servitude for the Third World," *Race & Class* 43, no. 4 (2002): 46.

48 Joseph Hanlon, "African Debt Hoax," *Review of African Political Economy* 25, no. 77 (1998): 490.

49 Hanlon, "African Debt Hoax," 490. According to Hanlon, NPV is the amount that would have to be put into the bank at present interest rates to repay a loan on schedule.

50 Hanlon, "African Debt Hoax," 490.

51 Hanlon, "African Debt Hoax," 490.

52 "How Europe Cancelled Germany's Debt," Jubilee Debt Campaign, January 2015, http://jubileedebt.org.uk/wp-content/uploads/2015/01/1501-Germany-Debt-Briefing-updated.pdf.

53 Hanlon, "African Debt Hoax," 490.

54 "How Europe Cancelled Germany's Debt," 2–4.

55 Hanlon, "African Debt Hoax," 490.

56 Amartya Sen, *The Idea of Justice* (Cambridge, Mass.: Harvard University Press, 2009), 233, emphasis in original.

57 Sen, *Idea of Justice*, 233.

58 Sen, *Idea of Justice*, 233.

59 Nussbaum, *Frontiers of Justice*, 74.

60 Sen, *Idea of Justice*, 402.

61 Paul Vallely, *Bad Samaritans: First World Ethics and Third World Debt* (Maryknoll, N.Y.: Orbis Books, 1990), 105.

62 Vallely, *Bad Samaritans*, 105.

63 Bruce Upbin, "The 147 Companies That Control Everything," *Forbes*, October 22, 2011.

64 Vallely, *Bad Samaritans*, 119.

65 Mokgethi B. G. Motlhabi, "An Ethical Appraisal of the Third World Debt Crisis," *Religion & Theology* 10, no. 2 (2003): 207.

66 Motlhabi, "Ethical Appraisal," 207.

67 Laurence Caramel, "Besieged by the Rising Tides of Climate Change, Kiribati Buys Land in Fiji," *Guardian*, June 30, 2014.

68 Christopher Pala, "Kiribati President Purchases 'Worthless' Resettlement Land as Precaution against Rising Sea," *Inter Press Service News Agency*.

69 Caramel, "Besieged by the Rising Tides."

70   African Forum and Network on Debt and Development, *Ecological Debt: The Case of Tanzania* (Harare, Zimbabwe: AFRODAD, 2011), 12.

71   World Bank, *International Debt Statistics 2016.*

72   African Forum and Network on Debt and Development, *Ecological Debt*, 12.

73   African Forum and Network on Debt and Development, *Ecological Debt*, 12.

74   African Forum and Network on Debt and Development, *Ecological Debt*, 13.

75   James Rice, "North-South Relations and the Ecological Debt: Asserting a Counter-Hegemonic Discourse," *Critical Sociology* 35, no. 2 (2009): 227.

76   Cynthia D. Moe-Lobeda, "Climate Change as Climate Debt: Forging a Just Future," *Journal of the Society of Christian Ethics* 36, no. 1 (2016): 29.

77   African Forum and Network on Debt and Development, *Ecological Debt*, 13.

78   U.S. Department of State, "COP21 Press Availability with Special Envoy Todd Stern," https://2009-2017.state.gov/s/climate/releases/2015/250363.htm.

79   U.S. Department of State, "COP21 Press Availability with Special Envoy Todd Stern."

80   African Forum and Network on Debt and Development, *Ecological Debt*, 14.

81   "The earth lies polluted under its inhabitants; for they have transgressed laws, violated the statutes, broken the everlasting covenant" (v. 5). "The earth is utterly broken, the earth is torn asunder, the earth is violently shaken" (v. 19).

82   Hans Ucko, "The Jubilee as a Challenge," in Ucko, *Jubilee Challenge*, 10.

83   Moe-Lobeda, "Climate Change as Climate Debt," 36.

84   Ucko, "Jubilee as a Challenge," 10.

85   Andrew Simms, *Ecological Debt: The Health of the Planet and the Wealth of Nations* (Ann Arbor, Mich.: Pluto Press, 2005), 92.

86   James P. Resor, "Debt-for-Nature Swaps: A Decade of Experience and New Directions for the Future," Food and Agriculture Organization (FAO).

87   Nicole Hassoun, "The Problem of Debt-for-Nature Swaps from a Human Rights Perspective," *Journal of Applied Philosophy* 29, no. 4 (2012): 359, 377, 359.

88   Hassoun, "Problem of Debt-for-Nature Swaps," 359, 377, 359.

89   Dal Didia, "Debt-for-Nature Swaps, Market Imperfections, and Policy Failures as Determinants of Sustainable Development and Environmental Quality," *Journal of Economic Issues* 35, no. 2 (2001): 484.

90   Didia, "Debt-for-Nature Swaps," 484.

91   Hassoun, "Problem of Debt-for-Nature Swaps," 365.

92   Researchers such as Catherine Kilbane Gockel and Leslie C. Gray, for instance, suggest that we should develop new methods of measuring success of the program. They write, "Although Tropical Forest Conservation Act projects may well have conservation effects, the current methods of measuring success do not reflect the types of conservation impacts of Tropical Forest Conservation Act projects." See their article, "Debt-for-Nature Swaps in Action: Two Case Studies in Peru," *Ecology and Society* 16, no. 3 (2011): 1.

93   Morris Miller, *Debt and the Environment: Converging Crises* (New York: United Nations, 1991), 154.

## CHAPTER 6

1   The commission was created by section 5 of the Fraud Enforcement and Recovery Act of 2009, which was signed into law by President Barack Obama on May 20, 2009.

2   Aliza D. Racelis, "Examining the Global Financial Crisis from a Virtue Theory Lens," *Asia-Pacific Social Science Review* 14, no. 2 (2014): 22.

3   Financial Crisis Inquiry Commission, *The Financial Crisis Inquiry Report*, January 2011, xxii, https://www.gpo.gov/fdsys/pkg/GPO-FCIC/pdf/GPO-FCIC.pdf.

4   Financial Crisis Inquiry Commission, *Financial Crisis Inquiry Report*, xvii.

5   Laura L. Hansen and Siamak Movahedi, "Wall Street Scandals: The Myth of Individual Greed," *Sociological Forum* 25, no. 2 (2010): 367.

6   Jeremy Bentham, *Defence of Usury*, 1787 (London: Routledge, 1992), 2.

7   Robert Mayer, "When and Why Usury Should Be Prohibited," *Journal of Business Ethics* 116, no. 3 (2013): 515.

8   Bentham, *Defence of Usury*, 9.

9   Bentham, *Defence of Usury*, 10.

10   Bentham, *Defence of Usury*, 11.

11   Bentham, *Defence of Usury*, 12.

12   Bentham, *Defence of Usury*, 12.

13   D. Stephen Long, Nancy Ruth Fox, and Tripp York, *Calculated Futures: Theology, Ethics, and Economics* (Waco, Tex.: Baylor University Press, 2007), 136.

14   Paul B. Rasor, "Biblical Roots of Modern Consumer Credit Law," *Journal of Law and Religion* 10, no. 1 (1993–1994): 172.

15   John Bobson, "Behavioral Assumptions of Finance," in *Finance Ethics: Critical Issues in Theory and Practice*, ed. John R. Boatright (Hoboken, N.J.: John Wiley & Sons, 2010): 45–59, 58, emphasis added.

16   Alyssa Labat and Walter E. Block, "Money Does Not Grow on Trees: An Argument for Usury," *Journal of Business Ethics* 106, no. 3 (2012): 385.

17   Labat and Block, "Money Does Not Grow on Trees," 385.

18   Milton Friedman, "Defense of Usury," *Newsweek*, April 6, 1970, 79.

19   Philip Goodchild, "Exposing Mammon: Devotion to Money in a Market Society," *Dialog: A Journal of Theology* 52, no. 1 (2013): 55.

20   Goodchild, "Exposing Mammon," 54.

21   Goodchild, "Exposing Mammon," 54.

22   Goodchild, "Exposing Mammon," 54.

23   Goodchild, "Exposing Mammon," 55.

24   Gordon Gekko is a fictionalized character played by Michael Douglas to dramatize Ivan Boesky, who was the convicted insider-trading felon.

25   Surendra Arjoon, "Narcissistic Behavior and the Economy: The Role of Virtues," *Journal of Market & Morality* 13, no. 1 (2010): 59.

26   Arjoon, "Narcissistic Behavior and the Economy," 60.

27   Racelis, "Examining the Global Financial Crisis," 25.

28   Racelis, "Examining the Global Financial Crisis," 25.

29   Bentham, *Defence of Usury*, 9.

30   James E. Crimmins, "Bentham and Hobbes: An Issue of Influence," *Journal of the History of Ideas* 63, no. 4 (2002): 677.

31  James E. Crimmins, "Bentham on Religion: Atheism and the Secular Society," *Journal of the History of Ideas* 47, no. 1 (1986): 95.

32  Crimmins, "Bentham on Religion," 95.

33  Crimmins, "Bentham on Religion," 95.

34  Maurizio Lazzarato, *The Making of the Indebted Man: An Essay on the Neoliberal Condition*, trans. Joshua David Jordan (Los Angeles: Semiotext, 2011), 38–39.

35  Hollis Phelps, "Overcoming Redemption: Neoliberalism, Atonement, and the Logic of Debt," *Political Theology* 17, no. 3 (2016): 266.

36  Margaret Atwood, *Payback: Debt and the Shadow Side of Wealth* (Berkeley, Calif.: Anansi Press, 2008), 81.

37  Atwood, *Payback*, 81.

38  Kathryn Tanner, "Economies of Grace," in *Having: Property and Possession in Religious and Social Life*, ed. William Schweiker and Charles Mathewes (Grand Rapids: Eerdmans, 2004), 356.

39  Tanner, "Economies of Grace," 361.

40  Tanner, "Economies of Grace," 363.

41  Tanner, "Economies of Grace," 363.

42  Tanner, "Economies of Grace," 364.

43  Tanner, "Economies of Grace," 369.

44  Tanner, "Economies of Grace," 369.

45  Tanner, "Economies of Grace," 369.

46  Tanner, "Economies of Grace," 369.

47  Tanner, "Economies of Grace," 370.

48  Tanner, "Economies of Grace," 371.

49  Tanner, "Economies of Grace," 371, emphasis added.

50  Tanner, "Economies of Grace," 372.

51  Tanner, "Economies of Grace," 374.

52  Tanner, "Economies of Grace," 374.

53  Stephen H. Webb, *The Gifting God: A Trinitarian Ethics of Excess* (New York: Oxford University Press, 1996), 9.

54  Webb, *Gifting God*, 10.

55  Webb, *Gifting God*, 11.

56  Webb, *Gifting God*, 11.

57  Webb, *Gifting God*, 31–32.

58  Webb, *Gifting God*, 32.

59  Webb, *Gifting God*, 32. Webb, however, finds Richard Titmus (*The Gift Relationship from Human Blood to Social Policy*) and Lewis Hyde (*The Gift*) somewhat favorable to his position. While Titmus is regarded as "one of the first scholars to try to argue that gift giving is an aspect of modern culture that needs to be cultivated and encouraged," Hyde is described as the one from whom "I [Webb] have learned a lot from his work" (32).

60  Webb, *Gifting God*, 90, emphasis in original.

61  Webb, *Gifting God*, 90.

62  Webb, *Gifting God*, 91.

63  Tanner, "Economies of Grace," 372.

64  Tanner, "Economies of Grace," 373.

65  Tanner, "Economies of Grace," 373.

66   Tanner, "Economies of Grace," 382.

67   Kathryn Tanner, *Economy of Grace* (Minneapolis: Fortress, 2005), 124.

68   Hyde, *Gift*, 50.

69   Hyde, *Gift*, 50.

70   Hyde, *Gift*, 51.

71   Ronald J. Colombo, "Toward a Nexus of Virtue," *Washington and Lee Law Review* 69, no. 3 (2012): 19.

72   William J. Bernstein, "Corporate Finance and Original Sin," *Financial Analysts Journal* 62, no. 3 (2006): 21.

73   Bernstein, "Corporate Finance and Original Sin," 21.

74   This list is excerpted from Seumas Miller's article, "Global Financial Institutions, Ethics and Market Fundamentalism," in *Global Financial Crisis: The Ethical Issues*, ed. Ned Dobos, Christian Barry, and Thomas Pogge (New York: Palgrave Macmillan, 2011), 25–26.

75   Johan J. Graafland and Bert W. van de Ven, "The Credit Crisis and the Moral Responsibility of Professionals in Finance," *Journal of Business Ethics* 103, no. 4 (2011): 605.

76   Thomas Aquinas, *Summa Theologica*, trans. Fathers of the English Dominican Province (New York: Benziger Brothers, 1947), II–II. Q. 118.8.

77   Mary L. Hirschfeld, "Reflection on the Financial Crisis: Aquinas on the Proper Role of Finance," *Journal of the Society of Christian Ethics* 35, no. 1 (2015): 68.

78   Thomas Aquinas, *Summa Theologica* I–II. Q. 2.1.

79   William Schweiker, "Reconsidering Greed," in Schweiker and Mathewes, *Having*, 268.

80   Thomas Aquinas, *Summa Theologica* II–II. Q. 141.1.

81   Jean Porter, "Perennial and Timely Virtues: Practical Wisdom, Courage and Temperance," in *Changing Value and Virtues*, ed. Dietmar Mieth and Jacques Pohier (Edinburgh: T&T Clark, 1987), 67.

82   Porter, "Perennial and Timely Virtues," 67.

83   Richard Hicks, "Markan Discipleship according to Malachi: The Significance of μὴ ἀποστερήσῃς in the Story of the Rich Man," *Journal of Biblical Literature* 132, no. 1 (2013): 199.

84   Thomas Aquinas, *Summa Theologica* III. Q. 7.3.

85   Thomas Aquinas, *Summa Theologica* II–II. Q. 133.4.

86   Thomas Aquinas, *Summa Theologica* III. Q. 7.3.

87   Aristotle, *Nichomachean Ethics* IV.1 (New York: Macmillan, 1962), 85.

88   Aristotle, *Nichomachean Ethics*, 84.

89   John Milbank, "Liberality vs. Liberalism," in *Evangelicals and Empire: Christian Alternative to the Political Status Quo*, ed. Bruce Ellis Benson and Peter Goodwin Heltzel (Grand Rapids: Brazos Press, 2008), 95.

90   Milbank, "Liberality vs. Liberalism," 95.

91   Milbank, "Liberality vs. Liberalism," 98.

92   Milbank, "Liberality vs. Liberalism," 98.

93   Kathryn Tanner, "Why Support the Occupy Movement?" *Union Seminary Quarterly Review* 64, no. 1 (2013): 28.

94   Tanner, "Why Support the Occupy Movement?" 29.

95   Tanner, "Why Support the Occupy Movement?" 30.

96   Thomas Aquinas, *Summa Theologica* I–II. Q. 61.2 & I. Q. 59.2.

97   Thomas Aquinas, *Summa Theologica* II–II. Q. 123.2.

98   Aristotle, *Nichomachean Ethics*, 71.

99   Elizabeth Agnew Cochran, "Jesus Christ and the Cardinal Virtues: A Response to Monika Hellwig," *Theology Today* 65, no. 1 (2008): 93.

100  Augustine, *On the Morals of the Catholic Church*, trans. Richard Stothert, in *Nicene and Post-Nicene Fathers of the Christian Church*, vol. IV, ed. Philip Schaff, 41–63. (Buffalo, N.Y.: Christian Literature, 1887), 48.

101  Cochran, "Jesus Christ and the Cardinal Virtues," 87.

102  Cochran, "Jesus Christ and the Cardinal Virtues," 93.

103  Thomas Aquinas, *Summa Theologica* II–II. Q. 106.1.

104  Thomas Aquinas, *Summa Theologica* II–II. Q. 106.1.

105  Thomas Aquinas, *Summa Theologica* II–II. Q. 106.1.

106  Thomas Aquinas, *Summa Theologica* II–II. Q. 106.4.

107  Hyde, *Gift*, 47.

108  Hyde, *Gift*, 47.

Conclusion

1   Philip Goodchild, *Theology of Money* (Durham, N.C.: Duke University Press, 2009), 13.

2   Goodchild, *Theology of Money*, xiv.

# BIBLIOGRAPHY

Aggarwal, Rajesh K., and Tarik Yousef. "Islamic Banks and Investment Financing." *Journal of Money, Credit and Banking* 32, no. 1 (2000): 93–120.

Ahmed, Habib. "Defining Ethics in Islamic Finance: Looking Beyond Legality," *New Horizon: Global Perspective on Islamic Banking & Insurance* 184 (2012): 20–26.

Ahn, Ilsup. "Deconstructing the Economy of Debt: Karl Marx, Jürgen Habermas, and an Ethics of Debt." *Trans-Humanities* 6, no. 1 (2013): 5–32.

———. "The Genealogy of Debt and the Phenomenology of Forgiveness: Nietzsche, Marion, and Derrida on the Meaning of the Peculiar Phenomenon." *Heythrop Journal* 51, no. 3 (2010): 454–70.

Al-Azhari, Manzoor Ahmad. "Credit Cards and Their Juristic Appraisal." *Homdard Islamicus* 34, no. 2 (2011): 29–56.

Allen, Katie. "Poor Nations Pushed into New Debt Crisis" *Guardian*, October 10, 2014. https://www.theguardian.com/business/2014/oct/10/poor-nations-debt-crisis-developing-countries.

Amstutz, Lorraine Stutzman. "Restorative Justice: The Promise and the Challenges." *Vision: A Journal for Church and Theology* 14, no. 2 (2013): 24–30.

Andrews, Edmund L. "Greenspan Concedes Error on Regulation." *New York Times*, October 23, 2008. http://www.nytimes.com/2008/10/24/business/economy/24panel.html.

Aquinas, Thomas. *Summa Theologica* I–II, II–II, and III. Translated by Fathers of the English Dominican Province. New York: Benziger Brothers, 1947.

Aristotle. *Nichomachean Ethics* IV.1. New York: Macmillan, 1962.

Arjoon, Surendra. "Narcissistic Behavior and the Economy: The Role of Virtues." *Journal of Market & Morality* 13, no. 1 (2010): 59–82.

Askari, Hossein, Zamir Iqbal, Noureddine Krichene, and Abbas Mirakhor. *Risk Sharing in Finance: The Islamic Finance Alternative*. Singapore: John Wiley & Sons, 2012.

Atwood, Margaret. *Payback: Debt and the Shadow Side of Wealth*. Berkeley, Calif.: Anansi Press, 2008.

Augustine. *On the Morals of the Catholic Church*. Translated by Richard Stothert. In *Nicene and Post-Nicene Fathers of the Christian Church*, vol. IV, edited by Philip Schaff, 41–63. Buffalo, N.Y.: Christian Literature, 1887.

Ayub, Muhammad. *Understanding Islamic Finance*. West Sussex: John Wiley & Sons, 2007).

Azzimonti, Marina, Eva de Francisco, and Vincenzo Quadrini. "Financial Globalization, Inequality, and the Rising Public Debt." *American Economic Review* 104, no. 8 (2014): 2267–302.

Bales, Kevin. *Disposable People: New Slavery in the Global Economy*. San Francisco: University of California Press, 2004.

———. *Understanding Global Slavery: A Reader*. San Francisco: University of California Press, 2005.

Barry, Christian. "Sovereign Debt, Human Rights, and Policy Conditionality." *Journal of Political Philosophy* 19, no. 3 (2011): 282–305.

Basso, Manuel Jordan, and Juan Pablo Hugues Arthur. "Argentina, Vulture Funds and a Sovereign Debt Convention." *Transnational Notes* (blog), July 20, 2015. http://blogs.law.nyu.edu/transnational/2015/07/argentina-vulture-funds -and-a-sovereign-debt-convention/.

Bataille, Georges. *The Accursed Share: An Essay on General Economy*. Vol. 1. Translated by Robert Hurley. New York: Zone Books, 1988.

Beitel, Karl. "The Subprime Debacle." *Monthly Review* 60, no. 1 (2008): 27–44.

Bensaid, Benaouda, Mohd Roslan Mohd Nor, and Mohd Yakub Zulkifli Mohd Yusoff. "Enduring Financial Debt: An Islamic Perspective." *Middle-East Journal of Scientific Research* 13, no. 2 (2013): 162–70.

Bentham, Jeremy. *Defence of Usury*. 1787. London: Routledge, 1992.

Bergsma, John Sietze. *The Jubilee from Leviticus to Qumran: A History of Interpretation*. Leiden: Brill, 2007.

Bernstein, William J. "Corporate Finance and Original Sin." *Financial Analysts Journal* 62, no. 3 (2006): 20–22.

Bigelow, Bill, and Bob Peterson, eds. *Rethinking Globalization: Teaching for Justice in an Unjust World*. Milwaukee, Wis.: Rethinking Schools Press, 2002.

Bobson, John. "Behavioral Assumptions of Finance." In *Finance Ethics: Critical Issues in Theory and Practice*, edited by John R. Boatright, 45–59. Hoboken, N.J.: John Wiley & Sons, 2010.

Boettcher, Jacques, Gerald Cavanagh, S.J., and Min Xu. "Ethical Issues That Arise in Bankruptcy." *Business and Society Review* 119, no. 4 (2014): 473–96.

Boorman, Jack. "Dealing Comprehensively, and Justly, with Sovereign Debt." In *Sovereign Debt at the Crossroads*, edited by Chris Jochnick and Fraser A. Preston, 226–45. London: Oxford University Press, 2006.

Bourdieu, Pierre. *The Logic of Practice*. Translated by Richard Nice. Stanford, Calif.: Stanford University Press, 1990.

———. "Marginalia—Some Additional Notes on the Gift." In *The Logic of Gift: Toward an Ethic of Generosity*, edited by Alan D. Schrift, 231–44. New York: Routledge, 1997.

Brueggemann, Walter. "Living with a Different Set of Signals." *Living Pulpit* 10, no. 2 (2001): 20–21.

Buchanan, James M. "The Ethics of Debt Default." In *Deficits*, edited by James M. Buchanan, Charles K. Rowley, and Robert D. Tollison, 361–73. Oxford: Basil Blackwell, 1987.

Buchholz, Todd G. "Biblical Laws and the Economic Growth of Ancient Israel." *Journal of Law and Religion* 6, no. 2 (1988): 389–427.

Campbell, Gwyn, and Alessando Stanziani, eds. *Bonded Labour and Debt in the Indian Ocean World*. London: Pickering & Chatto, 2013.

———, eds. *Debt and Slavery in the Mediterranean and Atlantic Worlds*. London: Pickering & Chatto, 2013.

Caramel, Laurence. "Besieged by the Rising Tides of Climate Change, Kiribati Buys Land in Fiji." Guardian, June 30, 2014. https://www.theguardian.com/environment/2014/jul/01/kiribati-climate-change-fiji-vanua-levu.

Chang, Shu-Sen, David Gunnell, Jonathan A. C. Sterne, Tsung-Hsueh Lu, and Andrew T. A. Cheng. "Was the Economic Crisis 1997–1998 Responsible for Rising Suicide Rates in East/Southeast Asia? A Time-Trend Analysis for Japan, Hong Kong, South Korea, Taiwan, Singapore and Thailand." *Social Science & Medicine* 68, no. 7 (2009): 1322–31.

Chase, Malcolm. "From Millennium to Anniversary: The Concept of Jubilee in Late Eighteenth- and Nineteenth-Century England." *Past & Present* 129 (1990): 132–47.

Cheru, Fantu. "Playing Games with African Lives: The G7 Debt Relief Strategy and the Politics of Indifference." In *Sovereign Debt at the Crossroads*, edited by Chris Jochnick and Fraser A. Preston. London: Oxford University Press, 2006.

Cochran, Elizabeth Agnew. "Jesus Christ and the Cardinal Virtues: A Response to Monika Hellwig." *Theology Today* 65, no. 1 (2008): 81–94.

Cokgezen, Murat, and Timur Kuran. "Between Consumer Demand and Islamic Law: The Evolution of Islamic Credit Cards in Turkey." *Journal of Comparative Economics* 43, no. 4 (2015): 862–83.

Colombo, Ronald J. "Toward a Nexus of Virtue." *Washington and Lee Law Review* 69, no. 3 (2012): 3–84.

Crimmins, James E. "Bentham and Hobbes: An Issue of Influence." *Journal of the History of Ideas* 63, no. 4 (2002): 677–96.

————. "Bentham on Religion: Atheism and the Secular Society." *Journal of the History of Ideas* 47, no. 1 (1986): 95–110.

Crotty, James. "The Neoliberal Paradox: The Impact of Destructive Product Market Competition and 'Modern' Financial Markets on Nonfinancial Corporation Performance in the Neoliberal Era." In *Financialization and the World Economy*, edited by Gerald A. Epstein, 77–110. Cheltenham, UK: Edward Elgar, 2005.

Curry, Pat. "How a Supreme Court Ruling Killed Off Usury Laws for Credit Card Rates." Creditcards.com, November 12, 2010. http://www.creditcards.com /credit-card-news/marquette-interest-rate-usury-laws-credit-cards-1282.php.

Davis, Bob. "What's a Global Recession?" *Wall Street Journal*, October 16, 2015. http://blogs.wsj.com/economics/2009/04/22/whats-a-global-recession/.

Dearden, Nick. "Jamaica's Decades of Debt Are Damaging Its Future." *Guardian*, April 16, 2013. http://www.theguardian.com/global-development/poverty -matters/2013/apr/16/jamaica-decades-debt-damaging-future.

DeBelder, R. T., and M. H. Khan. "The Changing Face of Islamic Banking." *International Financial Law Review* 12, no. 11 (1993): 23–29.

Didia, Dal. "Debt-for-Nature Swaps, Market Imperfections, and Policy Failures as Determinants of Sustainable Development and Environmental Quality." *Journal of Economic Issues* 35, no. 2 (2001): 477–86.

Dodd, Randall. "Derivatives Markets: Sources of Vulnerability in US Financial Markets." In *Financialization and the World Economy*, edited by Gerald A. Epstein, 149–80. Cheltenham, UK: Edward Elgar, 2005.

Drinan, Robert F. "Jamaica, Entire Third World in Bondage to American Banks." *National Catholic Reporter* 30, no. 8 (1993): 18.

Dworkin, Ronald. *Taking Rights Seriously*. Cambridge, Mass.: Harvard University Press, 1978.

El-Erian, Mohamed. "Who Is to Blame for Greece's Crisis?" *Guardian*, May 18, 2012. http://www.theguardian.com/business/economics-blog/2012/may/18 /who-blame-greece-crisis.

El-Gamal, Mahmoud A. "An Economic Explication of the Prohibition of Gharar in Classical Islamic Jurisprudence." Paper prepared for the 4th International Conference on Islamic Economics, Leicester, August 13–15, 2000. http:// instituteofhalalinvesting.org/content/el-gamal/gharar.pdf.

————. *Islamic Finance: Law, Economics, and Practice*. New York: Cambridge University Press, 2006.

Ellis, Jessica R. "The Absolute Priority Rule for Individuals after *Maharaj*, *Lively*, and *Stephens*: Negotiations or Game Over?" *Arizona Law Review* 55, no. 4 (2013): 1141–69.

Epstein, Gerald A. "Introduction: Financialization and the World Economy." In *Financialization and the World Economy*, edited by Gerald A. Epstein, 3–16. Cheltenham, UK: Edward Elgar, 2005.

Farooq, Muhammad. "Interest, Usury and Its Impact on the Economy." *Dialogue* 7, no. 3 (2012): 265–76.

Fitzpatrick, William M., and Samuel A. DiLullo, "Bankruptcy: A Stakeholder Analysis," *Advances in Competitiveness Research* 20, nos. 1–2 (2012): 4–28.

Foster, John Bellamy. "The Age of Monopoly-Finance Capital." *Monthly Review* 61, no. 9 (2010): 1–13.

Foster, John Bellamy, and Fred Magdoff. *The Great Financial Crisis: Causes and Consequences*. New York: Monthly Review Press, 2009.

Freeman, Edward R. "Stakeholder Theory of the Modern Corporation." In *Ethical Theory and Business*, edited by Tom L. Beauchamp and Norman E. Bowie, 7th ed., 38–48. Englewood Cliffs, N.J.: Prentice Hall, 2003.

Frefield, Karen. "NY Court Lets Lawsuit against Goldman over Timberwolf CDO Proceed." Reuters, January 30, 2014. http://www.reuters.com/article/2014 /01/30/us-goldman-basisalpha-idUSBREA0T1VN20140130.

Friedman, Milton. "Defense of Usury." *Newsweek*, April 6, 1970, 79.

Gillespie, Michael Allen. "On Debt." In *Debt: Ethics, the Environment, and the Economy*, edited by Peter Y. Paik and Merry Wiesner-Hanks, 56–71. Bloomington: Indiana University Press, 2013.

Gnuse, Robert. "Jubilee Legislation in Leviticus: Israel's Vision of Social Reform." *Biblical Theology Bulletin* 15, no. 2 (1985): 43–48.

Gockel, Catherine Kilbane, and Leslie C. Gray. "Debt-for-Nature Swaps in Action: Two Case Studies in Peru." *Ecology and Society* 16, no. 3 (2011): 1–16.

Gohain, Manash Pratim. "New Evidence of Suicide Epidemic among India's 'Marginalized' Farmers." *Times of India*, April 17, 2014. http://timesofindia .indiatimes.com/india/New-evidence-of-suicide-epidemic-among-Indias -marginalized-farmers/articleshow/33867066.cms.

Goodchild, Philip. "Exposing Mammon: Devotion to Money in a Market Society." *Dialog: A Journal of Theology* 52, no. 1 (2013): 47–57.

———. *Theology of Money*. Durham, N.C.: Duke University Press, 2009.

Graafland, Johan J., and Bert W. van de Ven. "The Credit Crisis and the Moral Responsibility of Professionals in Finance." *Journal of Business Ethics* 103, no. 4 (2011): 605–19.

Graeber, David. *Debt: The First 5,000 Years*. Brooklyn, N.Y.: Melville House, 2012.

———. "Debt, the Whole History." *Green European Journal* 7 (2014): 24–29.

Greenstone, Michael, and Adam Looney, "Rising Student Debt Burdens: Factors behind the Phenomenon." *Brookings*, July 5, 2013. http://www.brookings.edu /blogs/jobs/posts/2013/07/05-student-loans-debt-burdens-jobs-greenstone -looney.

Gritsenko, Liliya. "Everybody Wins! Elimination of the Absolute Priority Rule for Individuals Under BAPCPA: A Middle Ground." *Cardozo Law Review* 35, no. 3 (2013): 1255–88.

Gross, Karen. *Failure and Forgiveness: Rebalancing the Bankruptcy System*. New Haven, Conn.: Yale University Press, 1997.

Guillot, Adéa. "Greece Struggles to Address Its Tax Evasion Problem." *Guardian*, February 24, 2015. http://www.theguardian.com/world/2015/feb/24/greece-collecting-revenue-tax-evasion.

Habermas, Jürgen. *Between Facts and Norms: Contributions to a Discourse Theory of Law and Democracy*. Translated by William Rehg. Cambridge, Mass.: MIT Press, 1996.

———. *Moral Consciousness and Communicative Action*. Translated by Christian Lenhardt and Shierry Weber Nicholsen. Cambridge, Mass.: MIT Press, 1990.

Hanlon, Joseph. "African Debt Hoax." *Review of African Political Economy* 25, no. 77 (1998): 487–92.

Hansen, Laura L., and Siamak Movahedi, "Wall Street Scandals: The Myth of Individual Greed." *Sociological Forum* 25, no. 2 (2010): 367–74.

Hartmann, Thom. "Private Debt—Not Government Debt—Will Destroy America." *Truthout*, February 14, 2013. http://www.truth-out.org/opinion/item/14566-private-debt-not-government-debt-will-destroy-america.

Harvey, David. "The Future of the Commons." *Radical History Review* 109 (2011): 101–7.

Hassan, M. Kabir, and Rasem Kayed. "The Global Financial Crisis and Islamic Finance." *Thunderbird International Business Review* 53, no. 5 (2011): 551–64.

Hassoun, Nicole. "The Problem of Debt-for-Nature Swaps from a Human Rights Perspective." *Journal of Applied Philosophy* 29, no. 4 (2012): 359–77.

Haugwout, Andrew, Donghoon Lee, Joelle Scally, and Wilbert van der Kalauw. "Student Loan Borrowing and Repayment Trends, 2015." *Federal Reserve Bank of New York*, April 16, 2015, 1–33. https://www.newyorkfed.org/media library/media/newsevents/mediaadvisory/2015/Student-Loan-Press-Brief ing-Presentation.pdf.

Hicks, Richard. "Markan Discipleship according to Malachi: The Significance of μὴ ἀποστερήσῃς in the Story of the Rich Man." *Journal of Biblical Literature* 132, no. 1 (2013): 179–99.

Hirschfeld, Mary L. "Reflection on the Financial Crisis: Aquinas on the Proper Role of Finance." *Journal of the Society of Christian Ethics* 35, no. 1 (2015): 63–82.

Hobbes, Thomas. *Leviathan*. London: Penguin Books, 1985.

Holland, Kelley. "The High Economic and Social Costs of Student Loan Debt." *CNBC*, June 15, 2015. http://www.cnbc.com/2015/06/15/the-high-economic-and-social-costs-of-student-loan-debt.html.

Hopper, Matthew S. "Debt and Slavery among Arabian Gulf Pearl Divers." In Campbell and Stanziani, *Bonded Labour and Debt in the Indian Ocean World*, 103–18. London: Pickering & Chatto, 2013.

Houle, Jason N., and Michael T. Light. "The Home Foreclosure Crisis and Rising Suicide Rates, 2005 to 2010," *American Journal of Public Health* 104, no. 6 (2014): 1073–79.

Hyde, Lewis. *The Gift: Imagination and the Erotic Life of Property.* New York: Vintage Books, 1983.

Issacharoff, Samuel, and Erin F. Delaney, "Credit Card Accountability." *University of Chicago Law Review* 73, no. 1 (2006): 157–82.

Jochnick, Chris. "The Legal Case for Debt Repudiation." In *Sovereign Debt at the Crossroads,* edited by Chris Jochnick and Fraser A. Preston, 132–57. London: Oxford University Press, 2006.

John Paul II. "Tertio Millennio Adveniente." https://w2.vatican.va/content/john-paul-ii/en/apost_letters/1994/documents/hf_jp-ii_apl_10111994_tertio-millennio-adveniente.html.

Johnston, Jake. "Partners in Austerity: Jamaica, the United States and the International Monetary Fund." Washington D.C.: Center for Economic and Policy Research, April 2005. http://cepr.net/documents/Jamaica_04-2015.pdf.

Jones, Tim. "A Legacy of Dodgy Deals: Auditing the Debts Owed to the UK." Jubilee Debt Campaign, June 2015. http://jubileedebt.org.uk/wp-content/uploads/2015/06/A-legacy-of-dodgy-deals.pdf.

Jospe, Raphael. "Sabbath, Sabbatical and Jubilee: Jewish Ethical Perspectives." In *The Jubilee Challenge: Utopia or Possibility?*, edited by Hans Ucko, 77–98. Geneva: WCC, 1997.

Jurgens, Rick, and Chi Chi Wu. "Fee-Harvesters: Low-Credit, High-Cost Cards Bleed Consumers." *National Consumer Law Center Report.* https://www.nclc.org/images/pdf/credit_cards/fee-harvesters-report.pdf.

Kant, Immanuel. *Groundwork of the Metaphysic of Morals.* Translated by H. J. Paton. New York: Harper & Row, 1964.

Kazi, Ashraf U., and Abdel K. Halabi. "The Influence of Qur'an and Islamic Transactions and Banking." *Arab Law Quarterly* 20, no. 3 (2006): 321–31.

Kennedy, Gavin. "Adam Smith and the Invisible Hand: From Metaphor to Myth." *Econ Journal Watch* 6, no. 2 (2009): 239–63.

Keynes, John Maynard. *General Theory of Employment, Interest and Money.* London: Macmillan, 1936.

Kilpi, Jukka. *The Ethics of Bankruptcy.* London: Routledge, 1998.

Kim, Bok-rea. "Debt Slaves in Old Korea." In *Bonded Labour and Debt in the Indian Ocean World,* edited by Gwyn Campbell and Alessando Stanziani, 165–72. London: Pickering & Chatto, 2013.

Krippner, Greta. "The Financialization of the American Economy." *Socio-Economic Review* 3 (2005): 173–208.

Krueger, Anne O. "A New Approach to Sovereign Debt Restructuring." *International Monetary Fund 2002.* https://www.imf.org/external/pubs/ft/exrp/sdrm/eng/sdrm.pdf.

Kunhibava, Sherin, and Balachandran Shanmugam. "Shari'ah and Conventional Law Objections to Derivatives: A Comparison." *Arab Law Quarterly* 24, no. 4 (2010): 319–60.

Kuran, Timur. "On the Notion of Economic Justice in Contemporary Islamic Thought." *International Journal of Middle East Studies* 21, no. 2 (1989): 171–91.

Labat, Alyssa, and Walter E. Block. "Money Does Not Grow on Trees: An Argument for Usury." *Journal of Business Ethics* 106, no. 3 (2012): 383–87.

Lazzarato, Maurizio. *The Making of the Indebted Man: An Essay on the Neoliberal Condition.* Translated by Joshua David Jordan. Los Angeles: Semiotext, 2011.

Lewison, Martin. "Conflicts of Interest? The Ethics of Usury." *Journal of Business Ethics* 22, no. 4 (1999): 327–39.

Li, Wenli. "The Economics of Student Loan Borrowing and Repayment." *Business Review* Q3 (2013): 1–10.

Locke, John. *Two Treatises of Government.* Edited by Peter Laslett. Cambridge: Cambridge University Press, 1988.

Long, D. Stephen, Nancy Ruth Fox, and Tripp York. *Calculated Futures: Theology, Ethics, and Economics.* Waco, Tex.: Baylor University Press, 2007.

Lorin, Janet. "Who's Profiting from $1.2 Trillion of Federal Student Loans?" *Bloomberg Business,* December 11, 2015. http://www.bloomberg.com /news/articles/2015-12-11/a-144-000-student-default-shows-who-profits-at -taxpayer-expense.

Lowery, Richard H. *Sabbath and Jubilee.* St. Louis, Mo.: Chalice Press, 2000.

Madslien, John. "Debt Relief Hopes Bring Out the Critics." *BBC News,* June 29, 2005. http://news.bbc.co.uk/2/hi/business/4619189.stm.

Malone, Andrew. "The GM Genocide: Thousands of Indian Farmers Are Committing Suicide after Using Genetically Modified Crops." *Daily Mail,* November 2, 2008. http://www.dailymail.co.uk/news/article-1082559/The-GM -genocide-Thousands-Indian-farmers-committing-suicide-using-genetically -modified-crops.html.

Marcaletti, Mariana. "Three Things to Know about the Supreme Court's Ruling on Argentine Debt—and Why It Matters to Argentina and the World." *Washington Post,* June 26, 2014. https://www.washingtonpost.com/news/worldviews /wp/2014/06/26/three-things-to-know-about-the-supreme-courts-ruling-on -argentine-debt-and-why-it-matters-to-argentina-and-the-world/.

Marx, Karl. *Capital.* Vol. 3. New York: International Publishers, 1967.

Matsui, Yoko. "The Debt-Servitude or Prostitutes in Japan during the Edo Period, 1600–1868." In *Bonded Labour and Debt in the Indian Ocean World,* edited by Gwyn Campbell and Alessando Stanziani, 173–86. London: Pickering & Chatto, 2013.

Mauss, Marcel. *The Gift: Forms and Functions of Exchange in Archaic Societies.* Translated by Ian Cunnison. Glencoe, Ill.: Free Press, 1954.

Mayer, Robert. "When and Why Usury Should Be Prohibited." *Journal of Business Ethics* 116, no. 3 (2013): 513–27.

McKenzie, Rex A. "Casino Capitalism with Derivatives: Fragility and Instability in Contemporary Finance." *Review of Radical Political Economics* 43, no. 2: 198–215.

Milbank, John. "Liberality vs. Liberalism." In *Evangelicals and Empire: Christian Alternative to the Political Status Quo*, edited by Bruce Ellis Benson and Peter Goodwin Heltzel, 93–103. Grand Rapids: Brazos Press, 2008.

Milgrom, Jacob. "Leviticus 25 and Some Postulates of the Jubilee." In *The Jubilee Challenge: Utopia or Possibility?*, edited by Hans Ucko, 28–32. Geneva: WWC, 1997.

Miller, Morris. *Debt and the Environment: Converging Crises*. New York: United Nations, 1991.

Miller, Seumas. "Global Financial Institutions, Ethics and Market Fundamentalism." In *Global Financial Crisis: The Ethical Issues*, edited by Ned Dobos, Christian Barry, and Thomas Pogge, 24–51. New York: Palgrave Macmillan, 2011.

Mitchell, Josh. "School-Loan Reckoning: 7 Million Are in Default." *Wall Street Journal*, August 21, 2015.

Moe-Lobeda, Cynthia D. "Climate Change as Climate Debt: Forging a Just Future." *Journal of the Society of Christian Ethics* 36, no. 1 (2016): 27–49.

Monaghan, Lee F., and Micheal O'Flynn, "The Madoffization of Society: A Corrosive Process in an Age of Fictitious Capital." *Critical Sociology* 39, no. 6 (2012): 869–87.

Moseley, Fred. "Marx's Economic Theory and Contemporary Capitalism." https://www.nodo50.org/cubasigloXXI/congreso/moseley_10abr03.pdf.

Motlhabi, Mokgethi B. G. "An Ethical Appraisal of the Third World Debt Crisis." *Religion & Theology* 10, no. 2 (2003): 192–223.

Murakami, Ei. "Two Bonded Labour Emigration Patterns in Mid-Nineteenth-Century Southern China: The Coolie Trade and Emigration to Southeast Asia." In *Bonded Labour and Debt in the Indian Ocean World*, edited by Gwyn Campbell and Alessando Stanziani, 153–64. London: Pickering & Chatto, 2013.

Nelson, Benjamin. *The Idea of Usury*. Chicago: University of Chicago Press, 1969.

Nelson, Julie A. "Ethics, Evidence and International Debt." *Journal of Economic Methodology* 16, no. 2 (2009): 175–89.

Nienhaus, Volker. "Islamic Finance Ethics and Shari'ah Law in the Aftermath of the Crisis: Concept and Practice of Shari'ah Compliant Finance." *Ethical Perspectives* 18, no. 4 (2011): 591–623.

Nietzsche, Friedrich. *On the Genealogy of Morals*. Translated by Walter Kaufmann and R. J. Hollingdale. New York: Vintage Books, 1989.

Noorzoy, M. Siddieq. "Islamic Laws on Riba (Interest) and Their Economic Implications." *International Journal of Middle East Studies* 14, no. 1 (1982): 3–17.

Norris, Floyd. "Card Act Cleared Up Credit Cards' Hidden Costs." *New York Times*, November 7, 2013. http://www.nytimes.com/2013/11/08/business /economy/a-credit-card-rule-that-worked-for-consumers.html.

Northcott, Michael. *Life after Debt*. London: SPCK, 1999.

Nussbaum, Martha. *Frontiers of Justice: Disability, Nationality, Species Membership*. Cambridge, Mass.: Belknap Press, 2006.

O'Neill, Onora. "Agents of Justice." *Metaphilosophy* 32, nos. 1–2 (2001): 180–95.

———. *Towards Justice and Virtue: A Constructive Account of Practical Reasoning*. Cambridge: Cambridge University Press, 1996.

Ong, Aihwa. "Neoliberalism as a Mobile Technology." *Transactions of the Institute of British Geographers*, n.s. 32, no. 1 (2007): 3–8.

Oxfam. "62 People Own the Same as Half the World, Reveals Oxfam Davos Report." Press release, January 18, 2016. https://www.oxfam.org/en/press room/pressreleases/2016-01-18/62-people-own-same-half-world-reveals -oxfam-davos-report.

———. "Working for the Few: Political Capture and Economic Inequality." Briefing paper, January 20, 2014. https://www.oxfam.org/sites/www.oxfam .org/files/bp-working-for-few-political-capture-economic-inequality-200114 -summ-en.pdf.

Pala, Christopher. "Kiribati President Purchases 'Worthless' Resettlement Land as Precaution against Rising Sea." *Inter Press Service News Agency*, June 9, 2016. http://www.ipsnews.net/2014/06/kiribati-president-purchases-worthless -resettlement-land-as-precaution-against-rising-sea/.

Payne, Dinah, and Michael Hogg. "Three Perspectives of Chapter 11 Bankruptcy: Legal, Managerial and Moral." *Journal of Business Ethics* 13, no. 1 (1994): 21–30.

Peterson, Matt, and Christian Barry. "Who Must Pay for the Damage of the Global Financial Crisis?" In *Global Financial Crisis: The Ethical Issues*, edited by Ned Dobos, Christian Barry, and Thomas Pogge, 158–83. New York: Palgrave-Macmillan, 2011.

Phelps, Hollis. "Overcoming Redemption: Neoliberalism, Atonement, and the Logic of Debt." *Political Theology* 17, no. 3 (2016): 264–82.

Piketty, Thomas. *Capital in the Twenty-First Century*. Translated by Arthur Gold-hammer. Cambridge, Mass.: Belknap Press of Harvard University Press, 2014.

Plumer, Brad. "How Greek Tax Evasion Helped Sink the Global Economy." *Washington Post*, July 9, 2012. https://www.washingtonpost.com/news/wonk/wp /2012/07/09/how-greek-tax-evasion-sunk-the-global-economy/.

Polland, Jane, and Michael Samers. "Islamic Banking and Finance: Postcolonial Political Economy and the Decentring of Economic Geography." *Transactions of the Institute of British Geographers*, n.s. 32, no. 3 (2007): 313–30.

Porter, Jean. "Perennial and Timely Virtues: Practical Wisdom, Courage and Temperance." In *Changing Value and Virtues*, edited by Dietmar Mieth and Jacques Pohier, 60–68. Edinburgh: T&T Clark, 1987.

Powell, Russell, and Arthur DeLong, "The Possible Advantages of Islamic Financial Jurisprudence: An Empirical Study of the Dow Jones Islamic Market Index." *Fordham Journal of Corporate and Financial Law* 19 (2014): 393–423.

Raaflaub, Kurt. *The Discovery of Freedom in Ancient Greece*. Translated by Renate Franciscono. Revised and updated edition. Chicago: University of Chicago Press, 2004.

Racelis, Aliza D. "Examining the Global Financial Crisis from a Virtue Theory Lens." *Asia-Pacific Social Science Review* 14, no. 2 (2014): 22–38.

Raffer, Kunibert. "The IMF's SDRM—Simply Disastrous Rescheduling Management?" In *Sovereign Debt at the Crossroads*, edited by Chris Jochnick and Fraser A. Preston, 246–66. London: Oxford University Press, 2006.

———. "Preferred or Not Preferred: Thoughts on Priority Structures of Creditors." Paper presented at the 2nd meeting of the ILA Sovereign Insolvency Study Group, October 16, 2009, Washington, D.C. https://homepage.univie.ac.at/kunibert.raffer/ila-wash.pdf.

———. "Risks of Lending and Liability of Lenders." *Ethics & International Affairs* 21, no. 1 (2007): 85–106.

Rasor, Paul B. "Biblical Roots of Modern Consumer Credit Law." *Journal of Law and Religion* 10, no. 1 (1993–1994): 157–92.

Rawls, John. *A Theory of Justice*. Cambridge, Mass.: Harvard University Press, 1971.

Resor, James P. "Debt-for-Nature Swaps: A Decade of Experience and New Directions for the Future." Food and Agriculture Organization (FAO). http://www.fao.org/docrep/w3247e/w3247e06.htm.

Reuveny, Rafael, and William R. Thompson. "World Economic Growth, Systemic Leadership, and Southern Debt Crises." *Journal of Peace Research* 31, no. 1 (2004): 5–24.

Rice, James. "North-South Relations and the Ecological Debt: Asserting a Counter-Hegemonic Discourse." *Critical Sociology* 35, no. 2 (2009): 225–52.

Risse, Mathias. "The Second Treatise in *On the Genealogy of Morality*: Nietzsche on the Origin of the Bad Conscience." *European Journal of Philosophy* 9, no. 1 (2001): 55–81.

Ritholtz, Barry. "What Caused the Financial Crisis? The Big Lie Goes Viral." *Washington Post*, November 5, 2011. http://www.dailymail.co.uk/news/article-1082559/The-GM-genocide-Thousands-Indian-farmers-committing-suicide-using-genetically-modified-crops.html.

Roe, Mark J., and Frederick Tung "Breaking Bankruptcy Priority: How Rent-Seeking Upends the Creditor's Bargain." *Virginia Law Review* 99, no. 6 (2013): 1236–90.

Sagiv, Yonatan. "The Gift of Debt: Agnon's Economics of Money, God and the Human Other." *PROOFTEXTS* 34, no. 2 (2014): 421–43.

Sahlins, Marshall. "The Spirit of the Gift." In *The Logic of Gift: Toward an Ethic of Generosity*, edited by Alan D. Schrift, 70–99. New York: Routledge, 1997.

Sambira, Jocelyne. "Borrowing Responsibly: Africa's Debt Challenge." *Africa Renewal Online*, August 2015, http://www.un.org/africarenewal/magazine /august-2015/borrowing-responsibly-africa%E2%80%99s-debt-challenge.

Schweiker, William. "Reconsidering Greed." In Schweiker and Mathewes, *Having*, 249–71.

Schweiker, William, and Charles Mathewes, eds. *Having: Property and Possession in Religious and Social Life*. Grand Rapids: Eerdmans, 2004.

Scott III, Robert H. "Credit Card Use and Abuse: A Veblenian Analysis." *Journal of Economic Issues* 41, no. 2 (2007): 567–74.

Sen, Amartya. *The Idea of Justice*. Cambridge, Mass.: Harvard University Press, 2009.

Sharma, Sohan, and Surinder Kumar. "Debt Relief—Indentured Servitude for the Third World." *Race & Class* 43, no. 4 (2002): 45–56.

Sherman, Matthew. *A Short History of Financial Deregulation in the United States*. Washington, D.C.: Center for Economic and Policy Research, 2009. http:// www.cepr.net/documents/publications/dereg-timeline-2009-07.pdf.

Simms, Andrew. *Ecological Debt: The Health of the Planet and the Wealth of Nations*. Ann Arbor, Mich.: Pluto Press, 2005.

Singer, Peter. "Famine, Affluence, and Morality." *Philosophy & Public Affairs* 1, no. 3 (1973): 229–43.

Smith, Adam. *The Wealth of Nations*. New York: Modern Library, 2000.

Smith, Helena. "Greece Erupts in Violent Protest as Citizens Face a Future of Harsh Austerity." *Guardian*, May 1, 2010. http://www.theguardian.com /world/2010/may/02/greece-violence-bailout-imf-euro.

Solomon, Norman. "Economics of the Jubilee: Putting Third World Debt in Context." *Church and Society* (September–October 1998): 58–67.

Sparks, Samantha. "Financing East-West Trade." *Multinational Monitor* 8 (1987): 54–55.

Stanziani, Alessandro, and Gwyn Campbell. "Introduction: Debt and Slavery in the Mediterranean and the Atlantic Worlds." In *Debt and Slavery in the Mediterranean and Atlantic Worlds*, edited by Gwyn Campbell and Alessandro Stanziani, 1–28. London: Pickering & Chatto, 2013.

Sternberg, Elaine. "Ethical Misconduct and the Global Financial Crisis." *Economic Affairs* 33, no. 1 (2013): 18–33.

Stewart, James B. "If Greece Defaults, Imagine Argentina, but Much Worse." *New York Times*, June 25, 2015. http://www.nytimes.com/2015/06/26/business /an-echo-of-argentina-in-greek-debt-crisis.html?_r=0.

Stiglitz, Joseph. *Free Fall: America, Free Markets, and the Sinking of the World Economy*. New York: W. W. Norton, 2010.

———. *The Price of Inequality: How Today's Divided Society Endangers Our Future*. New York: Norton, 2013.

Suchitra, M. "Crop of Debt." *Down to Earth*, August 1, 2015, 18–21. http://www .downtoearth.org.in/coverage/crop-of-debt-50630.

Sullivan, Bob. "Like a Drug: Payday Loan Users Hooked on Quick-Cash Cycle." *NBC News*, May 11, 2013. http://www.nbcnews.com/feature/in-plain-sight /drug-payday-loan-users-hooked-quick-cash-cycle-v18088751.

Sy, Amadou. "Trends and Developments in African Frontier Bond Markets." *Brookings Institution*, March 2015. http://www.brookings.edu/~/media/Research /Files/Papers/2015/03/03-trends-development-african-frontier-bond -markets-sy/Sovereign-Debt-Africa-Final.pdf.

Talib, M. T., and Jamiu A. Oluwatoko. "Islam and the Debt Question in Nigeria." In *The Church and the External Debt: Report on a Conference Held in Jos, Nigeria, November 26–30, 1990*, edited by Jan H. Boer, 60–68. Jos, Nigeria: Institute of Church and Society, 1992.

Tanner, Kathryn. "Economies of Grace." In Schweiker and Mathewes, *Having*, 353–81.

———. *Economy of Grace*. Minneapolis: Fortress, 2005.

———. "Why Support the Occupy Movement?" *Union Seminary Quarterly Review* 64, no. 1 (2013): 28–35.

Thesnaar, Christo. "Restorative Justice as a Key for Healing Communities." *Religion & Theology* 15, nos. 1–2 (2008): 53–73.

Titmus, Richard. *The Gift Relationship: From Human Blood to Social Policy*. New York: Vintage Books, 1971.

Tomaskovic-Devey, Donald, and Ken-Hou Lin. "Income Dynamics, Economic Rents, and the Financialization of the U.S. Economy." *American Sociological Review* 76, no. 4: 538–59.

Ucko, Hans. "The Jubilee as a Challenge." In *The Jubilee Challenge: Utopia or Possibility? Jewish and Christian Insight*, edited by Hans Ucko, 1–14. Geneva: WCC, 1997.

Upbin, Bruce. "The 147 Companies That Control Everything." *Forbes*, October 22, 2011. http://www.forbes.com/sites/bruceupbin/2011/10/22/the-147 -companies-that-control-everything/#45db52827638.

Vallely, Paul. *Bad Samaritans: First World Ethics and Third World Debt*. Maryknoll, N.Y.: Orbis Books, 1990.

Veerkamp, Ton. "Judeo-Christian Tradition on Debt: Political, Not Just Ethical." *Ethics & International Affairs* 21, no. 1 (2007): 167–88.

Visser, Wayne A. M., and Alastair McIntosh. "A Short Review of the Historical Critique of Usury." *Accounting, Business and Financial History* 8, no. 2 (1998): 175–89.

Webb, Stephen H. *The Gifting God: A Trinitarian Ethics of Excess*. New York: Oxford University Press, 1996.

White, Michelle J. "Bankruptcy Reform and Credit Cards." *Journal of Economic Perspectives* 21, no. 4 (2007): 175–200.

Wu, Jonathan. "Average Credit Card Interest Rates (APR)—2017." Value Penguin, http://www.valuepenguin.com/average-credit-card-interest-rates.

Young, Iris Marion. *Responsibility for Justice*. Oxford: Oxford University Press, 2011.

Zaman, M. Raquibuz, and Hormoz Movassaghi. "Interest-Free Islamic Banking: Ideals and Reality." *International Journal of Banking* 14, no. 4 (2002): 2428–42.

# Author Index

# Subject Index